Tourism Management Dynamics

Prediction is very difficult, especially of the future.
                                        – Niels Bohr

Tourism Management Dynamics

Trends, management and tools

Edited by Dimitrios Buhalis and
Carlos Costa

ELSEVIER
BUTTERWORTH
HEINEMANN

AMSTERDAM   BOSTON   HEIDELBERG   LONDON   NEW YORK   OXFORD
PARIS   SAN DIEGO   SAN FRANCISCO   SINGAPORE   SYDNEY   TOKYO

Elsevier Butterworth-Heinemann
Linacre House, Jordan Hill, Oxford OX2 8DP
30 Corporate Drive, Burlington, MA 01803

First published 2006

British Library Cataloguing in Publication Data
A catalogue record for this book is available from the British Library

Library of Congress Cataloguing in Publication Data Control Number: 2005928727

ISBN 0 7506 6378 2

For information on all Elsevier Butterworth-Heinemann
publications visit our website at www.elsevier.com

Typeset by Charon Tec Pvt. Ltd, Chennai, India
www.charontec.com
Printed and bound in Great Britain by MPG Books Ltd, Bodmin, Cornwall

Cover photographs by D. Buhalis

Contents

Contents

List of Figures

List of Tables

List of Case Studies

Editors

Dimitrios Buhalis, University of Surrey, UK

Dr Dimitrios Buhalis is Course Leader MSc in Tourism Marketing and Leader of e-Tourism Research at the School of Management, University of Surrey. Dimitrios is also Adjunct Professor at the MBA in Hospitality Management at IMHI (Cornell University-ESSEC) in Paris. Dimitrios has been an active researcher in the areas of ICTs and Tourism and also serves as Vice-Chairman on the International Federation of Information Technology and Tourism (IFITT) Board. He has editorial roles in a number of academic journals and he has written, edited or co-edited 8 books on eTourism, Tourism Strategic Issues and Distribution Channels of Tourism.

Carlos Costa, University of Aveiro, Portugal

Dr Carlos Costa is Associate Professor at the University of Aveiro. He has been Director of the Tourism teaching programme since 1996, which includes a BSc on Tourism Planning and Development and an MSc on Tourism Management and Development. He holds a PhD and MSc on Tourism Management from the University of Surrey. He is also Editor of the *Tourism & Development Journal*, the first Tourism Journal to be launched in Portugal. Dr Costa has also been involved in several projects and consultancy for the Portuguese government and other Portuguese organizations. He is currently a Visiting Professor in several universities around the world and has taught tourism courses in Finland, the UK, Greece, Cuba, Brazil and Goa.

Contributors

Tom Baum, University of Strathclyde, Glasgow, UK
Tom Baum is Professor of International Tourism and Hospitality Management at the University of Strathclyde in Glasgow. Tom has Bachelor's and Master's degrees from the University of Wales and a PhD in tourism labour markets from Strathclyde. He is author of books and scientific papers on tourism, with a particular focus on HRM, education and training. He has taught and consulted across six continents, working with both governments and the private sector.

Bill Bramwell, Sheffield Hallam University, UK
Bill Bramwell is Reader in Tourism in the Centre for Tourism and Cultural Change at Sheffield Hallam University. He has edited books on rural tourism, collaboration and partnerships in tourism, sustainable tourism in Europe and Southern European tourism and he is the founding editor of the *Journal of Sustainable Tourism*. His research interests include discourses of sustainable, cultural and environmental tourism policies.

Peter Burns, University of Brighton, UK
Professor Burns is Director of the Centre for Tourism Policy Studies at the University of Brighton, UK. He has published widely and his latest book on tourism and anthropology has been a particular success. His consulting work has encompassed many regions of the world covering a variety of institutions including the European Union and United Nations. He is a member of the World Tourism Organization's Education Council.

Po-Ju Chen, University of Central Florida, USA
Po-Ju Chen is an Assistant Professor at the Rosen College of Hospitality Management, University of Central Florida. She received her Doctor of Philosophy from the Pennsylvania State University. Her research interests have been focused on marketing and methodology, with an emphasis on hospitality and tourism.

Frank Go, Erasmus University, The Netherlands
Frank Go is the Bewetour Chair of Tourism Management Research at the Rotterdam School of Management, Erasmus University. Previously, he served

within business faculties at universities in Toronto and Calgary in Canada and in Hong Kong. The focus of his current research examines network marketing management, sustainable business development and e-learning, projected and perceived destination images and brand identity.

Colin Hales, University of Surrey, UK

Colin Hales is Professor of Organisational Behaviour at the University of Surrey School of Management. He holds a Bachelor's degree in Economics from the University of Cambridge and an MA and PhD in Sociology from the University of Kent at Canterbury. He is the author of two books and publishes widely in management journals.

Michael Hall, University of Otago, New Zealand

Michael Hall is Professor and Head of the Department of Tourism, University of Otago and a visitor in the Department of Social and Economic Geography, Umeå University, Sweden. Co-editor of *Current Issues in Tourism*, he is the author of a number of publications in the areas of tourism, mobility and regional development.

Atsuko Hashimoto, Brock University, Canada

Dr Hashimoto is Associate Professor in the Department of Recreation and Leisure Studies at Brock University and teaches in the Bachelor of Tourism Studies Degree programme. She lectures on the areas of international tourism and social psychology of tourism. Her research interests lie in cross-cultural studies in tourism, sociocultural impacts and tourism development and environmental issues in tourism.

Tazim Jamal, A&M University, Texas, USA

Tazim Jamal is an Associate Professor in the Department of Recreation, Park and Tourism Sciences at Texas A&M University. Her main research areas are community-based tourism planning, collaborative processes for sustainable development, and theoretical/methodological issues related to tourism and sustainability.

Ute Jamrozy, A&M University, Texas, USA

Ute Jamrozy is a Research Associate in the Department of Recreation, Park and Tourism Sciences at Texas A&M University. Her main research interests are sustainable marketing, communication and sustainability in tourism, consumer psychology and community tourism development.

Rok Klancnik, World Tourism Organization, Madrid, Spain

Rok Klancnik has been Chief of Press and Communications at the World Tourism Organization since June 2002. Among others, he edited the third edition of the 'Shining in the Media Spotlight' handbook, organized the First World Conference on Tourism Communications (TOURCOM) and is editor of the publication *Observations on International Tourism Communications*.

Gang Li, University of Surrey, UK
Gang Li is a Lecturer in Economics in the School of Management, University of Surrey, UK. His research interests include applied econometric modelling and forecasting, with an emphasis on international tourism demand analysis. He is also interested in econometric studies of Chinese economic issues, such as income inequity.

Roger March, University of New South Wales, Australia
Roger March is Head of the Tourism and Hospitality Management Unit at the University of New South Wales in Sydney. His research focuses on Asian and Japanese tourism markets, distribution in international tourism and cross-cultural tourist behaviour.

Antonio Massieu, World Tourism Organization, Madrid, Spain
Antonio Massieu is Chief of the Department of Statistics and Economic Measurement of Tourism at the World Tourism Organization (WTO), Madrid. He is responsible for developing support systems for member countries. Following the World Conference on the Measurement of the Economic Impact of Tourism, he led the adoption of the 'Tourism Satellite Account: Recommended Methodological Framework' by the United Nations Statistical Commission (UNSC).

Graham Miller, University of Surrey, UK
Dr Graham Miller is a Lecturer in Management at the University of Surrey, where he teaches issues relating to business ethics and the tourism industry. Graham has a PhD and Master's degree in Tourism Management from the University of Surrey and his undergraduate degree from the University of Salford. Beyond indicators for sustainability, Graham's main research interest is in the forces that enable and prevent the drive for a sustainable transition.

Sarah Nicholls, Michigan State University, USA
Sarah Nicholls is an Assistant Professor with a joint appointment between the Departments of Community, Agriculture, Recreation, & Resource Studies, and Geography, at Michigan State University. She is interested in the impacts of climate change on international tourism, as well as tourists' knowledge and perceptions of this issue and its potential impacts on their leisure activities.

Outi Niininen, La Trobe University, Australia
Outi Niininen is currently at the La Trobe University, having recently moved from the University of Surrey in the UK. Her research focuses on consumer behaviour in tourism and impacts of electronic business on tourism.

Peter O'Connor, Institut de Management Hôtelier International, Paris, France
Peter O'Connor is co-Director and Professor of Information Systems at Institute de Management Hotelier International (IMHI), an MBA program in international hospitality management administered by ESSEC Business School, Paris. His research interests focus on information technology in hospitality (particularly on

electronic channels of distribution) and he has authored two textbooks – *Using Computers in Hospitality* and *Electronic Information Distribution in Hospitality and Tourism* – as well as numerous articles in the trade and academic press. He is also a past winner of the prestigious Best Research Paper award at the ENTER Information Technology in Tourism conference.

Andreas Papatheodorou, University of Oxford, UK

Dr Papatheodorou is an economic geographer with a DPhil from the University of Oxford. He is actively engaged in lecturing and tourism research, focusing on competition, pricing and corporate strategies in air transport and travel distribution. Most of his work is related to the Mediterranean Region and has been published in international academic journals.

Mike Peters, University of Innsbruck, Austria

Dr Mike Peters is Assistant Professor at the Center for Tourism and Service Economics at the University of Innsbruck. His main areas of research include internationalization of service enterprises, problems and challenges of small businesses in tourism, entrepreneurship in tourism and innovation and product development in tourism.

Abraham Pizam, University of Central Florida, USA

Abraham Pizam is Dean and Linda Chapin Eminent Scholar Chair in Tourism Management at the Rosen College of Hospitality Management, the University of Central Florida. Professor Pizam is the author of 145 scientific publications and four books and is on the editorial staff of fourteen academic journals.

Michael Riley, University of Surrey, UK

Michael Riley is Professor of Organisational Behaviour at the School of Management at the University of Surrey. His work of two decades centres upon the labour aspects of tourism and he has written extensively about human resource management in the industry.

Roslyn Russell, RMIT University, Australia

Dr Roslyn Russell is a Senior Research Fellow at RMIT University, Melbourne. Most of her tourism research has focused on models of destination development, entrepreneurship, chaos theory and mountain tourism. Roslyn is also currently researching in the areas of social entrepreneurship, entrepreneurship in the arts, biotechnology and generational differences in the workforce.

Haiyan Song, Hong Kong Polytechnic University, China

Haiyan Song is a Chair Professor of Tourism in the School of Hotel and Tourism Management, The Hong Kong Polytechnic University, Hong Kong. Professor Song has a background in Economics. His main research area is tourism economics with a particular focus on tourism demand modelling and forecasting. He has extensive research and consultancy experience in such areas as foreign direct investment in China and economic issues related to China's tourism sector.

Edith Szivas, University of Surrey, UK
Edith Szivas is a Senior Lecturer in Tourism at the School of Management at the University of Surrey. Her research interests and publications are in the fields of labour economics, economic transition and tourism planning and development. She is a consultant too.

David J Telfer, Brock University, Canada
Dr Telfer is Associate Professor in the Department of Recreation and Leisure Studies at Brock University and teaches in the Bachelor of Tourism Studies Degree programme. He teaches in the areas of tourism planning, heritage tourism and themes in tourism development. His research interests include linkages between tourism and development theories, economic linkages of tourism with host communities, strategic alliances and rural tourism.

Dallen Timothy, Arizona State University, USA
Dr Dallen Timothy is Associate Professor at Arizona State University and Visiting Professor of Heritage Tourism at the University of Sunderland, UK. He is editor of the *Journal of Heritage Tourism* and has authored many articles, books and chapters on tourism and political boundaries, heritage, shopping and consumption, planning, community-based development and developing country dynamics.

Tony Tse, Hong Kong Polytechnic University, China
Tony S M Tse is the Industry Partnerships Director at The Hong Kong Polytechnic University's School of Hotel & Tourism Management. His interest in crisis management began with the outbreak of severe acute respiratory syndrome (SARS) in Asia and its impact on tourism. Tony has spoken on crisis management in tourism at the University's Winter School, UNESCAP and PATA seminars. Tony was previously the General Manager of Marketing Communication at the Hong Kong Tourism Board.

Louise Twining-Ward, New York, USA
Dr Louise Twining-Ward is a New York based tourism consultant specializing in tourism management and development. She has a PhD and Masters from the University of Surrey and undergraduate degree from the University of Durham. Her doctoral studies specialized in techniques for monitoring sustainable tourism, using the case study of Samoa, where she lived for eight years. Her research interests include complex adaptive systems, resilience, monitoring sustainable tourism development and stakeholder participation.

Erik van't Klooster, Erasmus University, The Netherlands
Erik van't Klooster is a PhD Candidate at the Rotterdam School of Management. The focus of his studies is on student preferences within interactive, distributed learning environments. He has co-authored a number of papers and has presented his research at the Bled eCommerce conference and the IFITT ENTER conference in Innsbruck.

David Viner, University of East Anglia, UK
David Viner is a Senior Research Scientist at the Climatic Research Unit, University of East Anglia. David specializes in the impacts of climate change on society and the

environment and is leading an international network of researchers and stakeholders who are addressing the interactions between climate change, the environment and tourism. He is also the course director of the Climate Change MSc in the School of Environmental Sciences at UEA.

Stephen Witt, University of Surrey, UK
Stephen Witt is a Visiting Professor in the School of Hotel and Tourism Management, The Hong Kong Polytechnic University, Hong Kong, and is also an Emeritus Professor at the University of Surrey, UK. His major research interests are econometric modelling of international tourism demand and assessment of the accuracy of different forecasting methods within the tourism context.

Karl Wöber, University of Economics and Business Administration, Vienna
Karl W. Wöber is Associate Professor at the Department for Tourism and Leisure Studies at the Vienna University of Economics and Business Administration. He is a consultant for the Austrian Society of Applied Research in Tourism and Technical Advisor of European Cities Tourism and the European Travel Commission. His main research activities include decision support systems, strategic marketing planning and evolutionary computation in city tourism and hospitality management.

Foreword

Over the past few years, the Travel and Tourism industry has had to contend with a series of unprecedented challenges. Political uncertainty, terrorism, consumer wariness and economic turbulence have all placed enormous pressure on our industry. These events have left their mark – not only on the balance sheets of industry players and on global employment, but also in terms of changes in consumer demand and behaviour. In an effort to adapt to the shifting marketplace, the Travel and Tourism industry has had to restructure and refocus its efforts. While business plans have become increasingly short term, more and more governments are realizing that they cannot leave Travel and Tourism growth to chance. This emerging global consciousness represents a great opportunity for our industry.

In response to this opportunity, the World Travel and Tourism Council (WTTC), the forum for global business leaders in Travel and Tourism, has created a new vision and strategy for Travel and Tourism. This vision of New Tourism is set out in the Council's *Blueprint for New Tourism* and calls for a coherent partnership between the private sector and public authorities. New Tourism is geared to delivering commercially successful products, but in a way that ensures benefits for everyone. It looks beyond short-term considerations and focuses on benefits not only for people who travel, but also for people in the communities they visit and for their respective natural, social and cultural environments.

Through the Blueprint, the Travel and Tourism industry has declared its readiness to do its part. Now we call upon other stakeholders to commit to the policies set out in the Blueprint and to join us in building a new vision of tourism which will bring benefits to the wider world. Therefore:

1   Governments should recognize Travel and Tourism as a top priority and
  - show leadership by defining coherent and streamlined management structures that can efficiently drive New Tourism
  - elevate Travel and Tourism to strategic national level with senior level policy making
  - factor Travel and Tourism into all policies and decision-making, to promote growth that respects both business needs and the well-being of citizens.
2   Business should balance economics with people, culture and environment and
  - adapt strategic thinking so as to develop tourism with benefits for everyone
  - extend and diversify product offerings to improve yields and social value

- spearhead innovative management and help spread best practice through corporate social responsibility.
3 Tourism and travel stakeholders should develop a shared pursuit of long-term growth and prosperity by
   - cooperating in identifying opportunities for growth
   - focusing on building Travel and Tourism that opens up prospects for people – from employment to development
   - working together to remove impediments to growth – from infrastructure shortcomings to pollution and from outdated legislation to unmet health and security concerns.

With these issues and priorities in mind we are particularly pleased to welcome the *Tourism Business Frontiers* and *Tourism Management Dynamics* books that explore not only developments in the supply and demand of tourism but also a wide range of trends and management tools. The books, written by renowned researchers from around the globe, provide contemporary thinking and contribute to the exploration of the future for empowering the tourism industry. The books provide an insight into the Travel and Tourism industry's transformation and support our vision for realizing our industry's potential for growth and ensuring maximum and sustainable benefits for everyone involved.

Jean-Claude Baumgarten
President, World Travel & Tourism Council
London

Preface

As this book was being written, The Athens 2004 Olympic Torch Relay travelled the globe proclaiming 'pass the flame, unite the world'. The Olympic flame is the primary symbol of the Olympic ideals: noble competition, friendship and peaceful coexistence. Apart from sports, education and tourism are the only other ideals that promote similar principles and can contribute to a more peaceful, prosperous and equitable world. Tourism is one of the most dynamic and challenging global industries. Its international nature, in combination with the need to coordinate the needs of a number of stakeholders, makes peaceful and constructive collaboration essential for the successful development of tourism products and destinations. Tourism is also increasingly responsible for poverty alleviation and for a greater understanding of our world – leading to peace and global prosperity.

Exploring the future of tourism not only enables businessmen, politicians, managers and academics better to understand the key trends and developments, but also prepares tourism organizations and destinations to devise strategies and policies to strengthen their competitiveness and ensure their future prosperity. *Tourism Management Dynamics*, together with its affiliate publication *Tourism Business Frontiers*, looks into the future of tourism and explores six key areas that will determine how the industry will develop globally. These include trends, management techniques, tools, consumers, products and industry. The books aim to provide analytical tools to enable both tourism professionals and researchers to identify trends and predict the future, in order to strengthen the competitiveness of the industry. They should also assist tourism destination organizations around the world in taking advantage of predictions and preparing their regions for enjoying better advantages from tourism. Finally the books aim to educate younger generations of tourism professionals who are currently studying in courses around the world.

We hope that you will enjoy the two books and we are looking forward to receiving feedback, contributions and debates that will inform future editions and meetings that we will organize on the topic. Predicting the future of tourism is a dynamic process that will keep all of us busy for many years to come.

Have a great tourism future! Happy 'pass the flame, unite the world…'

Dimitrios Buhalis and Carlos Costa
March 2005

Acknowledgements

These books have a history of many years. Carlos and Dimitrios first met at the University of Surrey looking for knowledge and challenging the world. Many people were instrumental to our professional development. We are particularly grateful to Chris Cooper for leading the development of our academic careers and for providing inspiration and solid frameworks for further research. Years later, over a beer at seaside Estoril, we were looking for material to systematize knowledge and explore the emerging global changes for our students. Ideas floated and the key concepts for the book projects emerged. Before we knew, colleagues, friends and leading researchers from around the world (most all three!) were invited to contribute to the project. Sally North, Kathryn Grant, Francesca Ford and their colleagues at Butterworth-Heinemann adopted the project, provided helpful guidance and offered a cheerful friendship that made the author–publisher relationship a great pleasure. A project of this nature is a huge undertaking and brings together 50 contributions from 72 authors spread across 20 countries. It has proven both an academic challenge and an immense pleasure. We are grateful to all colleagues and friends who contributed to this project and would like to thank them for the academic debates and stimulation we enjoyed throughout the process.

During the preparation period of these books a number of things developed us personally and professionally. The project survived the best ever organized EURO2004 Football Cup in Portugal … when the Greeks won the cup after beating the Portuguese team twice. Both nations celebrated together! – demonstrating in practice what noble competition, friendship and peaceful coexistence is all about. We were also saddened by the premature loss of Dr Felix Martins of the University of Algarve, a great friend and colleague, reminding us where the future lies for all humans. We were also extremely sad to experience the tragic loss of life of both tourists and local residents and the disaster that the tsunami effect caused in Asia, demonstrating the power of nature. And we watched our children grow, bringing hope, dreams and inspiration for the future. We should acknowledge the contribution of our families, Maria and Stella in Guildford and Graça, Sebastião and Lourenço in Aveiro who have suffered from our absence, looked after us when we were editing and often reminded us that there is more to life than tourism research.

1

Introduction

Carlos Costa and Dimitrios Buhalis

Anticipating and predicting the future has always been among men's main wishes. To know what people will like most, and what sort of products and services will be sold and consumed in the future, are key questions that businessmen, politicians, managers and academics would love to have an answer to, if they could. When looking at the way in which tourism will be shaped in the future, there are two dimensions one should take into account. Tourism businesses will undergo major changes as a result of new trends observed in the new emerging consumers. Inevitably new and innovative products will change industry structures and operational requirements. Such a discussion is expanded in the accompanying book entitled *Tourism Business Frontiers – Consumers, Products and Industry*.

It is on the second dimension of change that this book will be concentrating. The external environment, and the way in which it is anticipated, understood, managed and planned, will decisively influence the success of tourism in the future. Planners, managers, politicians and academics ought to be aware of their external environment and develop techniques and tools to improve their performance. The success of tourism, both at the micro and macro levels, will very much depend on the way organizations and destinations as a whole are planned, managed and marketed.

This book does not deal with the 'art' of guessing the future. On the contrary, it attempts to predict the future by using a wide range of trends and scientific methods. *Tourism Dynamics: Trends, Management and Tools* proclaims that the future of tourism should be predicted through the observation of key trends and indicators. Decision-makers, researchers, academics, politicians, managers and planners can then design and launch suitable tools for improving their competitiveness. The book examines empirical evidence and seeks to provide vision by looking at some of the main trends that are already emerging in society and shaping the future of tourism. The idea that the success of the future tourism industry will depend on the way in which entrepreneurs, politicians and academics understand and explore these changes is right in the heart of the book.

Tourism Management Dynamics also provides an insight into the future management techniques and tools that will be utilized in the tourism industry in order for tourism organizations and destinations to address the emerging trends. This edited publication has been written by some of the most renowned tourism academics and researchers who, based on empirical evidence, analyse past trends, describe the state of the art and provide vision for the future of tourism as it is emerging around the globe. As shown in Figure 1.1, an understanding of the demand and supply trends, as demonstrated in *Tourism Business Frontiers*, is leading to an appreciation of the emerging realities in the marketplace. *Tourism Management Dynamics* explores the most significant trends on the external environment, while a number of managerial techniques and tools that will enable tourism organizations to address these challenges are explored. The focus of this

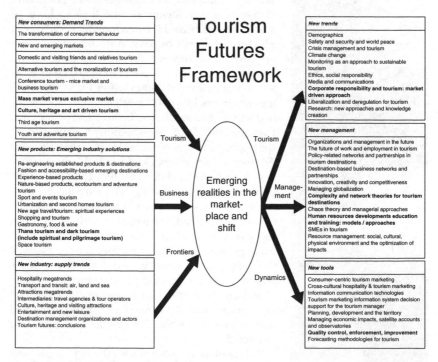

Figure 1.1 Tourism futures framework.

book is therefore geared towards explaining the significance of those external environment trends that will shape the future and also towards identifying and discussing suitable management instruments for the future.

One of the central arguments is that the success of future tourism is intrinsically interconnected with the way in which the industry and the tourism system understand and incorporate the emerging critical trends that support its expansion. Tourism is undergoing major changes so far as its demographics are concerned. The ageing of the world's population and the active lifestyle of older travellers, the emerging new markets, the growing disposable incomes of the youth market and an increasing awareness of the implications of the greenhouse effect, will decisively influence the number, motivations, destination and product choices, as well as activities of future travellers.

Nonetheless, these demographic trends will also be accompanied by major changes in the characteristics of the travel itself. New forms of activities, products, consumption patterns and interaction with both locals and fellow travellers will be observed at the destination areas. Climatic change will also alter the attractiveness of destinations, as temperatures are expected to rise, making Mediterranean destinations for example uncomfortably hot, while affecting the snowfall in alpine regions. Issues related to ethics and sustainability need to be incorporated into the destination planning and management. Safety and security will grow in importance, especially since many terrorism attacks deliberately target tourism honeypots in order to take advantage of international media coverage. Increasingly, destinations and tourism organizations will need to develop crisis management plans to be able to avoid and/or handle disasters. The emerging trends will also be influenced by an increasing visibility of the travel market, which is a result of the globalization of the world media and the transparency that introduces globally. The rapid liberalization and deregulation of markets will bring fierce competition, based not only on price, but also on the quality and the characteristics of the products supplied to clients. These developments will have a strong impact on the way tourism will attempt to capitalize on competitive advantages, by differentiating supply and by offering travellers new, diversified and customer-oriented products.

These new trends will bring profound changes in the management and planning of tourism businesses and destinations. In face of ferocious competition, destinations will need to increase their awareness of the way the industry, processes and systems ought to be analysed and organized. The monitoring of the global tourism system will need to provide information about industry directions, which organizations will need to utilize for developing proactive and reactive responses. Key indicators in important markets should therefore be monitored constantly to provide early warnings about trends and developments in order to trigger both strategic and tactical management mechanisms. Close interaction with research centres, observatories and think tanks will ensure knowledge transfer while it will provide tourism organizations with needed intelligence and strategic tools. Establishing these mechanisms will determine the way in which the tourism industry learns how to plan and react to unforeseen events and also how it may become more innovative, differentiated, authentic and competitive.

As a result, new managerial and planning orientations will gradually be brought into the tourism sector. Increasing competition will require managers to implement new forms of strategic management, capable of maximizing not only direct economic benefits emerging from the operation of individual businesses, but also the optimization of indirect and induced spin-offs that may emerge if a properly networked tourism industry is set up. Contemporary approaches which exploit knowledge, networks, partnerships, SME (small and medium-sized enterprise) clusters and globalization will then emerge. Alongside internal strategies, such as new managerial and organizational approaches, innovation, creativity and learning organizations will also emerge to enhance organizational efficiency and competitiveness. The creation of interconnected and networked regional businesses will be looking for collective competitive advantages within their destinations. They will also strengthen their positioning in the world's market through competition, i.e. simultaneous collaboration and competition. The globalization of the tourism industry will require not only the expansion of businesses to operate on an international level, but will also demand strategies and tactics that will support businesses and destinations to build their brand and image worldwide.

Academics and entrepreneurs should introduce innovative managerial and planning approaches that will provide the industry with intelligence, knowledge and tools that may bring public and private tourism organizations competitive advantages. Under this wave of development, human resources will also need to gain renewed importance. As tourism is labour (rather than capital) intensive, education and training have to assume centre-stage to prepare the intellectual capacity that will be required for the future. Hence, new directions for tourism education and research need to emerge and mechanisms for closer interaction between academia and practice need to be established.

While global trends push forward new managerial approaches, planners and managers ought to be aware of the emerging tools that will help them to plan, manage and market businesses and destinations. Future trends point towards three strategic directions, namely: satisfying consumers, destination management and territory organization. First, with regard to consumers, tourism marketing will evolve from a classic product-centred approach, to an emphasis placed on tailor-made products that meet the demands of particular niche markets and individuals. Traditional marketing orientations will therefore give place to consumer-centred marketing practices, where ultimately organizations aim to please the market segment of one customer. One-to-one (121) marketing will be required in the future. However, to make this financially viable, advanced technology and customer relationship management (CRM) systems, in particular, will need to facilitate the interaction and to ensure that the cost of production and delivery of customized products remains competitive. Meeting, satisfying and exceeding customer's expectations, while remaining profitable, will be critical for determining the success and the quality of the products provided by the tourism industry. The enforcement and the monitoring of such marketing practices will also be most important to meet forms of sustainable and competitive growth. In an increasingly globalized industry, where both the workforces and clientele are coming from a diverse background, cross-cultural marketing will be significant for the success of both destinations and businesses.

Secondly, along with the new marketing orientations, the success of the tourism industry will depend on the way destinations are managed and planned. The quality of the infrastructures, facilities and amenities assumes critical importance in the way in which consumers are pleased and satisfied and affects the economic benefits for the destination. New planning and development approaches emphasizing regional development, host communities and economic structures of tourism destinations are emerging worldwide. Thirdly, the organization of the territory is increasingly determined by economic forces rather than by formal plans set up by public sector organizations. Driving social and economic forces should be managed within innovative organizational structures capable of bringing together public and private sector organizations. The development of the satellite accounts methodologies and supply side definitions by The World Tourism Organization (WTO), as well as the research undertaken by several observatories that are already flourishing in a number of countries, provide more comprehensive evaluations of the value of tourism and also its impact on national and regional economies. To perform a comprehensive analysis of the impact and contribution of tourism, research tools such as the satellite accounts and forecasting methodologies are required. These will ensure that destinations have scientifically sound approaches for ensuring that they can plan their macro economic benefits based on accurate future predictions. They also have the research tools not only to identify which prospective markets they should target but also to evaluate the economic, sociocultural and environmental impacts of those markets.

The main objective of this book is therefore to discuss future trends of tourism and identify new management and planning tools to enable tourism businesses and destinations to benefit. The book provides an overview of the historical evolution of these areas, so far as knowledge, issues, trends, managerial implications and paradigms are concerned. The 'state of the art' is also discussed and emerging trends, approaches, models and paradigms are also introduced. The book provides vision for the future of the tourism industry and analyses emerging and leading practices. Support discussion questions and pedagogic aids and literature are available on the accompanying website to provide further intellectual stimulation and to support additional study and continued pursuit of knowledge.

A companion website containing material for both tutors and students can be found at: http://books.elsevier.com/hospitality?ISBN=0750663782

Part One: New Trends

2

Demography

C Michael Hall

Introduction

Demographics are an important factor in assessing tourism production and consumption. Demography is the study of the characteristics of human populations. This may be done at both a macro level, e.g. in relation to population characteristics in general, or at a micro level, which looks at the characteristics of specific populations either for identified locations or communities or for defined sample populations, such as consumers of particular tourist products, the characteristics of destination residents, or the characteristics of the tourism workforce. Indeed, almost any tourist survey collects the demographic profile of its respondents in order to provide empirical data. The present chapter concentrates on the implications of macro-level demographic data and trends for the future of tourism. However, it also provides an outline of the life-course concept which is central to much discussion of demographic change as well as its implications for tourism consumption.

Demographic theory: from life cycles to life courses

Demography, along with psychographic information, has long been used to assess tourism market trends. Much of the understanding of demographic information, particularly in the western world, has been influenced by ideas that there are normal stages in life through which humans pass and that these stages influence the nature of consumption. These ideas have been most pronounced in the idea of a 'life cycle'.

As originally conceived, the life cycle referred to individuals moving through certain stages of life, e.g. school, university, work, marriage, children, retirement, at certain ages, and that these stages then influence particular patterns of consumption due to the nature of family and work commitments as well as overall well-being (Glick, 1947). However, such a model has been subject to substantial criticism in recent years. For example, the notion of family life cycle as it was (and still is) usually elaborated, refers to the family circumstances of white urban middle-class Americans in the 1950s and 1960s, which was a far more child-oriented period in the developed world than at present as, since the 1970s the birth-rate in developed countries has slowed substantially (Murphy, 1987). The notion of a family life cycle was therefore time and space specific (O'Rand and Krecker, 1990). Moreover, human life paths are not constituted by the endless repetition of orderly sequences, 'the deterministic implication that life is irreversibly leading something back to where it came from' (Bryman et al., 1987, p.2); personal time, like historical time, is linear not cyclical. Therefore, attention is increasingly being given to the notion of a life-course perspective.

The life-course approach

The essence of the life-course approach is that the unit of analysis becomes the individual sited in geographical, social, historical and political space and time and that the study of the individual, household or family becomes the study of conjoined or interdependent life courses or paths (Elder, 1994). This perspective suggests that the timing and order of major life events (e.g. partnership (marriage), separation (divorce), birth of children, retirement), be considered with respect to 'the interplay between individual life stories and population ageing, as well as the relationships among the individual, age cohorts, and the changing social structure' (McPherson, 1998, p.7). The life course is therefore a social construct.

A life-course approach seeks not to impose a normal or ideal life path as articulated in traditional life-cycle models; instead what is central to the concept of the life course is not the concept of stage but that of transition. Early transitions have implications for later ones with transitions occurring in 'personal time', 'historical time' and 'family time'. The life-course paradigm therefore emphasizes that changes in one dimension of the household-ageing process, for example, are necessarily linked to changes in other dimensions. Different personal, historical or societal events create variations within and between cohorts and individuals in the timing and sequencing of events as people age (Nelson and Dannefer, 1992) in different parts of the world. For example, economic depression and war are likely to have substantial impacts on specific age cohorts but not on others, or even on specific individuals within an age cohort depending on specific circumstances. Similarly, McPherson (1998) has noted that the feminist movement has had different impacts on the ageing process throughout the life course for different age cohorts of women, with it having relatively little effect on women who are presently in the later stages of their life but having a substantial effect on age cohorts from the 1970s onwards. Taking a temporal standpoint to analyse behaviour in the life course therefore 'shifts the focus from static spatial or group-based comparisons of the life course (e.g. current socioeconomic status, residence, education) to more dynamic analysis of the evolving, natural, constructed and data-related aspects of time' (Mills, 2000, p.93).

Cohort membership

Membership in a cohort is a central factor in life-course opportunities such as partnership, employment or the capacity to raise a family. However, the temporal category of birth cohort, which is an epistemological tool used by many researchers in examining consumer behaviour, may also be a factor related to value shifts (Mills, 2000) with the cohort size 'likely to leave an imprint on the cohort as well as on society' (Ryder, 1965, p.13). As Mills (2000, p.101) noted, 'Although one's spatial or physical location, for instance, may change as a consequence of migration, persons are born into not only a particular historical, but also a unique cultural and social context'. For example, Foot and Stoffman (1996) examined the Canadian postwar 'baby boom' generation born between 1946 and 1966. In 1996, this generation born in a relatively economically prosperous period comprised approximately 33 per cent of the Canadian population and therefore had a major influence on the political, social and cultural agenda of the country. Significantly, Foot and Stoffman argued that the 'return to family values' phenomenon in Canadian life could be attributed to a cohort effect, rather than a value shift due to the fact that this cohort was in the 'family' life stage of mortgages and children. Interestingly, Foot and Stoffman (1996, p.189) predicted that in the new millennium, when the large 'baby boom echo' cohort born from 1980 to 1995 begins to leave the parental home (Figure 2.1), values will shift to sex, drugs and new music: 'Social observers will herald the arrival of yet another value shift,

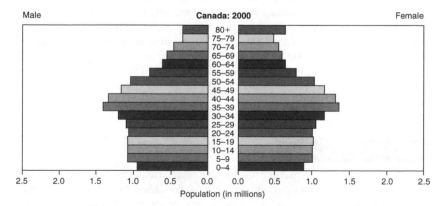

Figure 2.1 Population pyramid for Canada 2000.
(Source: US Census Bureau, International Data Base)

but the real reason will be the demographic shift'. This particular group is now usually referred to as Generation Y with some of the characteristics predicted by Foot and Stoffman being identified in several studies (e.g. Shepherdson, 2000; Bakewell and Mitchell, 2003).

Clearly, events and transitions over the life course as well as population cohorts can have substantial impacts on leisure, travel and mobility as well as other aspects of consumption. In Australia, as with many other countries, leisure time varies by age group and gender, with the most 'leisure-rich' age group (those aged 65 and over) having 60 per cent more leisure time than the most 'leisure-poor' age group (35–44) (Lynch and Veal, 1996). Such a situation clearly relates to the extent of the influence of work demands on overall available time as well as the time available for certain types of travel. Given the changing demographics of Australia's population in terms of people living longer and staying active and healthy as well as the regulatory and institutional context of retirement, it is likely that the retired and semi-retired market, from 60 to 65 on, will become of increasing importance as a target market. Moreover, changes in demographic behaviour with respect to marriage and children are also influencing tourism. For example, many people in the 20–30 age cohort are getting married later and having children later than previous cohorts or choosing not to have children at all. Such decisions within cohorts have substantial impacts on travel because of the amount of disposable incomes people will therefore have at various stages of their lives with tourism and leisure being one of the major beneficiaries of such disposable income. More and more younger people from developed countries postpone the entrance into 'real life' through an intensive and longer travel period than previous cohorts (Williams and Hall, 2002). Moreover, cohort differences may have substantial implications, not only for travel lifestyles but also in terms of use of technology or receptivity to particular marketing techniques. For example, research has indicated that there are significant generational differences in the use of Internet travel services (Furr et al., 2002). However, while such information is potentially useful in determining tourism futures, it must be remembered that the life-course approach emphasizes the particular context of the individual within certain cultural, economic, institutional, spatial, physical and gendered constraints. For example, women's and men's perceptions and uses of time often differ substantially, ranging from basic biological differences to distinct patterns of managing public and private time and space (Mills, 2000), with gender also providing a constraint to travel mobility (Kwan, 2000; Hall, 2005). Therefore, in examining demographic characteristics and their potential implications for tourism, it is important to recognize the limitations of aggregated data. Nevertheless, certain broad trends can be identified.

Demographic change

Probably the key demographic factor that will affect the future of tourism is the ageing of the world's population (Hall, 2005). This substantial demographic change has occurred because of dramatic improvements in health care and a decline in the birth rate in the developed world and is predicted to continue well into the coming centuries, so long as the world's resources are able

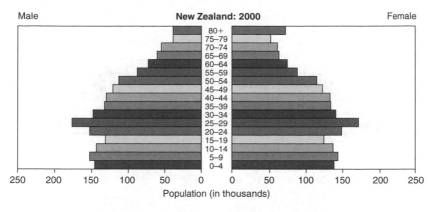

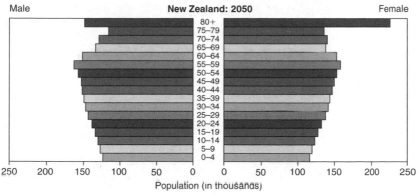

Figure 2.2 Population pyramids for New Zealand 2000–50.
(Source: US Census Bureau, International Data Base)

to support the increases in population. At the end of the twentieth century 11 per cent of the world's population was aged 60 and above. By 2050, it is estimated that 20 per cent will be 60 years or older; and by 2150, approximately one-third will be 60 years or older (United Nations Population Division, 1998).

Just as significantly the older population itself is ageing (United Nations Population Division, 1998). The increase in the number of very old people (aged 80+ years) between 1950 and 2050 is projected to grow by a factor of from 8 to 10 times on the global scale. As well as general ageing of the world's population there are also substantial regional differences in the aged population. For example, currently 20 per cent of Europeans are 60 years or older, but 5 per cent of Africans are 60 years or older. In some developed countries today, the proportion of older persons is close to 20 per cent. According to the United Nations Division for Social Policy and Development (1998) by 2050 that proportion will reach one in four and, in some countries, one in two (see Figures 2.2, 2.3 and 2.4).

Given that the vast majority of the world's tourists come from the developed countries, an ageing population will clearly have substantial implications for the international tourism industry. Not only may particular types of tourism favoured

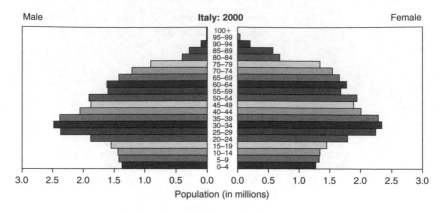

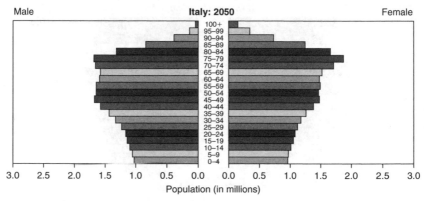

Figure 2.3 Population pyramids for Italy 2000–50.
(Source: US Census Bureau, International Data Base)

by older travellers continue to grow in popularity, such as cruising, but second homes and retirement homes and the provision of health facilities for retirees may become increasingly important in destination development strategies (Hall and Müller, 2004). For example, areas of Mediterranean Europe and the Iberian Peninsula and south-west USA and Florida are already subject to substantial seasonal and permanent retirement migration (e.g. King et al., 2000; Williams and Hall, 2002). Yet the longer term implications of transnational second home purchase and retirement migration are relatively unclear, particularly when individuals become infirm. Moreover, a critical factor in the tourism, leisure and second home patterns of retirees is not only their time budget but also their level of income. Growth of retirement tourism therefore requires continued economic growth in order to maintain pension and superannuation packages. Yet, in many western countries, the retirement age is now being increased by governments, e.g. New Zealand, or such increases are being debated, e.g. France, Germany, Italy and the UK, because of concerns over the affordability of pensions. In addition, many retirees are continuing to work either out of choice or of necessity because of the inadequacy of retirement savings.

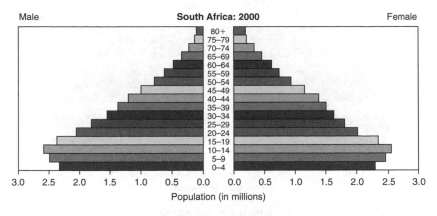

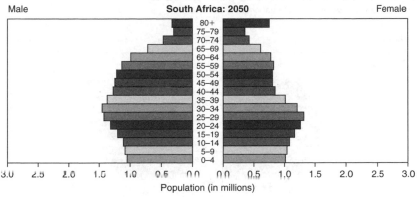

Figure 2.4 Population pyramids for South Africa 2000–50.
(Source: US Census Bureau, International Data Base)

A further influential factor with respect to demographic change and tourism is that it is estimated that, among the major industrialized countries, only the USA is estimated to have significant population growth by 2050 (Population Reference Bureau, 2004). The USA is expected to have reached a population of 420 million by 2050, an increase of 43 per cent (Figure 2.5), but Europe is expected to have 60 million fewer people than today and some countries could lose more than a third of their populations. Japan, which currently has only 14 per cent of its current population under 15, may have shrunk in size to approximately 100 million people by 2050. Over the same period Eastern Europe is also predicted to experience major population loss. Bulgaria is expected to return to pre-1914 population levels, losing 38 per cent of its people, while Romania could have 27 per cent fewer and Russia 25 million fewer people. Germany (Figure 2.6) and Italy are expected to shrink by approximately 10 per cent. In contrast, developing countries are predicted to expand dramatically in population. Although the world's developed countries are expected to grow in total population by about 4 per cent to over 1.2 billion, population in developing countries is predicted to

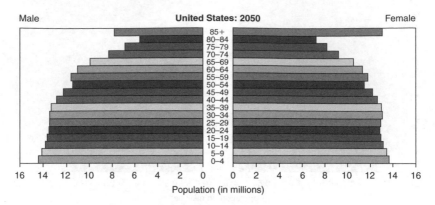

Figure 2.5 Population pyramid for the United States 2050.
(Source: US Census Bureau, International Data Base)

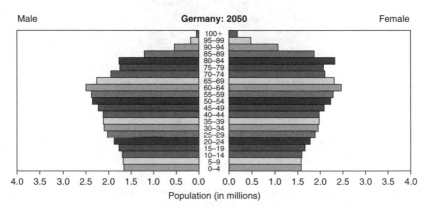

Figure 2.6 Population pyramid for Germany 2050.
(Source: US Census Bureau, International Data Base)

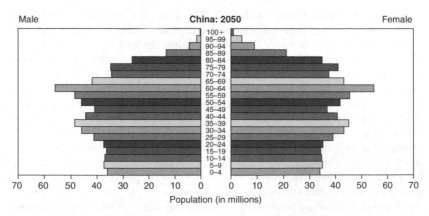

Figure 2.7 Population pyramid for China 2050.
(Source: US Census Bureau, International Data Base)

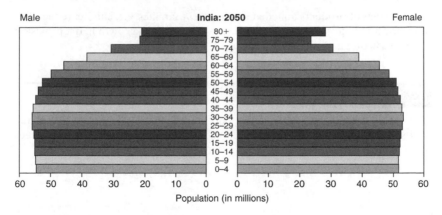

Figure 2.8 Population pyramid for India 2050.
(Source: US Census Bureau, International Data Base)

grow by up to 55 per cent to more than 8 billion. In this scenario Western Asian nations are expected to gain about 186 million people by 2050 and sub-Saharan African countries more than one billion people. By 2050, India will be the largest country in the world, having long passed China (Population Reference Bureau 2004) (Figures 2.7 and 2.8).

Conclusions

Although the ageing of the population will be a dominant demographic factor in tourism trends in the future, other factors will also be significant. For example, the breakdown of the traditional nuclear family in many western countries marked by increased single parenting, people marrying later, more people never marrying and many people never having children, not only influences demographic characteristics but will also affect the pattern of holiday taking and leisure travel (Hall, 2000a). In addition, the growth of large migrant populations in many developed countries, particularly as labour may be required to sustain economic growth within an ageing population, is also expected to contribute to the development of new transnational tourism patterns as migrant groups seek to retain relationships to 'home' (Williams and Hall, 2002). In fact one of the greatest predictors of future mobility patterns is previous mobility (Hall, 2005).

The implications of these predicted changes for tourism are incredibly complex and need to be seen in relation to other factors discussed in this book, particularly with respect to global environmental change. Even assuming the world's environmental systems can sustain such population growth, the economic and political instability that may result as a result of resource insecurity may severely damage tourism growth in the less developed world. Indeed, a major constraint on population growth as well as tourism may be the cost of energy, as the Worldwatch Institute (2004) argues that people usually only have as many children as they can afford (Abernathy, 2004). However, in terms of direct tourism industry response to demographic change it is likely that we will see the ongoing

17

development of products aimed at single parent families, e.g. child-care facilities at resorts and hotels and, more significantly, a substantial growth in the provision of infrastructure and services for the aged.

Acknowledgements

The author would like to note the contribution of Iris Ljubicic, Madelaine Mattson and Judit Sulyok to his understanding of European demographic issues and their tourism implications.

3

Safety and Security Issues in Tourism

Dallen J Timothy

Introduction

Tourism is volatile. Even the slightest whispers of political discontent, disease and natural disaster typically send tourist arrivals plummeting. When people feel unsafe they will either choose to alter their travel plans to safer destinations or cancel altogether, until public memory of the episode begins to pale. This chapter provides a brief overview of crisis and disaster situations that call tourist safety and security into question. It examines tourist, business and government responses to catastrophes and highlights the future directions of tourist security.

Safety and security issues

Observers have noted differences between crises and disasters. In most cases, crises are unexpected, although potentially predictable, management failures that might have been averted with proper management. Disasters on the other hand, are unpredictable, catastrophic events that cannot be foretold (Faulkner, 2001; Prideaux et al., 2003). Both crises and disasters significantly affect tourists' choice of destination and even people's decision whether or not to travel. While there are acknowledged differences between the two concepts, in this chapter both terms are used interchangeably to indicate major destructive events that jeopardize tourist safety and security. Broadly speaking, these events can be classified as either human-induced or naturally occurring incidents.

Human-induced security threats

Several types of negative events occur relatively often and have major impacts on tourist flows and tourism economies. Table 3.1 highlights several of the most common threats to tourist safety, both human-induced and natural. The common recurrence of accidents, where visitors are severely injured or killed, can create a negative image associated with specific destinations even when most of the accidents are caused by the tourists themselves (Bentley and Page, 2001).

Crime in destination areas also contributes to tourists' reluctance to visit. In most cases, as tourism grows, so does crime, resulting in a negative, but interdependent, relationship (de Albuquerque and McElroy, 1999). Criminals often prey on tourists, because the outsiders are seen as having more money to spend and less time in the destination to pursue the perpetrators. Most crimes against tourists are economics-based, including robberies and pickpocketing, although crimes of passion (e.g. rape and murder) are not uncommon either. There are many destinations in the world today (e.g. Rome and Hong Kong) that are stigmatized owing to a long record of crimes committed against tourists.

Ethnic unrest creates uncertain conditions, especially when violence erupts and hostage taking is involved. Fighting between ethnic groups, such as in Rwanda in the 1990s, and insurgencies by minority groups against dominant groups or governments (e.g. the Chiapas uprisings in Mexico) deter many people from visiting.

Another important security threat is political unrest, which usually undermines any cost savings associated with less-expensive destinations (Soemodinoto et al.,

Table 3.1 Major threats to tourist safety and security

Threats	Examples
Accidents	Car accidents, airplane crashes, skydiving
Crime	Pickpocketing, robberies, murders, rapes
Ethnic unrest	Fighting between ethnic groups, conflict between religious groups, ethnic rebellions
Health concerns	Unrefrigerated dairy products and meats, uncooked fruits and vegetables, food-borne illnesses, insanitary water, diseases
Natural disasters	Earthquakes, floods, hurricanes, volcanic eruptions
Political unrest	Coups, border closures, corrupt administrations, political scandals, riots
Terrorism	Bombings, shootings, mass destruction, kidnappings
War	Military altercations, cross-border armed conflicts, multi-national wars

2001). For instance, Maoist rebels have threatened Nepal's political stability since the mid-1990s. Their efforts to create a 'People's Democratic Republic' have resulted in many lives lost, government takeovers and the destruction of much of the country's infrastructure (Thapa, 2003). These events, like the repeated coups in Fiji and Ghana over the years and the Tiananmen Square standoff in China, have resulted in major downturns in tourist demand to places that might otherwise be very desirable destinations.

Terrorism, a form of political instability and war, attempts to enact changes in policy and practice through intimidation and fear. The most common forms of terrorism today include hostage taking, murder and mass destruction of people and property. The best recent examples include the Al Qaida attacks on New York City and Washington in 2001 (see Case study 3.1), the embassy bombings in eastern Africa, the recent bombings in Bali and Jakarta and the 1990s murders of tourists in Egypt (Pizam and Mansfeld, 1996).

Case study 3.1 The World Trade Center, New York City

On 11 September, 2001 (9-11), four commercial airliners were hijacked; two were used by terrorists to strike the World Trade Center in New York City, which subsequently collapsed, killing nearly 3000 people. The immediate effects of the act on tourism were profound. All border crossings and ports were closed for several hours and air travel was grounded for several days. At first the US travel industry was most affected, but the ripple effects soon spread to other economic sectors and to other parts of the world. In the first two days following the attack, the airlines lost over US $100 million, with many more billions of dollars in lost revenue in the weeks and months that followed. As a result, tens of thousands of people lost their jobs, profits plummeted and several airlines filed for bankruptcy, not just in the USA, but worldwide. Hotel companies were hit hard as well, with most reporting a significant decline in occupancy in the weeks and months following the event (Goodrich, 2002; Blake and Sinclair, 2003; Chen and Noriega, 2003). While consumer spending declined and people stayed closer to home, resulting in increased levels of car-based domestic tourism, in the end, billions of dollars and thousands of jobs were lost in tourism.

The effects of war on tourists' perceptions of safety and security are another major issue (Pizam and Mansfeld, 1996). As noted with political instability generally, civil war in one country or battles between countries can tarnish the image of an entire region. Wars are among the most violent of all political conflicts and involve the killing of enemy fighters and innocent bystanders. Not only does war destroy natural and cultural resources upon which tourism may depend, but it also diverts people to other destinations and, in most cases, causes downturns in international travel throughout the entire world. During the Gulf War of the early 1990s (and the current war in Iraq) international travel was affected everywhere, not just in the Middle East.

Natural security threats

Health problems also affect tourists' perceptions of safety and are in effect a combination of nature and human behaviour. Diseases such as malaria, hepatitis and yellow fever are common ailments in many developing regions against which travellers must be immunized. During the past few years, the outbreak of SARS (severe acute respiratory syndrome) in Asia and Canada and the foot-and-mouth disease (FMD) in England (see Case study 3.2) contributed to significant declines in visitation to those regions and countries (Coles, 2003; Ritchie et al., 2003). Food and water safety is another health-related concern of utmost importance for tourists visiting the developing world where food preservation practices are different from those of their home countries and where many fruits and vegetables should be peeled or well cooked to avoid spreading bacteria. Diarrhoea is the most prominent disease encountered by tourists and its primary cause is improper hygiene and improperly prepared foods and drinks.

Case study 3.2 Foot-and-Mouth Disease, UK

The outbreak of foot-and-mouth disease (FMD) in southwest England in February 2001 had a considerable impact not only on agriculture, but on tourism as well, even though the disease is known to affect only animals. Several areas were quarantined and visitors to those areas were required to disinfect their cars, shoes and clothing. Images of burning animal carcasses and disinfection procedures, coupled with the declaration of certain rural precincts as 'off-limits' had a dramatic effect on tourist arrivals in Britain (Beirman, 2003b). Rural attractions, farm-based accommodations, coastal footways and rural hiking trails were closed to prevent spreading the disease. While recovery began in May, in most of the region affected business was down between 74 and 98 per cent by the end of March at an economic loss of approximately £300 million (Coles, 2003, p.184).

The next set of safety concerns results from natural disasters. While not fully substantiated empirically, the impacts of natural disasters on tourists' travel decisions have a shorter duration than those of human-created disasters. Destinations affected by hurricanes, volcanic eruptions and earthquakes typically do not take as long to recover as destinations rocked by human-induced catastrophes (see Case study 3.3). Natural disasters often function as major tourist attractions in their aftermath (e.g. Mount St Helens, earthquakes in San Francisco and Italy).

All of these situations cause a spillover effect wherein entire regions are tainted. Thapa (2003), for example, noted that the prolonged negative images of political discord, natural disasters and military skirmishes in and between India, Pakistan, Bangladesh and Sri Lanka have influenced the world's view of the entire region. Perhaps an even better example of this is the Middle East.

Case study 3.3 The 2004 Asian Tsunami

Strong earthquakes in Southeast Asia on 26 December, 2004, resulted in one of the most devastating natural disasters in recorded history in terms of lives lost, geographical coverage and number of countries involved. The death toll resulting from the consequent tsunami was estimated to be over 200 000 people, with Indonesia, Sri Lanka, and India being the hardest hit. Major effects were also felt in Thailand, Malaysia, Myanmar, Bangladesh, the Maldives, and as far away as Somalia, Tanzania, Kenya and the Seychelles in eastern Africa. In addition to the thousands of lives lost in local communities, many tourists were also killed as huge waves washed over beaches, crumbled hotels and carried away other buildings and vehicles. Providing information and assistance to relatives and next of kin was a major challenge for the destinations hit.

Tourism and fishing, the two leading economic mainstays in many of the affected areas, were devastated by the event. While tourism and fishing were the industries most negatively affected by the disaster, there are optimistic observations that suggest tourism will be quick to recover. Billions of dollars in foreign aid have been poured into the twelve countries to help feed the people, rebuild roads and reconstruct schools, hospitals and homes for devastated families. However, calls have been put out by government officials in places like the Maldives, Thailand and Sri Lanka for tourists to return, suggesting that, while the international assistance is deeply appreciated, the best gifts would be for tourists to begin visiting once again, so that rebuilding can take place and jobs re-created as the industry regains its momentum and strong foundation.

Disaster responses and the future of tourist security

Traveller responses

Among tourists, the most common response to catastrophes is avoidance. As noted above, the exception to this is people who travel to view disaster sites to satisfy their curiosity. Typically, when travellers perceive unsafe and insecure conditions, they cancel their plans or select alternative, safer destinations. For example, while inbound and outbound travel from the USA suffered after 9-11, domestic tourism grew. Likewise, safer foreign destinations were selected in lieu of prior selections. For example, Thailand became a more popular destination when many western tourists changed their itineraries from Malaysia and Indonesia, two predominantly Muslim nations, to a country that was not involved in the war on terrorism (McKercher and Hui, 2003). As with the 9-11 example, FMD in the UK was blamed for dramatic declines in tourist arrivals from around the world (Beirman, 2003b).

According to a study in Hong Kong, 40 per cent of the respondents made changes to their travel plans immediately following 9-11. Most of them changed their destination, although a smaller proportion cancelled or postponed their travels.

People preferred postponing their travel to cancelling it outright (McKercher and Hui, 2003, p.108). Similarly, in Chen and Noriega's (2003) study, some one-third of their student traveller population changed travel plans following the event. McKercher and Hui (2003) found that immediately following 9-11, 50 per cent of the population felt that travel was as safe as or safer than before the attack. A year later, three-quarters of their survey population felt travel conditions were as safe as or safer than before 9-11. Nonetheless, there seems to be a relationship between the gravity of the incident and the duration of its negative effects on tourism (Pizam, 1999; McKercher and Hui, 2003).

Business responses

Prideaux et al. (2003, p.479) contend that long-term crises can provide a degree of predictability, whereas disasters can best be addressed only after the event has occurred. Even when crisis situations can be averted to some degree, in most cases they are addressed only after the crisis unfolds.

Generally, the first response in the business community should be, and usually is, to decide what actions would be most helpful in the situation and provide care for the needy. In New York, restaurateurs noted that their first reaction was to provide shelter, water, food, toilets, telephone service, and comfort to people in need, including police officers and firefighters. Their response to employees included assuring them that their jobs were secure and many business owners took large profit reductions to keep people employed. The restaurants' approach to their customers involved menu and price changes, changing indoor ambiance and assessing the new needs of the community (Green et al., 2003). Many tourism firms reduced prices to encourage the public to continue using their services (Blake and Sinclair, 2003).

Government responses

Government responses to negative events will influence the rate of recovery of the tourism industry (Prideaux et al., 2003). In the short term, governments typically try to maintain law and order, provide disaster relief, implement security measures and effect changes in negative public perceptions (Beirman, 2003b; Blake and Sinclair, 2003). Likewise, in the aftermath of catastrophes, some national governments issue official travel warnings for parts of the world affected most by turmoil and shock. For instance, the US government regularly publishes travel warnings for countries it recommends its citizens to avoid (see Table 3.2). This usually causes damage to the tourism industries of the countries listed (Sönmez, 1998; Thapa, 2003). Perhaps the most notable long-term responses by governments are policy changes. In the USA, for instance, the government has established many new policies aimed at protecting public safety at home and abroad, involving tourism workers, suppliers and tourists themselves (Table 3.3). Nearly all of these focus on improving security and offering financial assistance to the people most affected by the events.

Table 3.2 Countries on the US Government's Travel Warning List, September 2004

Country	Reason
Afghanistan	Terrorist threat, crime, political instability
Algeria	Terrorist threat
Bahamas	Natural disaster (hurricanes)
Bosnia-Herzegovina	Political instability, ethnic conflict
Burundi	Civil war, political instability
Cayman Islands	Natural disaster (hurricanes)
Central African Republic	Political instability
Colombia	Narcoterrorism, crime
Cote d'Ivoire	Civil war, political instability
Cuba	Natural disaster (hurricanes)
Democratic Republic of the Congo	Civil war, political instability
Grenada	Natural disaster (hurricanes)
Haiti	Political instability, crime
Indonesia	Terrorist threat, political instability
Iran	Terror threat
Iraq	Terror threat, war, political instability, crime
Israel	Political instability, terror threat
Jamaica	Natural disaster (hurricanes)
Kenya	Terror threat
Lebanon	Terror threat, crime
Liberia	Crime, political unrest, ethnic disputes
Libya	Terror threat
Nepal	Political instability
Nigeria	Political instability, crime, ethnic disputes
Pakistan	Terror threat
Palestinian Territories	Political instability, terror threat
Saudi Arabia	Terror threat
Somalia	Ethnic disputes, crime, political instability
Sudan	Civil war, ethnic disputes, terror threat
Turks and Caicos	Natural disaster (hurricanes)
Yemen	Terror threat
Zimbabwe	Political instability, crime

Source: US Department of State, 2004.

Planning for threats to tourist security

Unfortunately, few businesses or governments have crisis management plans in place, creating emergency conditions that are more reactive than proactive (Green et al., 2003; Ritchie et al., 2003). Research shows that institutions and destinations with crisis plans are better able to re-establish their image, restore consumer confidence, and sustain a faster recovery (Sönmez, 1998). The key is to have a pre-emptive plan that will allow destinations and organizations to respond quickly, cope with the problems and control the damage (Ritchie et al., 2003).

Several scholars have suggested various survival strategies, or crisis management approaches/plans, to address security problems and catastrophes in tourist destinations (e.g. Faulkner, 2001; Beirman, 2003b; Ritchie et al., 2003). The most

Table 3.3 Current and Proposed Policy Changes in the USA after 9-11

- Fingerprinting incoming visitors
- Implementing biometric technologies (e.g. eye scans/DNA checks)
- High-tech passports that provide additional data on individuals
- Increased video surveillance in airports, high-rise hotels, harbours and convention centres
- Tracking and monitoring all foreign students in the USA
- Excluding some students from enrolling in university classes or enrolling part time
- Reinforcing cockpit doors
- Stationing more armed sky marshals on flights
- Tightening border controls and immigration procedures
- Increased funding for security-related government agencies
- Establishment of the Department of Homeland Security
- Loans for airlines and other travel industry suppliers
- Airport security forces added, including military presence
- Private security companies replaced by government employees
- Additional personal security checks
- New security equipment and detectors on ships, trains and buses
- Additional airline employee security training
- Military aircraft patrolling the skies over large cities
- Limiting the legal liability of the airlines in the case of terrorist attacks
- Compensation for the victims of terrorism
- Tax credits for tourism-related economic sectors
- Tax breaks to travellers and travel-related businesses

common elements in these approaches include information dissemination, marketing and publicity, public relations efforts and post-disaster analysis. Most tourism catastrophe management plans focus on information dissemination and counteracting the negative effects of the media. Media reports inevitably exaggerate problems, resulting in perceived risks associated with a destination prevailing over real conditions (Sönmez, 1998; Green et al., 2003; Floyd et al., 2003; Ritchie et al., 2003). Information dissemination, or balanced crisis communication, is an important part of the recovery process. It allows destinations to provide honest and accurate reports about what has occurred to counteract the damage often caused by media hype. The Internet plays a very important role in this exercise.

Similarly, aggressive marketing and other publicity efforts can help comfort potential tourists and promote image recovery. This often takes place in the form of product repositioning, special prices, familiarization tours for travel professionals and financial support, although one of the most successful measures often utilized is intense promotional campaigns aimed at mitigating negative images. For example, in response to the negative press Nepal has received in the global media, the National Tourism Board launched its 'Destination Nepal' campaign in 2002 to instil the image of Nepal as a safe, reliable and interesting destination (Thapa, 2003). After the outbreak of FMD, the British Tourist Authority (BTA) initiated the 'UK OK' and 'Only in Britain: Only in 2002' campaigns to inform the world that tourists were safe and the situation under control (Ritchie et al., 2003). According to Beirman (2003b), marketing efforts should be implemented during and after the event.

Public relations tactics are also important and should be implemented as soon as possible. These inform the public that business will go on as usual and that the destination is still a desirable place to visit (Pizam, 1999; Sönmez et al., 1999; Faulkner, 2001; Green et al., 2003; Ritchie et al., 2003).

Understanding the causes of the event, its impacts and how the responses were handled is an important part of evaluating the success of recovery efforts. This should be done after each crisis and evaluated to make improvements for future contingency plans.

As part of the recovery efforts, most advocates suggest that the crisis management plan should include pre-established, separate committees in charge of public relations, recovery marketing, information distribution, fund raising and post-incident analysis (Sönmez et al., 1999). During security duress these committees can spring into action, giving the recovery process a head start.

Conclusion: the future

What will the future bring for safety and security issues in tourism? There will no doubt continue to be tourism crises as long as tourism exists, but the ways in which travellers, the industry and governments respond to various security threats will likely undergo change. Travellers should expect to see intensified security measures being implemented in areas of high population density and in transportation centres. Decreased levels of personal privacy will likely result and highly sophisticated security implements, such as DNA-testing devices and face scanning equipment, will be employed (Goodrich, 2002).

There have always been crises and disasters. However, given the intensity of security threats during the past 15 years and because current forecasting methods are imperfect and, in many cases, entirely unable to predict most security threats (Prideaux et al., 2003), there will also likely be an increased awareness of the need for crisis and disaster management plans and contingency operation approaches. Places that have experienced major events in recent years (e.g. Egypt, Indonesia, Israel, Croatia, Mexico, Bosnia-Herzegovina, Fiji, UK, USA, China, etc.) will hopefully be more ready to address safety and security issues by establishing contingency plans that determine short- and long-term responses. With any luck, other destinations will learn from the experiences of their neighbours.

Hall et al. (2003) contend that the future will also bring a new security agenda in tourism that focuses more broadly on the causes of threats and a larger diversity of potential problems. Poverty, human rights, economics, social welfare, food, water, and the environment, for instance, must all be seen now as major threats to world security (Hall et al., 2003). It is not just the outward manifestation of these (e.g. terrorism, crime, etc.) that must be considered in understanding instability and security questions. Issues like bio-security, environmental security and economic security need to receive more attention by tourism scholars commensurate with the issues' importance.

It is clear that changes are occurring in the industry and among government ministries in charge of tourism. Hopefully, recent catastrophic events have created more prepared destinations and better informed tourists who know how to travel more safely and who are less inclined to believe everything they see and hear from media sources.

4

Crisis Management in Tourism

Tony S M Tse

Introduction

Tourism is traditionally associated with leisure and vacation, and tourists look for rejuvenation and relaxation in a holiday. Therefore, for a long time, the focus of tourism management has been how to enhance the experience of tourists, and tourism management has branched into different disciplines such as cruise management, theme park management, sustainable tourism, urban tourism, adventure tourism and attraction management, etc. There have been crises in history, such as war and terrorism, which interrupted the growth of tourism, but the study of crisis management in tourism began only recently.

The argument for using a crisis management plan as a management tool in the hospitality industry was first put forward by Barton (1994), just over ten years ago. Barton stressed the importance of anticipating crises and argued that a well-thought-out plan can help hotel management respond and control the damage to the organization's reputation, financial condition, market share and brand value. Everyone in the organization has a predetermined role to play in an anticipated crisis.

Sönmez et al. (1999) argued that tourist destinations should also incorporate crisis management planning into their overall sustainable development and marketing strategy to protect and rebuild their image of safety/attractiveness, to reassure potential visitors of the safety of the area and to aid local travel and tourism industry members in their economic recovery. Sönmez and Graefe (1998) studied terrorist attacks since 1993 and examined international tourist decisions made within the context of terrorism risk. Study results have demonstrated that factors that directly influence risky international decisions include attitude towards foreign travel, risk perception level and income. Leslie (1999) studied tourism in Northern Ireland and how the country suffered by hiding behind the veil of terrorism and argued for the need to consider the demand for tourism in the province and for the market share to be accorded to the main categories of tourists.

Faulkner (2001) put forward a comprehensive tourism disaster management framework and advocated the need for disaster contingency plans. The three prerequisites of effective tourism disaster management planning identified were: coordination, consultation and commitment.

In more recent years, studies in tourism crisis management were mostly prompted by and related to specific events. Stafford et al. (2001) examined the response of hotels in Washington, DC to the 11 September terrorist attack to illustrate how the local hospitality industry worked closely with other tourism partners to manage this unprecedented situation and to develop recovery strategies. Beirman (2003a) put together a comprehensive review of the impact of the following major crises on their respective countries: terrorist attack of 11 September in the USA; terrorist killings in Egypt; political violence in Israel; civil war in Sri Lanka; political coup in Fiji; earthquake in Turkey; foot-and-mouth disease in Britain; crime in South Africa; Port Arthur massacre in Australia; war in Croatia, and terrorism, natural disaster and political instability in the Philippines. Chien and Law (2003) provided an overview of the impact of severe acute respiratory syndrome (SARS) on the hotel industry in Hong Kong and why government should step in to support the industry.

In fact, it was not until the occurrence of a series of incidents, beginning with the terrorist attacks in New York and Washington, DC in September 2001, followed by the war in Afghanistan in 2002, the bombing of a night club in Bali in 2002, the bombing of J W Marriott in Jakarta in 2003 and the outbreak of severe acute respiratory syndrome (SARS) in Asia in 2003, that the tourism industries began to realize the ramifications and serious impact of a crisis on tourism. These events triggered a lot of concern among the tourism industries and governments. It is now well recognized that tourism management should not only examine the positive events, but also include the study of crisis: its impact on tourism businesses, how it can be prevented, how to contain the damage should it happen and how to ensure recovery as soon as possible.

Types of tourism crisis

A simple definition of tourism crisis by the World Tourism Organization is:

> … any unexpected event that affects traveller confidence in a destination and interferes with the ability to continue operating normally (Luhrman, 2003).

A more elaborate definition of tourism crisis is:

> ... any occurrence which can threaten the normal operations and conduct of tourism related businesses; damage a tourist destination's overall reputation for safety, attractiveness, and comfort by negatively affecting visitors' perceptions of that destination; and, in turn, cause downturn in the local travel and tourism economy, and interrupt the continuity of business operations for the local travel and tourism industry, by the reduction in tourist arrivals and expenditures (Sönmez et al., 1994).

There are four types of crisis which may affect tourism. They are crises related to (1) nature, (2) civil conflicts, (3) epidemics, or (4) technology failures.

1. *Disasters related to nature* include avalanche, flood, earthquake, bush fire, and hurricane, etc. Such natural disasters may lead to disruption to communication and transportation and even damage to infrastructure. Tourists could be stranded in the areas affected and it takes some time before the affected areas are cleared and tourist confidence and interest restored.
2. *Civil conflicts* can be confined within a country such as community unrest, demonstration, street violence and guerilla threat, etc., or they can be international in nature. The threat by Maoist activists in Nepal, for example, caused a tourism downturn in Nepal in 2003. Wars in Afghanistan and Iraq are examples of international conflict, which affect not just tourism in the countries at war, but neighbouring countries as well. Terrorist attack or the potential of terrorist attack is even worse because the threat is unspecific and lingering. Tourists normally do not take the risk of visiting countries in danger of terrorist attack.
3. *Epidemics* affecting tourism are rare because of the advances in medical science and effective control of the spread of diseases on a worldwide basis. The foot-and-mouth disease outbreak in the UK in 2001 caused a serious downturn in tourism, particularly rural tourism. The severe acute respiratory syndrome (SARS) dealt a severe blow to the tourism industry in Asia in 2003.
4. *Technology failures* are related to aircraft crashes, power blackouts and computer irregularity, etc. The fear of computer failure in the transition from 1999 to 2000 raised questions whether it was safe and desirable to travel away from home then. Huge investments were made to ensure computer systems were able to recognize the transition, and it turned out to be safe to travel during the transition.

A tourism crisis could be totally unexpected as in the case of a tourism downturn caused by a terrorist attack or epidemic. A tourism crisis could also be looming or threatening as in the case of war and social unrest. In either case, a tourism crisis tends to cause sudden disruption in tourism arrivals and spending. Decisions have to be made in a relatively short period of time to address the crisis. It is the time compression and the need to respond quickly which make crisis management different from other forms of management and difficult to handle.

Tourism risk versus tourism crisis

It is important to differentiate between the terms *tourism risk* and *tourism crisis*. A tourism organization may identify a potential risk based on experience and get prepared for it. Once the tourism risk has been identified and dealt with, the chance of something undesirable happening is reduced and, should something undesirable occur, the negative impact can be minimized. Therefore, most of the time, we are talking about risk management, i.e. addressing the potential crisis before it actually happens. Risk is expected and predictable.

However, a risk may materialize despite the best efforts to prevent it from happening. In most cases, the tourism industry has been caught unprepared by disastrous events. When something undesirable happens, the risk becomes a crisis and tourism arrivals and confidence can be negatively affected. Crisis management should then be activated to address the specific crisis. Theoretically speaking, if we can be better prepared for any risk identified, the chance of a risk turning into a crisis is minimized. Risk management refers to the planning before a crisis happens and crisis management refers to the actions after a crisis happens. However, risk management and crisis management are used interchangeably in much of the literature. The ultimate success of risk management is to avoid having to turn to crisis management altogether.

Risk management model

Zamecka and Buchanan (2000) designed a disaster risk management process, which is represented in Figure 4.1.

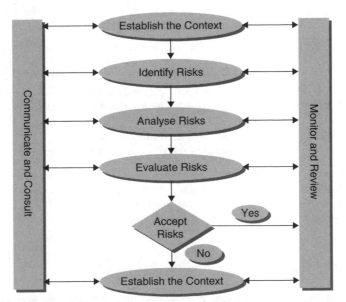

Figure 4.1 Disaster risk management process.
(Source: Zamecka and Buchanan, 2000)

Establish the context

The first step of the disaster risk management process is to identify the scope and nature of the issues that should be addressed to ensure safety and well-being. In the context of tourism, we should be clear as to what are the types of crisis we are trying to manage. Are we talking about risks related to nature, civil conflicts, epidemics or technology failures? A hotel within the tourism industry might be more concerned with fire and food poisoning as potential threats to its reputation and business. A destination might be more concerned with terrorist attack and natural disaster as potential threats to visitor arrivals and safety. In any case, the risk management begins with establishing the context.

Identify risks

The identification of risks begins with developing an understanding of the legislative, regulatory, political, social and physical environment. A close examination of the environment can reveal the potential risks associated with employee relationship, social disorder, attack and technology failure. Examination of historical records and case studies can also help identify risks. Identification of risks also includes the identification of clients and stakeholders. In the case of an epidemic outbreak, for example, the issue of visitor safety has to be considered in the context of community health, medical resources and communication with the World Health Organization.

Analyse risks

The identified risks are then examined in terms of likelihood and consequence and rated according to level of risk. The likelihood of the occurrence of a specific risk is categorized as *Almost certain, Likely, Possibly, Unlikely* or *Rare*. The consequence of the occurrence of a specific risk is categorized as *Insignificant, Minor, Moderate, Major* or *Catastrophic*. The matrix of likelihood and occurrence is constructed as a risk classification (Figure 4.2), with levels of risk classified into the following categories: *Extreme, High, Moderate, and Low*.

The four levels of risk identified in the risk classification are explained below:

(E) Extreme risk   Immediate action required
(H) High risk   Senior management attention needed
(M) Moderate risk   Management responsibility must be specified
(L) Low risk   Manage by routine procedure

Evaluate risks

After analysis, the risks should be assessed and classified as *Acceptable* or *Unacceptable*. Acceptable risks will need to be documented and revisited in the next cycle of the risk management process. Once unacceptable risks have been

Likelihood	Consequences				
	Insignificant	*Minor*	*Moderate*	*Major*	*Catastrophic*
Almost certain	H	H	E	E	E
Likely	M	H	H	E	E
Possibly	L	M	H	E	E
Unlikely	L	L	M	H	E
Rare	L	L	M	H	H

Figure 4.2 Risk classification.
(Source: Zamecka and Buchanan, 2000)

identified, they should be examined and categorized so that they are dealt with in priority order.

Treat risks

The last step of the disaster risk management process is to treat the unacceptable risks by developing operations in the areas of *Prevention*, *Preparedness*, *Response* and *Recovery*. The best thing that can happen in tourism crisis management is the prevention of a risk becoming a crisis altogether, thus preventing any damage to the tourism industries and the community.

Prevention consists of adopting structural and non-structural measures to prevent the crisis from happening. An example of a structural measure is the putting up of warning signs and barriers to prevent people from getting close to hazardous sites. An example of a non-structural measure is providing staff training to increase surveillance and security checks.

Preparedness refers to any contingency planning and public awareness campaign taken. An example of preparing for a crisis is a public education campaign to raise awareness of any potential disaster and advise on measures to be taken by concerned parties.

Response refers to the coordination of action in the case of crisis. The focus is on issuing warnings to the stakeholders and providing immediate relief to those affected. Communication with stakeholders is crucial at this stage. Stakeholders should be identified well beforehand to avoid time wasting in searching for contacts in the middle of a crisis. Stakeholders could include the government, owner, senior management, media, staff members, customers and families of the victims.

Recovery refers to the actions to be taken to return a community or business to normality. Judgement will have to made as to when normality could be resumed, taking into consideration the negative impact created and the possibility of another crisis occurrence. From a commercial point of view, business operation should be resumed as soon as possible. However, care should be taken in making the decision to resume advertising and promotion, as public emotion is likely to be sensitive immediately after a disaster.

Communicate and consult

Good communication is an essential feature of successful risk management activities. Good communication begins with communication within the risk management team. The team should receive adequate and the same information before and during a crisis, for the team members to make decisions quickly and consistently.

Communication and consultation with the senior management and government ensures that they are aware of the progress and support can be provided promptly if required.

Communication within an organization ensures that individual staff are kept informed of the 'big picture' and they can render help if appropriate and necessary.

Communication with clients is essential to minimize disruption to service and business and avoid any repercussion in the longer term.

Communication and consultation with the community helps people avoid risks and cope with crisis when it happens and also helps an organisation answer questions of responsibility.

Monitor and review

Risk management is a dynamic process. The physical environment and political situation may change and hence continual monitoring and review of the context is necessary. A risk considered low at one point in time might be considered high in the future due to a change in circumstances. New risks might surface as a result of new epidemics, latest political confrontation, or fresh travel patterns. New risk treatments might be available with advances in communication and technology. Continual monitoring and review of risk and its evaluation helps keep the risk management process up to date.

Expect the unexpected. Be prepared

Prompted by the effects of the terrorist blasts in Bali in October 2002, the Pacific Asia Travel Association (2003) put forward the 'Four Rs' of crisis management, representing four distinct phases in dealing with a crisis. The 'Four Rs' are a guide through the steps to prepare and protect an organization or destination. The 'Four Rs' are:

Reduction Detecting early warning signals
Readiness Preparing plans and running exercises
Response Executing operational and communication plans in a crisis situation
Recovery Returning the organization to normal after a crisis.

Reduction

The key to crisis management is to identify a potential crisis and then seek to reduce its impact. Managers need to perform a survey of their organization's internal strengths and weaknesses and external opportunities and threats (SWOT analysis). Based on the SWOT analysis they can evaluate the likely impact on the organization of a particular type of crisis, devise continuity and contingency plans and work out how to reduce the possibility of crisis.

Readiness

'Being ready' involves more than making plans and running an occasional drill. Organizations need to evaluate their crisis exposure and develop strategic, tactical and communication plans. Managers must regularly audit the plans, conduct crisis response exercises and continually acquire crisis management skills. Managers and staff need to be psychologically and physiologically prepared for the impact and stresses that crisis events may impose upon them. Readiness also nips potential crises in the bud.

Response

Response is dedicated to the immediate aftermath of an event when everything is at its most chaotic. It will become apparent very quickly whether the reduction and readiness phases have developed continuity and contingency plans that are effective. The emphasis of the initial operations will be on damage control for both lives and property. The crisis communication strategy should already be in play, pre-empting and reassuring stakeholders and the public.

Recovery

The best assessment of effective crisis management is if a crisis has been avoided. However, many crises are 'acts of the gods' – seemingly unavoidable. In this case, a crisis management system's effectiveness can be gauged in three ways:

1. The speed with which an organization resumes or continues full business operations
2. The degree to which business recovers to pre-crisis levels
3. The amount of crisis-resistance added since the crisis.

Contingency planning

The need for a contingency plan for each organization in the tourism industry cannot be stressed enough. The plan would help the management think and prepare before a risk becomes a crisis. Specifically, the contingency plan helps identify the following:

- signals of a crisis
- stakeholders: customers, staff, supplier, media, victims, owners, etc.

- crisis management team members and their contacts
- meeting venue for the crisis management team
- measures to prevent a crisis
- measures to reduce the impact should a crisis happen
- chain of command
- spokesperson
- need for making a public statement
- communication channels with the stakeholders
- training required
- relief measures for the victims
- additional financial and non-financial resources available
- signals of an end of a crisis, and
- recovery measures.

The UK government, after the outbreak of foot-and-mouth disease in 2001, had the Lessons Learnt Inquiry looking into the disaster. The inquiry report stressed the importance of contingency planning, the need to react with speed and certainty and the importance of clear and consistent communication with interested parties. The Department for Environment, Food & Rural Affairs (2004) put together a 163-page contingency plan which sets out the structure and systems that would be immediately implemented in an outbreak and describes the capability that would enable the speedy provision of resources to bring into operation the government's control policies.

Another aspect of contingency planning is communication with the media. Nowadays, the general public expect transparency and therefore the media demand immediate information and explanation in case of a disaster outbreak. The media sometimes play the role of investigator and pre-judge a case and their influence should not be underestimated. It is therefore important to keep the media fully informed of a crisis, so that they can provide accurate reporting of the incident. The media should be provided with the facts as timely as possible and it is not advisable to provide speculation of any sort. Facts and figures can help the media put things in perspective and avoid an incident being blown out of proportion. It is desirable for an organization to accept responsibility once the facts are established, show sympathy and care for the victims and their families and promise what actions will be taken.

The communication associated with the crash of Singapore Airlines flight SQ006 in 2000 in Taipei, Taiwan, killing 82 people and injuring another 81, demonstrated very well the importance of handling such a crisis with speed and dealing sympathetically with the victims. Henderson (2003) reported in her analysis of the tragedy that:

> Special attention has been given to communications strategies adopted
> in the event and intermediate periods, with some reference to longer
> term actions. The company is shown to have moved from avoiding
> questions of responsibility to accepting responsibility, making amends
> and offering reassurance, before looking ahead. These strategies required
> communications with many interested parties through provision of news to
> the media and individuals affected, demonstrations of concern for survivors
> and relatives, and a display of confidence and belief in the future.

Case study 4.1 Severe Acute Respiratory Syndrome (SARS)

The World Health Organization (WHO) imposed a travel advisory against non-essential travel to Hong Kong and parts of China from April to June 2003, because of the then unknown lethal virus causing SARS. Visitor arrivals in Hong Kong dropped by 57.9 per cent in the three months, compared to the same period the year before, and the hotel industry suffered an unprecedented low occupancy of 17 per cent in May (Hong Kong Tourism Board, 2003). The epidemic crippled tourism not just in Hong Kong, but mainland China, Taiwan, Singapore, Vietnam, Thailand and most Asian countries. The following are what the countries have learnt in terms of the 'Four Rs': reduction, readiness, response and recovery:

Reduction: After SARS, most countries in Asia put up measures to detect the possible outbreak, both at the border and within the community. In many airports, visitors are required to complete a health declaration form to indicate if the visitor has symptoms associated with SARS on arrival. Some airports install infra-red facilities to measure the temperature of arriving visitors to detect any possible SARS carrier entering a destination.

Readiness: After SARS, the hygiene level and community hygiene awareness in many Asian cities are much higher than before. Should there be a SARS outbreak again, hotels know exactly how to control cost by adopting more flexible staff deployment, reducing operational outlay by suspending less crucial services such as recreational facilities and overnight room service. Most hotels would have a crisis management team and crisis management plan in place.

Response: Hotels now know when to issue a hygiene checklist and step up hygiene standards during crises similar to SARS. Communication with customers is crucial. Hotels would put letters in guest rooms to provide information regarding the SARS situation and advise guests of all the precaution measures taken by the hotel.

Recovery: The tourism industries in Hong Kong suffered heavy losses during the SARS outbreak in 2003. The hotel industry alone lost US$250 million of business. The Hong Kong Tourism Board worked with the industry to help make up for the loss in business during SARS. The Board got an additional budget of US$20 million in 2003 to market Hong Kong. They staged the first major event *'Hong Kong Welcomes You'* in July, followed by a daily outdoor evening show *Strato-Fantasia* to add colour to the city in August and a *Super Draw* to stimulate spending in September. Pacific Asia Travel Association undertook a recovery campaign called Project Phoenix on television and in print media to promote the back-to-normal situation in Asia with the support of many destinations, hotel chains and regional media, when SARS was under control in Asia in August 2003 (Jong, 2004). With the collective efforts of the industries, visitor arrivals and hotel room occupancy were restored to pre-SARS level in August. The case clearly demonstrated the importance of the tourism industries working together to ensure speedy recovery after a crisis.

Lettenblicher (2004), Chairman of the Hong Kong Hotels Association, summarized the lessons learnt in the SARS saga as follows: 'This crisis brought unification to our entire community. It transpired a level playing field for all. Within the hotel and tourism industries in Hong Kong, we certainly came together for countless hours of meetings, strategizing and contingency planning. This crisis sparked a need – a need for concern, a need for safety and a need to be involved, from Government, Tourism Commission, Hong Kong Tourism Board, airlines, Travel Industry Council, Chambers of Commerce, Consular Corp, the business community and of course, Hong Kong Hotels Association became united like never before. It brought us greater synergies, stronger relationships and a better understanding between us.'

Conclusion

Crisis management in tourism is a subject of conflict, contradiction and dissonance. On the one hand, tourism promotes visa-free travel and more extensive airline access, but on the other hand, crisis management advocates security measures and tighter scrutiny. While nature-based and cultural tourism is being promoted, we are also concerned about the sustainability of natural resources and heritage as a result of such development. Tourists certainly want their holiday and travel to be worry-free, but it is good crisis management to issue warnings and remind travellers of necessary precautions related to their activities, reminding them of possible dangers.

There is nothing sure about crises – except that there will be another one. The only certain way of handling the next tourism crisis is by working together and supporting each other. The level of interest in getting prepared is usually very high right after a crisis and then the enthusiasm slowly fades away and gets overwhelmed by other more pressing issues. The tourism industries should try to harness the goodwill and sensitivity after a crisis to become better prepared. The chapter provides a framework for tourism organizations to develop their own crisis management plan. If there is anything positive about a crisis, it is the willingness of the industries to work together afterwards.

5

Climate Change and its Implications for International Tourism

David Viner and Sarah Nicholls

Introduction

Despite the highly intuitive nature of the relationship between tourism activity and the typical climatic conditions of both origin and destination regions, this area has received relatively little consideration by either tourism practitioners or researchers. This absence of activity has been attributed in part to a historical lack of communication between climatologists and meteorologists on the one hand, and leisure specialists on the other (Smith, 1993). In addition, the large number and complex interactions between the many influences on tourism, from economic and political conditions, to fashion and media attention, complicate the identification and measurement of the exact effect of any one.

Nevertheless, it can safely be said that tourism development has long been concentrated in environments that offer specific climatic conditions. The Mediterranean region has been attracting Northern Europeans looking for the traditional, sun, sea and sand-based summer holiday for well over a century.

Similarly, the long-standing popularity of skiing holidays in resorts in the European Alps and the US Rockies has been based to a large extent on the predictability and abundance of their annual natural snowfall.

Given the increasing amount of evidence regarding global warming and climate change, however, and the potential impacts of such change on many forms of tourism, whether winter or summer, and based on land or sea, the topic of climate–tourism interactions warrants immediate and substantial consideration by both researchers and the industry.

Climate and climate change

The Intergovernmental Panel on Climate Change (IPCC) was formed in 1988 by the World Meteorological Organization (WMO) and the United Nations Environment Programme (UNEP) in order to assess climate change and its potential impacts. According to the IPCC (2001), the average surface temperature across the globe has increased by approximately 0.6°C ± 0.2°C since 1861. Records suggest that the majority of this warming occurred during two periods, 1910–1945 and 1976–2000, that the 1990s was the warmest decade and 1998 the warmest year since these records began (Figure 5.1). In the course of the twentieth century, global average sea level has risen between 10 and 20 cm and noticeable reductions have occurred in both snow cover and ice extent.

While estimates vary widely depending upon the modelling procedures used, climate change scenarios suggest that the global average surface temperature will increase by between 1.4 and 5.8°C between 1990 and 2100. Projections regarding global mean sea level indicate a rise of between 9 and 88 cm over the same period (Figure 5.2). An increase in the frequency and intensity of extreme weather events (floods, droughts, heatwaves, etc.) is also expected (IPCC, 2001).

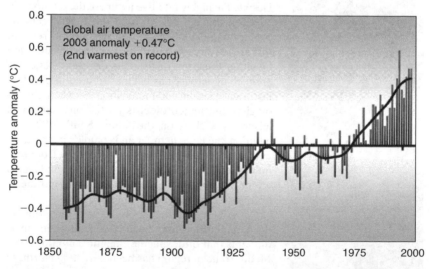

Figure 5.1 Observed global air temperature (1856–2003), deviation from mean (1961–1990). (Source: Jones et al., 1999; Jones and Moberg, 2003)

Causes of climate change

The world's changing climate is a result of both natural and anthropogenic factors. A stable climate requires a balance between incoming solar radiation and outgoing radiation. Fundamental to this stable state is the natural greenhouse effect, the process whereby greenhouse gases such as carbon dioxide, methane and nitrous oxide absorb and emit infrared radiation, trapping heat within the atmosphere and maintaining a suitable temperature for human habitation. Natural variations in climate have historically been associated with a number of factors, including variations in solar output, changes in the orbital characteristics of the Earth and volcanic eruptions, the ash and sulphur dioxide emissions from which alter the reception and reflection patterns of solar radiation.

In recent decades, however, increasing attention has focused on human-induced climate change. The principal cause of anthropogenic climate change has been the rising concentration of greenhouse gases and aerosols in the atmosphere resulting from various human activities carried out in increasing intensity since the beginning of the Industrial Revolution. Table 5.1 illustrates the rises in the concentration levels of the major greenhouse gases since 1750, as well as their major sources.

Table 5.2 outlines the changes predicted in temperature, precipitation and other key climatic and environmental variables at both global and regional scales for the next 50–100 years.

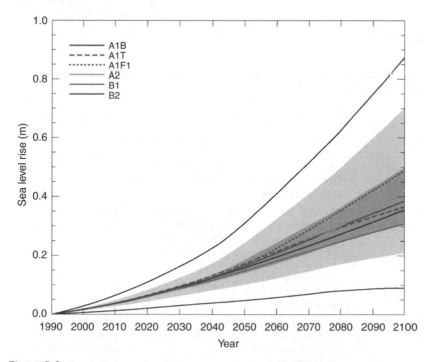

Figure 5.2 Projected sea level rise, 1990–2100, under various climate change scenarios. Note: the four main scenario storylines – A1, A2, B1, B2 – are discussed on p. 44. (Source: IPCC, 2001)

Table 5.1 Greenhouse gas concentrations and sources

Gas	Increase in atmospheric concentration since 1750	Major sources
Carbon dioxide (CO_2)	31%	Three-quarters of anthropogenic emissions in last 20 years due to burning of fossil fuels; remainder due mainly to land use change, e.g. deforestation
Methane (CH_4)	151%	Just over 50% of CH_4 emissions are human-induced, primarily from the use of fossil fuels, the raising of cattle, the cultivation of rice and landfills
Nitrous oxide (N_2O)	17%	Approximately 1/3 of N_2O emissions are human-induced, primarily from agricultural fertilizers, cattle feed lots and the chemical industry
Ozone (O_3)	36%	Ozone is not emitted directly into the air; rather, it forms when heat and sunlight interact with nitrogen oxides and volatile organic compounds

Source: IPCC, 2001.

Table 5.2 Summary of projected changes in temperature, rainfall and key environmental variables (1990–2100)

	Temperature	Rainfall (precipitation)	Other key variables
Global	0.2–0.6°C rise in temperature per decade Decrease in diurnal temperature range	Increase in rainfall by 3–10% by 2050 Increase in droughts over continental areas	4–10 cm increase in sea-level per decade
Northern Europe	0.4–0.8°C rise in temperature per decade Increase in winter and summer temperatures Decrease in frost days	Increase in amount and intensity of winter rainfall Decrease in summer rainfall	Summers become 'better' and appear 'more reliable'
European Alps	Increase in winter temperatures Snowline increases in altitude by up to 100 m per decade	Increase in winter snowfall	Increased risk of avalanches due to combination of higher temperatures and increase in snow

(Continued)

Table 5.2 (*Continued*)

	Temperature	Rainfall (precipitation)	Other key variables
Mediterranean basin	0.3–0.7°C rise in temperature per decade Increase in heat index Increase in number of days over 40°C	Decrease in summer rainfall (−15%) Increase in desertification Increase in winter rainfall Increase in runoff and erosion	Increased risk of forest fires Increased risk of flash floods Water resource pressures Coastal areas and infra-structure vulnerable to sea level rise
Middle East/ North Africa	0.3–0.7°C rise in temperature per decade Increase in number of very hot days	Slight decrease in annual rainfall Rainfall and convective activity become more intense	Increased pressure on water resources Increase in flash floods and erosion Sea level rise threatens beaches Increased sea surface temperatures
Sub-Saharan Africa	0.3–0.7°C rise in temperature per decade	10–15% increase in winter rainfall	Wetter, warmer winters Drier, more intensely hot summers
North America	0.3–0.7°C rise in temperature per decade	Slight increase in annual rainfall Rainfall and convective activity become more intense	Increased rainfall and hurricane activity over Pacific states associated with El Niño events
Caribbean	0.2–0.6°C rise in temperature per decade	Slight increase in annual rainfall Rainfall and convective activity become more intense	Increased rainfall and hurricane activity associated with La Niña events
Central/South America	0.2–0.6°C rise in temperature per decade	Decrease in annual rainfall (−3%)	Decrease in hurricane activity associated with El Niño events
North East Asia	0.4–0.8°C rise in temperature Increase in winter and Summer temperatures Decrease in frost days	Increase in amount and intensity of winter rainfall Decrease in summer rainfall	Summers become 'better' and appear more 'reliable'
South Asia	0.1–0.5°C rise in temperature per decade	Little change in rainfall	Coastal areas vulnerable to erosion
Far East/ Pacific	0.1–0.5°C rise in temperature per decade	Little change in rainfall	Small island states and coastal areas vulnerable to sea-level rise

Climate change scenarios

The future of the planet as a result of continued climate change can be assessed using scenarios. Scenarios are descriptions of alternative world futures that reflect various combinations of future demographic, socioeconomic, techno-logical and environmental change. Different scenarios therefore suggest different futures for greenhouse gas emissions and, hence, climate change. Since the future is inherently uncertain, scenarios cannot predict; rather, they paint pictures of possible future situations and allow the exploration of the potential outcomes of each.

The IPCC has developed a series of 40 emissions scenarios based on four major families of storylines or narratives about future world development (IPCC, 2000). These four major families of scenario are labelled A1, A2, B1 and B2 and they contain 17, 6, 9 and 8 scenarios, respectively.

Under the A1 storyline, the world experiences rapid economic growth, a global population that peaks in the mid-twenty-first century and the introduction of new, more efficient technologies. A key theme of this scenario family is significant reductions in income disparities across regions. The A1 family is subdivided into three groups based on alternative sources of energy, namely A1FI (fossil inten-sive), A1T (non-fossil) and A1B (a balance of sources).

According to the A2 storyline, economic growth and technological change are slower than in other sets of scenarios. The A2 world is heterogeneous, with an emphasis on regional differentiation and the preservation of local identity. Global population continues to increase. The B1 storyline is somewhat similar to A1 in terms of a global population that peaks mid-century and then falls into decline; however, it suggests a much more equitable world dominated by a service-based, information economy and cleaner, resource-efficient technology.

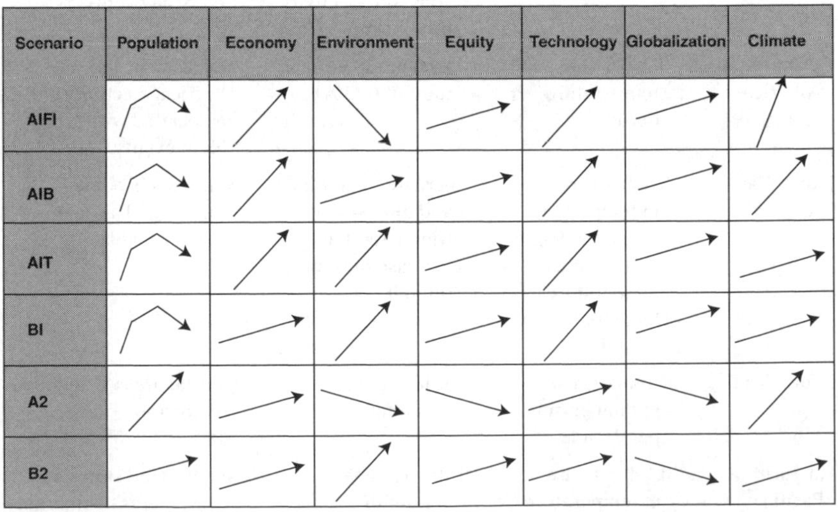

Figure 5.3 Qualitative description of IPCC SRES scenarios.

The B2 storyline also suggests improvements in environmental protection and social equity, but at a local and regional, rather than global level. In the B2 future, the world's population continues to increase, though at a rate lower than in A2, while economic development and technological change occur less rapidly than in the B1 and A1 scenarios.

Figure 5.3 demonstrates the direction of impact of each of the six major groups of scenario (A1FI, A1B, A1T, B1, A2, B2) on population, economy, environment, equity, technology, globalization and climate. It is important to emphasize that there is no single, 'most likely' future and that statistical probabilities can be assigned neither to families of, nor individual, scenarios.

Climate change and tourism

The relationship between climate change and tourism is bidirectional, in that tourism activity is both impacted by, as well as being a major contributor to, this phenomenon.

Implications of climate change for tourism

Climate change may have important consequences for tourism activity in what are currently the dominant origin and destination areas in the world. By far the largest, climate-induced flow of tourists is the mass movement from the colder, northern regions of Europe southwards to countries bordering the northern coast of the Mediterranean – the annual search for summer sun. In 2000, this flow accounted for 116 million arrivals, approximately one sixth of all international trips globally. Other flows that tend to be dominated by tourists in search of warmer climes include the 8 million North Americans and 4 million Europeans who visited the Caribbean in 2000.

Table 5.3 indicates the types and extents of climate change likely to occur over the next 100 years in Northern and Southern Europe, North America, South East Asia and the Caribbean. As it shows, climate change will likely create both winners and losers in the tourism industry. In Northern Europe, for example, summer conditions are likely to become not only more pleasant, but also more reliable, which may lead to a reduction in the traditional summer exodus to the Mediterranean and a con-comitant increase in regional and domestic summer travel. Giles and Perry (1998) have demonstrated the potential impacts of climate change on the British tourism industry, using the summer of 1995 as a temporal analogue for future conditions. Southern Europe, however, is likely to become too hot for human comfort in the summer months, but any losses may well be offset by increases in travel in the current shoulder seasons. Case study 5.1 describes likely changes in southern Spain.

One sector which is likely to suffer under projected climate conditions is the winter tourism market. Research in Canada (Scott et al., 2003), Scotland (Harrison et al., 1999) and the European Alps (Elsasser and Messerli, 2001) suggests that the ski industries in these regions should expect reductions in natural snowfall and a substantial shortening of season length, even with improved snow-making capabilities. Climate change may also have especially negative impacts on small islands and other low-lying areas, including loss of land, increased storm

Table 5.3 Summary of climate changes and their anticipated impacts on major tourism regions over the next 50–100 years

Region	Projected climate changes	Environmental implications	Potential impacts on tourism activity
Northern Europe	Much warmer, wetter winters Warmer, drier summers More 'reliable' summers	Potential stress on ecosystems sensitive to warming Damage to some ecosystems as a result of increased tourism activity	Improvement of Northern European summers triggers more domestic holidays Warmer, more reliable summers also provide increased incentive for southern Europeans to travel to northern Europe
Mediterranean/ Southern Europe	Warmer, wetter winters Much warmer, drier summers Eastern region sees especially sharp changes Increased heat index More days above 40°C More arid landscape Small tidal range means greater impact of sea level rise	Greater risk of drought and fire Rise in water shortages Greater personal heat stress Beach degradation and habitat loss due to sea level rise Increased vulnerability to tropical disease (e.g. malaria) More flash floods Reduced air quality in cities	Reduction in traditional Mediterranean summer holidays due to excessive heat, but increase in visits in current shoulder seasons Increased incentive for southern Europeans to travel to northern Europe
North America	Warmer winters Warmer summers Rise in heat index Slight rainfall increases	SE USA at greater risk from storms and beach erosion Sea level rise damages Florida coast and Everglades Risk of coastal erosion and storm damage on east coast Pacific coast at greater storm risk with higher rainfall and risk of coastal damage Risk of tropical disease rises	Florida may become less attractive Carolina coast may become more attractive Cities in Canada and along Eastern coast may become too hot to visit in summer, but general, sightseeing travel unlikely to be greatly affected Potential for stronger winter ski market due to reduced capacity in Europe, subject to suitable conditions in USA

(Continued)

Table 5.3 (*Continued*)

Region	Projected climate changes	Environmental implications	Potential impacts on tourism activity
South East Asia	Little change in rainfall Relatively little change in temperatures	No dramatic climatic changes foreseen Islands and coastal areas vulnerable to sea level rise Coral bleaching	Limited influence on travel patterns, though decline in dive and beach markets possible
Caribbean	Warmer winters Warmer summers Small decrease in rainfall	Particularly vulnerable to sea level rise Increased beach erosion Coral bleaching and damage to reef Salinization of aquifers Higher energy costs for air conditioning Greater need for sea defences and flood control More tropical disease	Beach product offering becomes less attractive due to increased heat index, beach erosion, sea and coral quality and decreased need/desire to escape northern climate Loss of confidence in destination due to increasing health risks

surge damage and saltwater intrusion into fresh groundwater aquifers. Though such locations do not dominate international tourism flows, tourism does frequently constitute a large proportion of the economic activity of such destinations. Case study 5.2 discusses the potential impacts of climate change for the Maldives.

Case study 5.1 Southern Spain

Southern Spain currently experiences a Mediterranean climate, with mild winters and warm, dry summers. Models of climate change indicate temperature increases for the area, but no significant changes in rainfall, such that summer months will remain dry but become warmer.

Travel and tourism employs approximately 25 per cent of the work force in Spain (approximately 3.3 million people) and in 1999 accounted for almost 23 per cent of GNP. South-eastern Spain is one of the major destinations for tourists from the UK as well as other European countries.

The summer of 2003 was characterized by very high temperatures. The figures below compare mean monthly temperatures as recorded at Valencia for 2003 with the long-term (1961–90) average (in °C). The summer months (June, July and August) recorded a seasonal temperature anomaly of 3.7°C compared to the long-term average. While this anomaly might appear relatively small it was the highest ever recorded, with the departure of maximum temperatures from the normal being even more pronounced.

	Jan	Feb	Mar	Apr	May	Jun	Jul	Aug	Sep	Oct	Nov	Dec
1961–90	10.2	11.2	12.8	14.7	17.9	21.7	24.7	24.9	22.6	18.2	13.5	10.5
2003	12.3	11.4	14.2	16.6	19.6	26.4	27.8	28.1	23.8	19.5	16.1	13.0

Impacts of climate change in this region are likely to include flash floods, an increased incidence of forest fires and heat stress following periods of extreme temperature. Forest fires already constitute a serious problem within the Mediterranean basin and are precipitated by hot, dry and windy conditions, when fires spread most rapidly. Furthermore, malaria has recently resurfaced in Spain and it is estimated that climate warming will result in this region becoming a more suitable habitat for certain species of mosquito by the 2050s.

Case study 5.2 The Maldives, Indian Ocean

The Maldives are located in the Indian Ocean, to the south-west of the Indian sub-continent. They consist of an archipelago of 26 coral atolls and their land area of less than $300\,km^2$ supports a human population of approximately 340 000. Many of the 1190 islands are less than one metre above sea level. During the 1980s, tourism became one of the fastest growing economic sectors and tourism is now one of the mainstays of the Maldives' economy.

The low elevation of the Maldives archipelago makes them particularly vulnerable to sea-level rise. As the oceans heat up they expand; moreover, warming temperatures also cause glaciers and ice caps to start to melt. Global mean sea level is projected to rise by between 0.09 and 0.88 metres between 1990 and 2100. At best, a rise in sea level in the Maldives would cause extensive coastal erosion, at worst, a sizeable proportion of the landmass could become submerged within the next 30 years.

In addition, coral bleaching (damage to or death of coral due to the loss of pigmented zooxanthellae from the polyps) could be induced by a warming of only 1 or 2°C. The 1997/1998 sea surface temperatures were the warmest in the observed record. The coral bleaching associated with this event impacted almost all species of corals and had a devastating effect on reefs in the Maldives. The combination of land loss and reef damage likely under warmer conditions could have severe negative impacts on the Maldives' tourism industry.

Source: Agnew and Viner, 2001

Impacts of tourism on climate change

It has been estimated that tourism activity may be responsible for 5.3 per cent of global CO_2 emissions (Gössling, 2002). This is a small but significant proportion given the World Tourism Organization's prediction that international arrivals will exceed 1.56 billion by the year 2020 (WTO, 2004). By far the largest tourism-related contributor to global warming is the transportation sector, accounting for 94 per cent of CO_2 emissions according to Gössling (compared to 4 per cent for accommodation, e.g. air conditioning and 2 per cent for activities, e.g. artificial snow-making). Of the various modes of transport typically used by tourists, air travel is the most polluting and it is estimated responsible for close to 40 per cent of all leisure travel emissions. It is important to note that the Kyoto Protocol, which sets legally binding targets for greenhouse gas emissions reductions for all countries that have ratified it (the United States and Australia being notable exceptions), does not cover aviation fuels.

Adaptation and mitigation

Adaptation to climate change implies the making of alterations in human and/or natural systems, whether in response to actual or anticipated adjustments in climatic conditions, so as to cope better with those changes. Adaptation can be proactive or reactive and occur in the private (individual or commercial) or the public (governmental) realm. Tourism-related adaptation to climate change is likely to involve changes in both the temporal and the spatial distribution of tourism patterns, with various shifts in both the location of destinations and the activities typically engaged in at tourism sites. At the site level, adaptation might take the form of various infrastructural alterations in architectural design, for example, exterior landscaping, water supply and conservation and energy efficiency. Successful adaptation will require a shift in the short-term planning horizon typical of most tourism providers, however. As shown by Byers and Slack (2001), small tourism businesses tend to engage primarily in adaptive decision-making, made in response to environmental contingencies or circumstances that have already occurred, rather than making long-term or strategically-oriented decisions.

Mitigation as it relates to climate change refers to the reduction of greenhouse gas emissions and/or the enhancement of greenhouse gas sinks, elements such as oceans and vegetation that absorb greenhouse gases, thereby removing them from the atmosphere. Probably the most relevant mitigation strategy for tourism is the reduction of emissions from the various modes of transportation this industry relies upon, whether through the adoption of more fuel-efficient technologies, fuel substitution, a carbon tax, e.g. a kerosene tax in the aviation sector, or voluntary reductions. Becken (2004) provides an examination of tourists' and tourism experts' perceptions of climate change and the use of forest carbon sinks as a means of offsetting CO_2 emissions.

An agenda for future research

Given the range and magnitude of potential impacts of climate change on tourism, and vice versa, the need to raise the profile of this issue among tourism stakeholders, whether in the industry or the academic community, is high. As identified at the European Science Foundation Exploratory Workshop on Climate Change, the Environment and Tourism, held in Milan, in 2003 (Viner and Amelung, 2003), key activities include the need to:

- Identify baseline conditions and relationships – analysis of the impacts of climate change on tourism first requires a far better understanding of historical and current relationships. Many important interrelationships between climate, the environment and tourism remain unclear
- Develop a database of indicators – a database of indicators of the impacts of climate change on tourism would help inform and advise tourism stakeholders
- Conduct more impact assessments – the number of studies that have identified and quantified the possible impacts of climate change on the tourism industry remains limited; analyses of tourists' perceptions of this issue are even more rare, yet their opinions and likely reactions to climate change are a vital element of the response; and
- Encourage increased communication and cooperation between all relevant individuals and organizations – this includes researchers (in both the physical and social sciences); tourism providers (from the largest multinationals that rely heavily on air transportation to the many small-scale, family-owned enterprises); public agencies at the local, national and international level; residents of tourism destinations; and tourists.

Conclusions

Projected climate change, including the shifts in temperature, precipitation and the frequency and severity of extreme weather events outlined above, is likely to create both winners and losers in the tourism industry. Alterations in the distribution of appropriate climatic conditions and, hence, tourists, may occur in both time and space, with significant implications for the provision of tourism infrastructure and services. There are many ways in which the tourism industry might adapt to such climatic changes. Further, the industry can help mitigate climate change, most notably through the reduction of greenhouse gas emissions. Both types of strategy will be vital to the long-term sustainability of tourism should warming continue as projected.

6

Monitoring as an Approach to Sustainable Tourism

Graham Miller and
Louise Twining-Ward

Introduction: monitoring for sustainability

Monitoring involves regularly assessing the state of an issue or phenomenon relative to particular goals, expectations and objectives. Simply the process of finding out what is to be measured can be instructive, as are the collective gathering of information, interpretation of results and the satisfaction of seeing these converted into positive action. Indicators can help a community, business, country or NGO (non-governmental organization) establish their sustainability objectives, define what they mean by sustainability, establish what progress they are making and prioritize areas for further work. In short, having a monitoring system in place can help transform sustainable tourism from a fuzzy concept to a clear set of measurable objectives against which progress is assessed, information is generated, knowledge enhanced and positive action taken to assist in a transition towards more sustainable tourism.

Nevertheless, monitoring such a multifarious concept as sustainable tourism also carries its share of risks, complications and challenges. It can be costly and time consuming to develop indicators and devise a monitoring system. It requires a degree of technical expertise and long-term commitment to monitor and report on indicators on a regular basis. Monitoring can also lead to 'targetitis', misplaced confidence in quantitative data and there is a risk important issues may be overlooked in favour of those that are most visible.

This chapter provides a brief account of the background to monitoring sustainability before examining the reasons why it may be advantageous for both public and private sector tourism bodies to establish monitoring programmes. Current techniques and practices are then reviewed together with case studies from recent sustainable tourism monitoring projects at international, regional and sector level. Lessons learned from this work are used as a basis from which to discuss future challenges facing tourism in general and monitoring in particular.

Historical background of monitoring

Monitoring is not a new invention. History suggests that the selection of indicators reflects the thinking of the time. The Romans conducted census surveys to assist in the accurate collection of taxes and the USA measured national income as an indicator of wealth and well-being in the 1920s. Despite the success of economic indicators in capturing and relaying key information to decision-makers and the general public, however, their deficiencies were also apparent. Henderson (in Hart, 1999, p.39) explains, '… trying to run a complex society on a single indicator like the GNP is … like trying to fly a 747 with only one gauge on the instrument panel'. During the mid-1960s to late 1970s there was a boom in social measurement, but it was not until the late 1980s, when the sustainable development movement effectively tied environmental conservation with poverty alleviation and economic welfare, that monitoring quality of life involved a more comprehensive set of instruments.

Since the Rio Earth Summit, many organizations, led by those associated with the United Nations, have begun to develop indicators as tools for monitoring progress made towards the broad goals of sustainable development. Agenda 21, the most important document to emerge from Rio, places considerable emphasis on the need to monitor sustainable development using indicators. Chapter 40, for example, notes that indicators can provide a solid base for decision-making at all levels. The UNCSD followed up on this interest in monitoring and approved a work programme on indicators of sustainable development, which came to fruition in 1996 with the publication of the UN's *Indicators of Sustainable Development Framework and Methodologies*.

As a result of this increased importance, many public and private sector bodies are looking to establish their own monitoring systems. Governments, as well as citizens, like to see the results of their efforts and indicators can act as a means of encouragement when times are tough, or to reveal the size and immediacy of a problem when change is needed. Indicators thus become evidence of professionalism and transparency. Following moves to strengthen trust and enable dialogue between stakeholders, another benefit of monitoring is the ability to bring stakeholders around the discussion table, identifying priority issues and highlighting ways to manage these – a solid and underlying principle of sustainable tourism.

NGOs have also shown an increasing interest in monitoring sustainable tourism. Organizations such as UKCEED have conducted assessments of the impacts of tourism in all-inclusive resorts on behalf of, and in conjunction with, British Airways Holidays. In this case, the monitoring is providing information to the company, creating awareness of the problems and enabling action to take place to ameliorate the problem. As well as NGOs, local communities and residents also stand to benefit from tourism monitoring if operational, structural and cultural difficulties can be overcome. With information comes empowerment; the process of indicator development enables a greater understanding of what is important and what needs to be sustained. The ability to measure and the knowledge of what to measure will reduce the reliance on outside 'experts', in terms of both finances and skills.

Current practices for sustainable tourism monitoring

Despite the new-found demand for sustainable tourism monitoring, there are as yet few examples of monitoring in practice. The tourism industry is no newcomer to monitoring, having measured its performance for many years using conventional tourism indicators such as arrival numbers, length of stay and tourist expenditure. However, the shift from using conventional indicators to indicators of sustainable tourism is a recent one. It was only in the second half of the 1990s that an increasing number of tourism researchers began to voice the need for the development of more comprehensive sustainable tourism indicators that make the important connection between tourism and the wider economic, environmental and social processes in the destination (Mowforth and Munt, 1998; Weaver, 1998; Swarbrooke, 1999; Sirakaya et al., 2001).

Early sustainable tourism indicator studies tended to be theoretical and focus on the impact assessment, e.g. Craik (1995). The University of Waterloo Heritage Resources Centre held a seminar on monitoring, planning and managing tourism and sustainable development in 1991 (Nelson et al., 1993). Few authors got as far as identifying possible indicators or indicator development processes and those that did were inward looking, heavily focused on economic issues and little different from conventional tourism indicators.

Over the last few years several publications have discussed the technicalities of indicator development notably Sirakaya et al. (1999), Miller (2001) and WTO (2004), but most authors adopt a parochial approach to indicators, focusing narrowly on the tourism industry and the resources on which it depends. Nevertheless, the World Tourism Organization has perhaps done more than any other body to advance the study of sustainable tourism indicators. From a rather narrow impact measurement approach adopted in initial studies of the Tourism and the Environment Committee, the latest addition to their work, *Indicators of Sustainable Development for Tourism Destinations – A Guidebook*, is much more comprehensive.

Case study 6.1 WTO Indicators for the Sustainable Management of Tourism

The World Tourism Organization (WTO) was one of the first international level organizations to develop and use indicators as an instrument to monitor and measure sustainable tourism. Since 1993 the organization has worked on numerous monitoring projects in different parts of the world. The results and evolution of the WTO indicator approach are to be found in three principal publications: 1993, 1996 and 2004.

The 1993 publication, entitled *Indicators for the Sustainable Management of Tourism*, focused primarily on indicators that would measure the impact of tourism on the natural and cultural environment. The potential indicators were divided into those intended for national use and those for local or 'hot-spot' application and then tested for usefulness in five locations worldwide. The better-known 1996 publication, *What Tourism Managers Need to Know*, is written for tourism industry decision-makers in order to assist them work towards enhanced sustainability. It identifies a set of 12 core indicators, suggests different destination-specific indicators and provides the results of the pilot studies. WTO's most recent work, *Signposts for Sustainable Tourism*, is much more extensive, produced with the input of more than 60 experts working on sustainable tourism in 20 countries. It details the process, practice and implementation of indicators with numerous practical examples as well as a practical step-by-step field guide for developing sustainable tourism indicators.

Although the WTO has done much to refine the process of indicator development, it still treats the economy, environment and society as large independent entities, expects variables from one place to suit another place, remains reliant on top-down expert input and focuses on the development rather than the use of indicators and how to maintain a monitoring system over time.

At a regional level the Tourism Optimization Management Model (TOMM) is an example of a sustainable tourism monitoring programme that addresses some of these shortfalls.

Case study 6.2 Tourism Optimization Management Model (TOMM) and Samoa Sustainable Tourism Indicator Programme

Developed in close consultation with community groups, local government and tourism businesses on Kangaroo Island, South Australia, the TOMM adopts a place-based, collaborative approach to monitoring which sees indicators as a tool to assist in the management of the area (Manidis Roberts Consultants, 1997).

TOMM involves envisioning optimal and sustainable outcomes for tourism and the community, from which acceptable ranges or scores for each indicator are drawn up. Indicators that score poorly are then earmarked for priority action. A central feature of the TOMM concept is the inclusion of a management response system that alerts key stakeholders, including the community, to those indicators that are not performing within their acceptable range and identifies other issues that may merit additional monitoring.

The Samoa Sustainable Tourism project is a national-level scheme run by the Samoa Tourism Authority. Based on the TOMM, Samoa takes a broader sustainable development approach to monitoring, identifying indicators that make the linkages between tourism and sustainability issues in the country and using the results to help prioritize tourism and policy and planning activities in the country as well as identify and access sources of donor funding. Despite its short-term success at raising awareness and understanding of sustainable tourism at the national authority level, the on-going maintenance of the scheme continues to pose problems specifically related to a lack of human capacity, expertise and industry backing.

Source: Miller and Twining-Ward, 2005.

Despite the logic and careful design of the TOMM process, it has also experienced difficulties in terms of resource constraints and scepticism within the business and resident community. Another weakness of the approach is the tourism-centric focus which, although conducive to industry involvement, risks overlooking other aspects of sustainable development. Similar difficulties face the UK-based Tour Operators Initiative (TOI) detailed in Miller and Twining-Ward (2005). The TOI is a voluntary industry scheme to promote more sustainable practices within tour operations from the selection of destinations to the management of suppliers. The scheme encourages operators to undertake detailed audits of a wide range of issues related to their business, but the complexity and level of detail required risk drowning the operator in a sea of figures rather than increasing their understanding and awareness of sustainability.

Emerging trends

Miller and Twining-Ward (2005) combine both theory and practice in a comprehensive discussion of the issues and considerations involved in the development and use of sustainable tourism monitoring systems. Sustainable tourism is approached from an interdisciplinary sustainable development perspective, looking at the significant progress made in the field of monitoring by scholars of the environment and development and applying this to tourism. Expanding on the work of Twining-Ward (2002) and Farrell and Twining-Ward (2004), tourism should be reconceptualized as a complex adaptive system, one which requires a comprehensive, stakeholder-driven and adaptive approach to indicator monitoring. From this theoretical stepping-stone future tourism managers should explore the sectoral, spatial and temporal boundaries of monitoring as well as what to measure, what types of indicators to use, how to identify and organize the indicators and the important issues concerning how to analyse and interpret indicator data and ensure monitoring programmes are linked to policy making.

The shift from the static indicator development approach to a more dynamic focus on adaptive and participatory monitoring is an important one that may reflect a wider change underway in the study and practice of tourism. Long-range tourism master plans worldwide are being replaced by strategic plans, static indicators replaced by adaptive ones, international consultants by local people and top-down approaches by participatory ones. It is becoming increasingly clear that tourism does not operate as a steady-state system, but as a complex system that is prone to surprise events. To cope with this, managers need broader interdisciplinary understanding, greater stakeholder collaboration and, above all, improved information about the place and context they are managing. Monitoring therefore becomes a key tool to new management practice – providing up-to-date information, enabling managers to develop the resilience and adaptive capacity in their business or organization to cope with the fast pace of change. Conventional indicators are failing to meet this need; improved information about the integrated social-ecological systems they are managing will enable managers to take better advantage of new opportunities and stay attuned to system change.

Challenges, risks and dangers for sustainable tourism monitoring

Despite the current popularity of indicators, however, there are also risks and dangers involved and not all scholars are entirely convinced of the validity of the approach. Hein (1997) suggests the indicator approach can result in misplaced confidence and over-reliance on a few quantitative measures. He also voices concern about devising strategies to address separate variables, without considering the complex dynamics of long-term socioeconomic change. Meadows (1998) comments that if indicators are poorly chosen, inaccurately measured, delayed or biased, they can result in serious malfunction of monitoring systems, resulting in reactions that are either too strong or too weak and produce ineffective decision-making.

These are all valid concerns. Indicator selection is bound to be a subjective undertaking and identifying just a few selected variables to describe the state of a complex system inevitably leads to a reduction in precision and a real risk of overlooking important elements of the tourism ecosystem. In this way indicators must be understood as a supplement, not a substitute, for rigorous scientific study of tourism development processes. However, rather than discouraging investigation of indicator methodologies, knowledge of indicator pitfalls may assist in the development of innovative solutions and improved monitoring systems and that, over time, can help advance the transition towards more sustainable tourism.

Conclusion: the future of monitoring for sustainable tourism

Although some small steps have been taken in the right direction, research on sustainable tourism indicators, like other areas of tourism, is still very parochial and constrained by disciplinary blinkers. Those monitoring projects that are in place are still in the process of development and few have sufficient data to identify trends over time. Nevertheless, there are already some common lessons to be learned from the practical examples discussed above.

The first is that monitoring appears to have a significant contribution to make to the movement from sustainable tourism principles to practice, especially with regard to what is now known about complex system behaviour. Indicators provide information that can enable improved decision-making, help develop and prioritize action plans and improve the general level of awareness and understanding of sustainable tourism issues. Where monitoring has been shown to be a most effective tool is when it focuses on developing consensus and constructive partnerships with communities, NGOs, tourism authorities and private sector business to provide a more informed, coordinated and multi-pronged approach to sustainability.

The case studies also help show the distinction between indicator development and the implementation and use of monitoring systems. One does not work without the other. Data are only of value if they can be applied and used by others; they cannot be the sole focus of the process. Similarly, indicator results do not create change in themselves. In order to promote positive change, it is essential that indicator results are communicated in a format and language understood by the intended audience.

Another important lesson is that priority issues change over time. Tourism systems are dynamic and subject to unexpected events. Sustainable tourism has therefore been presented as a journey or *transition* which will occur over varying space and time scales. Despite the enormous value in longitudinal data, indicators cannot be cast in stone; they need to be reviewed on an ongoing basis and ineffective indicators adapted or replaced. Finally, both the TOMM and the Samoa Indicator projects found that the challenge is not just in developing the indicators or monitoring them but in maintaining them in the long term, avoiding burnout of key project drivers, securing funding and the political will to continue monitoring and creating positive action as a result. To this end, it is important to establish the reasons why different stakeholders are interested to pursue sustainability and to determine how indicators can seek to increase this motivation and maintain efforts when difficult decisions are needed.

The development and use of indicators may not be infallible; there are risks and dangers, explained above, involved such as the replacement of ideology with managerialism. There are also barriers to the development of indicators such as technical expertise, know-how, resources and short-term political, business and personal horizons. Despite these constraints, indicators have proven themselves to provide a useful and pragmatic addition to what has to date been a rather grey and fuzzy process characterized by a lack of tools, empirical understanding and theoretical unity. But in order for indicators not to become tarnished as an instrument of unwarranted bureaucracy, there is a need for more monitoring action and practical on-going research. An important challenge to those charged with developing indicators in the future will be to ensure that the science continues to keep pace with the increased role indicators are being asked to perform, as well as with progress in areas related to sustainable development.

It is clear that indicators cannot be a goal in their own right; they are a technical approach to a human problem and like other techniques need careful, adaptive management. Nevertheless, when indicators are carefully chosen to reflect the place-specific issues facing stakeholders in a destination, adapted as these issues changes over time and the results are used to help steer tourism policy, it is suggested here that monitoring can become invaluable as an approach to sustainable tourism.

7

Media and Communications

Rok V Klancnik

Background: tourism in a volatile environment

A wave of global changes in the tourism industry began in the 1990s and marked the entry to the new millennium. New markets emerged, including the Russian, Chinese and Indian markets. The collapse of centrally planned economies gave rise to market economies, mergers, acquisitions and alliances – all bringing powerful new players to the game. The expansion of post-modern information technology and the emergence of global media, such as CNN and many others, have accelerated all these processes. It was inevitable that tourism would be affected by these developments.

Until the early 1990s, there was a certain '*laissez faire, laissez passer*' tendency in tourism and tourism communications, at least so long as there was sufficient growth, because 'one simply does not mend what is not broken'. Some governments felt that their role was unnecessary in this remarkable period of tourism growth. Many ministries of tourism ceased to exist or were incorporated into other ministries. National tourist boards were established with a mere promotional and research and development role. At the dawn of the twenty-first century, new macro-economic rules emerged with a need for economic

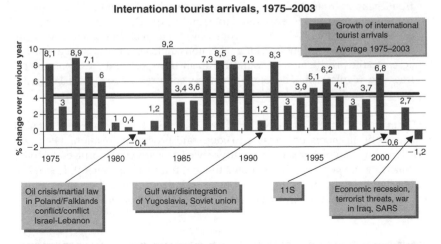

Figure 7.1 International tourist arrivals, 1975–2003.

restructuring. Supply exceeded demand and all of a sudden consumers had end-less choice, which substantially increased competition in the markets. The 'new normality', as the situation was called by Peter de Jong, CEO and President of Pacific Asia Travel Association (PATA, 2004), was compounded by new political and security issues and even unexpected health problems.

Figure 7.1 demonstrates that these challenges resulted in a series of crises in international tourism, even worse than those at the beginning of the 1980s, marked by the oil crisis and martial law in Poland, or those in the early 1990s, with the dis-integration of the Soviet Union and Yugoslavia. In 2003, when the whole world was still recuperating from the shock of the 11 September 2001 attack on the USA, which affected the tourism industry dramatically, overall tourism growth was down by 1.2 per cent, which was the biggest decline since 1950.

Globalization of the tourism industry

Tourism grows exponentially and rapidly spreads worldwide, although it seems to be slowing down somewhat, especially in Europe. According to the World Tourism Organization (WTO) statistics, there were twenty-five million international arrivals in 1950, 165 million in 1970, 703 million in 2002 and a 1.5 billion forecast for 2020 (WTO, 2001). There is no evidence of saturation of demand, at least on a global level.

The industry is becoming globalized. In 1950, the top fifteen destinations in the world accounted for 87 per cent of foreign visitor arrivals, in 1970 for no more than 75 per cent and in 2000 for only 62 per cent. When there is too much pres-sure on a region, tourists travel to another, neighbouring or comparable region or turn to domestic tourism. What drives this growth? Is tourism a natural force mushrooming on its own? Is it pursuing dreams, escape, sympathy or strategically planned business?

Besides man's insatiable curiosity about the world in which he lives, three developments caused international tourism to explode and then become widespread: the increase in purchasing power and in discretionary income, in particular, of middle- and working-class households in the developed world; access to the private motor car and cheap air transport; and the expansion of free time, regulated and developed in many countries by social legislation in favour of employees (Frangialli, 2001).

The major effects of globalization on a tourism destination are increased demand and competition, increased pressure to cooperate, product innovation, specialization, branding and higher service quality as well as a growing shortage of capital for financing the necessary investments to meet future goals (Smeral, 1996). The author highlights branding, but could have included as well all communication techniques, since they are indispensable in the globalization process.

Building the communication bridge between organizations and the media

Media relations are only a part of communications. Nielsen (2001) suggests that the tourism industry engaged with the media mainly in public relations (the monitoring and promoting of uncommissioned information in the public media with the intention that an interested party be presented favourably) and advertising (commissioned formal communications). Communications, on the other hand, stand for transmitting ideas and information to several parties and in many ways (Reilly, 1990).

Tourism requires hard work, beginning with strategy, careful product development, lobbying for support of the policy-makers and a never-ending battle on an international market. All these processes require constant communications flows.

National Tourism Administrations (NTA) took care of the tourism policy and international relations, but often were not responsible for marketing and media relations. Most of the National Tourism Organizations (NTO) were established in the 1990s to become 'official tourism communicators' of destinations. They had to perform and learn at the same time. Until mid-1990s only very few NTOs had a public relations manager (Luhrman, 1999). However, by 2004, the situation had altered almost completely.

There are several ways of categorizing tourism and tourism-related organizations. Perhaps the most useful typology is based on the membership of an organization (WTO, 1997b). It provides the clearest indication of its purposes and objectives (Table 7.1).

As tourism becomes increasingly sophisticated, competitive and global, the international and national organizations provide one means for those involved in tourism to keep abreast of the rapidly changing market. Through organizations, members can create networks, share capacity and resources and benefit from efficiencies in scale and size that might otherwise be unattainable by them individually. The major areas of concern to international tourism organizations are promotion of industry interests, marketing and promotion, regional cooperation, data and capacity transfer, direct assistance, trade issues (liberalization of trade and services

Table 7.1 Types of tourism organizations by membership

	Public sector		Private sector	Regional organizations
	International	*National*		
Organizations	Inter-governmental organizations	National Tourism Administrations (NTA) National Tourist Organizations (NTO)	International or national tourist associations of common goals or interests	Tourist organizations based on regional proximity or affiliation
Character	United Nations specialized or related agencies; they serve as a forum for discussion of issues related to laws, regulations, agreements, policy, on inter-governmental level	NTA is a government body responsible for national tourism policy, legislation, investments, classifications etc. NTO or tourist boards are mainly concerned with marketing and promotion function	They serve as a forum for their members to identify issues of importance to the different sectors, creating standards and guidelines, increasing public awareness and lobbying	Formed initially for the purpose of marketing and increasing the travel market's awareness of their regions. They often enable destinations to pool their resources and mount more effective marketing campaigns, but some expanded their goals to include travel facilitation and policy coordination
Composed of	Member states (represented by government representatives), affiliate members and associate members	NTAs are usually directorates or secretariats. NTOs may be government owned or mixed and often involve representatives of the private sector	Hotel chains, tour operators, spas, airlines, theme parks etc.	National tourism administrations, national tourist boards, influential representatives of the private sector, sometimes individuals
Examples	World Tourism Organization (WTO) International Civil Aviation Organization (ICAO)	VisitBritain, Canadian Tourism Commission, Tourism Authority of Thailand, Austrian National Tourist Board	World Travel and Tourism Council (WTTC), International Air Transport Association (IATA), International Hotel and Restaurant Association (IH&RA), national hotel associations	Pacific Asia Travel Association (PATA), European Travel Commission (ETC), African Travel Association (ATA)

in tourism) and sustainable tourism development issues (environmental protection, cultural awareness and social development).

Communication has become one of the strategically important activities among the stakeholders as well as in media relations. Heads of communications, corporate communications, public affairs etc. are used in both the public and private sectors and regional organizations. They have become indispensable high-level officers (even CIOs: Chief Information Officers) often with technical responsibility, usually reporting directly to the chief executive. Their duty is no longer only to write press releases, but also to act as strategic advisors on the positioning of the organization or company. They are also responsible for media management, reputation management, web editing, negotiating, corporate branding, crisis communications, agenda-setting, raising awareness, cross-cultural communications and communication of ethical issues.

Like other industries, the tourism process simply cannot be realized without a global communication exchange. There is an international market of tourist information, in which senders are communicating encoded messages through the media, decoded by the receivers, who send back their feedback and create their own messages. National and international, public and private organizations in tourism act both as senders and receivers, while millions of potential and active tourists are mainly perceived as receivers of mediated information.

Technological development has rapidly expanded the range of mass media. Still, Wilbur Schramm's definition (1960) remains practically unchanged: 'A mass medium is essentially a working group organized round some device for circulating the same message at about the same time, to large numbers of people'. Mass media underscore other, non-institutionalized media, such as word-of-mouth (for many the most

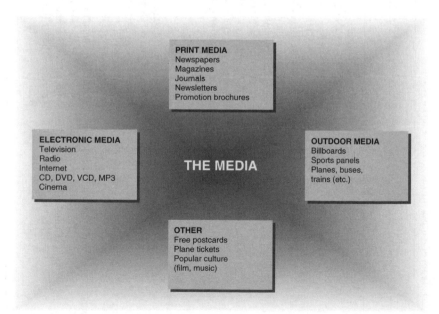

Figure 7.2 Media formats. (Source: adapted from Nielsen, 2001)

efficient promotion of destinations), brochures/pamphlets, travel agent and tourist packages (Hsieh and O'Leary, 1993). Mass media complement travellers' personal experiences, the web-based information (the Internet) and education.

Tourism organizations communicate with the majority of these media. However, 'traditional' media like print and electronic, mainly television and, since the 1990s the Internet, are still and will probably remain dominant. Following the great success of the Lord of the Rings films (Mintel, 2003), a focus has also been put on the film industry. What has changed is the content and the form of the messages, expansion from simple press releases to a great variety of messages, many of them carefully aimed at different target groups. While paid advertising is more popular among hotel chains, tour operators and travel agents that can afford it, most NTOs prefer other, non-payable communications techniques, due to financial reasons.

The magic pyramid?

The 'magic pyramid', as demonstrated in Figure 7.3, represents a different communications model for the future. It consists of tourism organizations (public sector and representative organizations and associations), the private sector (companies), destinations and the media. Good functioning of this pyramid means that the messages are articulated through efficient, professional, comprehensive communications among all stakeholders. This process can boost tourism, resulting in economic, cultural and social wealth. It can also accentuate the dangers of possible unfair globalization practices, such as leakages, negative environmental impacts and unwelcome cultural uniformity.

The 'magic pyramid' foresees several parallel information flows, along which the senders want to convey their messages that are either commercial or corporate (non-commercial). The media 'observe' these information flows 'from the top' and use those that appear most attractive. A decisive factor is very often whether the sender of the message is ready to increase their own commercial performance

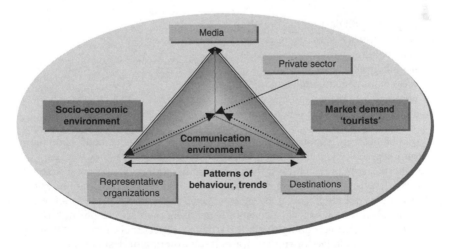

Figure 7.3 Pyramid of tourism communications.

by means of advertising. The senders usually have attractiveness of the messages for the recipients as a priority; however, if the recipients are business decision-makers, they also pay a great deal of attention to the patterns of behaviour of the market demand and the socioeconomic environment, in the frame of which this market demand exists.

The private sector tries to detect trends in the international (and national) tourist market and strives to adapt its offer to them, especially with the help – be it financial, informational or educational – of destination management organizations. International organizations observe the process, offer their guidelines and sometimes serve as a 'watchdog' (e.g. protection of children against sexual exploitation in tourism, WTO, Ecpat etc.). Building awareness on positive economic, environmental and social impacts of tourism is high on their list of priorities.

With the ever-growing importance of tourism as a 'smokeless' industry, with new emerging markets and destinations, the importance of communications began to be recognized and, at the same time, media interest in the tourism industry increased rapidly forcing these organizations to realize the need for specialized personnel in this area.

Tourism organizations in the past believed that building awareness should be linked to public relations only. On the other hand, the private sector and destinations understood the media to be a bridge to the demand side of the market and thus promotion. Media relations, however, evolved to be a part of an integrated communication process. Media attention on the world's fastest growing industry has also intensified. This is due to the increased demand and supply, issues related to safety and security in tourism (terrorist threats and SARS) and also to the realization of the importance of tourism following major crises between 2001 and 2004.

Development of the communications mix

Tourism communication activities expanded from simple public relations and media relations to a range of new tasks including:

- corporate and destination branding
- cross-cultural communication
- stakeholder relations
- negotiations
- crisis management and communication
- new media management and communication, and
- shift from traditional advertising to strategic PR.

Traditionally, professional communicators were informing the media about news of tourism products or simply about marketing programmes that they were carrying out and performance achieved. Now they must address issues in sustainable tourism development, product differentiation, ethics and crisis communications. They must master the *jargon* of the various stakeholders: trade partners, politicians, financiers and the public, while constantly updating their knowledge of how and what the competition is doing. Their needs mainly reflect their mission statement, which is often a pledge for support for better marketing of destinations, but also lobbying in favour of certain tourist sectors, such as air carriers and hotels.

The language of the messages is thus adapted, although there is always a lingua franca in the international tourism community, as dictated to the tourism industry by the international business media. Some of the activities mentioned overlap the traditional activities of marketing departments, which more than ever started to focus on research and development. Practices differ and marketing and communications departments must work in close cooperation to achieve the strategic objectives.

The nature of tourism destinations: relationships with the media

There appear to be three different groups globally, which have different communications needs:

1. The *positive group* of destinations looking for marketing and PR opportunities through various channels – the media (TV, Press, PR, Internet) – intermediary marketing opportunities – tour operators/travel agents and other representation companies. This refers to established tourism destinations that are under constant pressure to retain their share of the source markets. Examples of such are France, Spain and other Mediterranean destinations, but also the UK, Germany, Austria and Scandinavian countries.
2. The *group concerned* with damage limitation following a crisis, image reversal and recovery, such as terrorist attacks, earthquakes or hurricanes. There is interaction between these two groups, especially in the time of crises, as has happened to the USA after September 11 and Indonesia.
3. The *group of destinations that are invisible* to consumers so that they are not included in the possible set of choices that a potential customer will make. This group wants to know how to be included in the first positive group. Unfortunately, they realize that first they need to establish their offer, invest in human resources, followed by aggressive and costly communications. All new destinations could be a part of this group, in Europe particularly former Eastern Europe, but especially several Asian, African and Latin American countries.

The nature of travel and tourism journalism

Travel and tourism journalists report about holiday options, business travels or economic performance of the operational sector. The sources and providers of tourism information are many and varied. The media receive information from the already mentioned organizations, but probably the most important source remains the journalist's own experience of a destination – as a Lufthansa passenger, for example, or as a diner at a Michelin-starred restaurant, as a guest enjoying a Sol Meliá bed in Madrid, as a backpacker in the state-of-art youth hostel *Celica* in Slovenia's capital Ljubljana, or as a tango dancer in Buenos Aires… Journalists experience the tourism product and put it to the test.

The media will not always agree with the provider of a tourism communication on what is important (Anderson, 2004). They have their own priorities and they will not renounce that they are also profit-oriented companies. Destinations are put in a position of seeking out interesting and unusual stories to pitch to the media along with many competitors doing the same thing. The media – public and private TV, press and the Internet – influence destination choice and consumer behaviour. The media have also taken note of environmental awareness and social responsibility; thus their role in tourism development is crucial.

Some critics, mainly from the camp of the news journalists, claim that 'travel journalism is corrupt'. They argue that press trips, sponsored flights, accommodation and *freebies* do not comply with the professional *codes of ethics* of journalists. However, one cannot imagine colourful stories about distant countries or even entire glossy magazines without such practices. The sponsoring of press trips is legitimate, so the word 'corruption' is not fair, at least when the journalists follow the basic rule of their profession, which is objective reporting.

Travel journalists are not public relations people. They are paid to pass on their own experiences, even if they are sponsored to travel to distant places for enjoyment. Consumer confidence boils down to the simple truth. Correct information on the quality–price ratio of a destination can have a bigger impact than glossy advertisements and slogans that include words like 'paradise', 'heart', etc. Tourists have become critical recipients of information and do not buy empty hype. This approach grows with their experience and quality of life, allowing them to be selective when choosing destinations and willing to pay more rather than be part of an anonymous tourist crowd.

But there is also a different group of journalists: those who focus on the news and 'hard facts', reporting on the trends, consumer confidence or lack of it, troubles or success stories in the airline industry and providing an ever-growing number of facts and figures. Both groups, which sometimes mix, are very important for the tourism industry. Journalists covering hard facts address a different target group from those reporting on destinations, since they are considered not as 'travel writers' but economic or business writers (broadcasters). Still, mastering both fields is an advantage for both groups of journalists and raises the quality and credibility of their output.

The future of communications and media in tourism

The future of communications and media in tourism will be determined by the following trends:

- Technological: both the media and destinations will take advantage of even more sophisticated technology (the Internet, broadband, WAP, interactive and digital television), while traditional print and electronic media will not go away. Tourism organizations and destinations also need to be able to address unfavourable comments and reviews in virtual communities on the websites, which publish consumer views.
- Geographical: tourism has already become globalized, yet more and more destinations will join the global media activity, start communicating and promoting and try to take their piece of the tourism cake. Liberalization of the world's economy not only foresees the lifting of trade barriers, but also helps less-developed countries and new destinations to enter the marketplace (Lipman, 2004). New destinations and new players are welcomed by both the

supply and demand side in the private sector and also by the organizations. The latter, regional and international organizations, pay a lot of attention to this issue, so they prepare plans for capacity sharing, education and cooperation when forming tourism master or marketing plans.

- Changes in content: the media will continue to specialize according to the different branches of travel industry and tourists' needs and motives for travel. Some media already specialize covering only business travel, meetings and conferences, health, i.e. spa tourism, or air transport. On the other side, the daily and Sunday newspapers, too, cover tourism-related issues, be it in the 'business section' or in special supplements or sections.
- Economic: the media will develop more alternative ways to generate profits and, since advertising budgets are not increasing, they will have to act more proactively in this endeavour.
- Ethics: both destinations and the media will be forced by market demand to accept the principles of the Global Code of Ethics for Tourism or at least socially responsible tourism practices.

Conclusion: the media will be critical for tourism success

The media have a key role in the constant search for trust. It is the media that build trust in the market by communicating attractive tourism offerings and disseminating statistics on the growth of all aspects of tourism. On the other hand, irresponsible media coverage can kill a destination. A tourism–media partnership is a precondition for building the values that are key to world tourism development, mitigating or preventing negative impacts and showing their commitment to the basic principles of peace, cooperation, friendship in the world, as well as to social, environmental and economic responsibility. These values are the fundamentals of the international tourism industry.

8

Liberalization and Deregulation for Tourism: Implications for Competition

Andreas Papatheodorou

Introduction

Economics have always praised competition for improving productive and allocative efficiency and therefore generating wider socioeconomic prosperity. Governments in advanced economies have long established policies aimed at stimulating competition and protecting consumers against market monopolization (Scherer and Ross, 1990). Still, until recently a number of industries were regulated, i.e. they operated under a specific institutional regime, which overviewed, controlled and imposed restrictions on the nature of market transactions. Regulation was deemed necessary on various grounds. Its advocates believed that *laissez-faire* would result in destructive competition among market participants, hence instability and loss of scale and scope economies, unit costs would be high and synergies in production would be lost. Moreover, regulation was expected to facilitate regional development: free competition would result in concentration of activities in a small number of places, enhancing core areas to the detriment of the periphery. Regulation in conjunction with overall protectionism and taxation was also used as a mechanism to direct productive resources towards selected industries (which would become national champions) and discourage consumption or other activities related to 'parasitic' or less serious economic sectors (Graham, 1998).

From regulation to liberalization and deregulation

Despite some interesting rationale behind regulation, such institutional regimes encountered significant difficulties in practice. They often resulted in inefficient industries, which lobbied constantly for subsidies that impeded general economic development. In many cases, regulation also led to income and foreign exchange leakage and failed to boost regional growth. For all these reasons, some economists and policy makers started advocating deregulation and liberalization in the early 1980s. They supported policy actions that would facilitate free market competition by reforming or even abolishing existing regulatory and other economic constraints. The rationale for such a regime change was the inherent belief in the superiority of market mechanisms: in thick markets (i.e. those involving many consumers), free entry and exit of producers would establish discipline, lower price and enhance service quality. But, even in cases of thin markets, which could sustain one producer at best, the threat of potential competition would be sufficient to persuade the monopolist to replicate the competitive outcome (Baumol, 1982).

The liberalization process has widely advanced in the western world. Developing nations have also gradually adopted similar measures encouraged by the World Bank, the International Monetary Fund and the World Trade Organization. China is undoubtedly the major country in this context and the liberalization of its markets will have a significant impact on the world economy. Nonetheless and despite the initial euphoria about market deregulation, most economists now acknowledge that liberalization has its caveats, as free markets occasionally fail to operate efficiently. Although few people nowadays support the re-regulation of the markets, it is widely argued that liberalization should be accompanied by a solid institutional framework that safeguards effective competition and consumer welfare. Main control areas should include the scrutiny of merger activity and the inspection of business practices such as contractual restraints that could prove anti-competitive especially when undertaken by dominant firms.

The tourism marketplace

The intervention of policy makers in tourism has been limited, being perceived as a 'pleasure' rather than serious economic sector (Papatheodorou, 2003). However, the industrial structure of tourism is quite complicated. More specifically, a market dualism seems to have emerged, where a multitude of small producers (competitive fringe) coexists with a small number of powerful transnational corporations. Size does matter as it enables the seizure of scale and scope economies and imposes barriers to market entry and exit through asset specificity and irreversibility.

Corporate network expansion and concentration in tourism seem to follow a self-reinforcing pattern through collaborative and integrative practices taking advantage of the current liberal policymaking worldwide (Ioannides and Debbage, 1998; Papatheodorou, 2004).

Although increased concentration does not necessarily imply restrictive conduct and abuse of market power, it is consistent with anti-competitive practices. Given the large size of the tourism industry and the subsequent potential detriment to consumer welfare, policy makers must be alert. This chapter studies competition issues that have emerged in the transport for tourism, accommodation and travel distribution sectors following deregulation and liberalization over the last two decades.

Applications of liberalization and deregulation in air transport

The passenger aviation industry became highly regulated in the aftermath of the second world war and, until thirty years ago, the International Air Transport Association (IATA) was acting as a legitimate cartel fixing prices and itineraries for its members, most of which operated as flag-carriers. As a counterpart, the International Civil Aviation Organization (ICAO) was the inter-governmental forum for discussing emerging issues and consulting member states. The regulatory regime was based on restrictive international agreements on a bilateral basis and essentially protected the national (and usually state-owned) airlines against other scheduled competitors and charter carriers. The national airlines were thought to act as factors of economic modernization which provided a stable and regular transport service, facilitated regional development and promoted international (tourism) recognition. In practice, however, this protectionism resulted in inefficient carriers, which constantly sought subsidies while offering low quality services at unjustifiably high fares. The emerging customer dissatisfaction led to the 1978 deregulation of the US domestic market and triggered similar practices worldwide: most notable examples are the completion of the European Single Aviation Market in 1997 and various open-skies agreements between the USA and European countries ever since (Papatheodorou, 2002). These gales of deregulation signified that market economics and subsequent competition came to the forefront of aviation policy making. Main issues to consider here include fare policy and service quality, selection of routes, creation of networks and collaborative agreements, management of airport slots and information technology. In the post 9/11 world, security and safety are also of primary importance.

Fares and service

When selecting services, passengers consider primarily the fare level (for a given class of ticket, e.g. business or leisure) and the service quality. This is conceived in terms of connection type (i.e. direct or indirect), frequency (i.e. scheduled or charter, number of itineraries) and timings of flights, airport choice (i.e. hub, satellite or regional) and in-flight catering and entertainment. Competition issues can then emerge either because of collusive behaviour among the airlines or due to predatory/excessive rivalry. In particular, overt market sharing and price wars might be regarded as anti-competitive in fare policy. For example, in July 2001, the European Commission fined the Scandinavian carrier SAS and the Danish Maersk €52.4 million for running a monopoly on the Stockholm–Copenhagen route and since mid-summer 2001, Ryanair and Go have occasionally engaged in ruthless promotional fare-cuttings between Ireland and Scotland. Although this practice benefits travellers in the short-term, it may prove detrimental in the long run as it induces the market exit of one carrier securing a quasi-monopoly for the other. The airlines may also follow a number of more implicit policies in route competition. Franchising, code-sharing and block-spacing (i.e. allocation by a carrier X of certain seats in its flights to carrier Y) might relax rivalry by effectively reducing the number of competitors (Hanlon, 1999).

Routes, networks and strategic alliances

In terms of network rivalry, Frequent Flyer Programmes (FFP) are likely to have anti-competitive features. By creating externalities, they induce passengers to use airlines with wide networks instead of cheaper, smaller ones for the sake of collecting points later redeemed for free flights. The large airlines can capitalize further on their network by establishing strategic alliances with other carriers around the globe. Three major global airline alliances exist, i.e. oneworld, Star Alliance and Sky Team. Such partnerships not only enhance the attractiveness of FFP, but can also create fortress airport hubs, when new carrier entry is impossible due either to a dearth of slots or restrictive international regulatory agreements. The airlines may also seek network enhancement directly through mergers with carriers of the same level (e.g. Japan Airlines and Japan Air System) or of a regional network, for example, Braathens accepted a take-over bid by SAS in November 2001 acknowledging the alternative of bankruptcy. Regulatory clearance should be granted to avoid all the above-mentioned anti-competitive effects.

Management of airport slots

Strategic control of airport slots (i.e. the aircraft arrival or departure time periods) may lead to market foreclosure. In particular, even if an airline is *de jure* allowed to serve a destination from a specific airport, this becomes *de facto* impossible if there are not available slots. Due to demand booming and supply rationalization following deregulation, most major airports in Europe are currently fully coordinated, i.e. formal procedures have been introduced for slot allocation (Graham, 2003). Some of them are related to the so-called 'grandfather rights' principle, where an airline is granted a slot perpetually if it is operated. This principle is clearly anti-competitive as it explicitly favours the market incumbents who were granted slots before the deregulation era, e.g. British Airways at London Heathrow. In addition to slot regulation, many airports, such as those controlled by the British Airports Authority (BAA), are subject to economic regulation (e.g. rate-of-return, price caps) as the policy makers are aware of their spatial monopoly characteristics. The European Commission has also recently issued a directive on the liberalization of ground handling services, which have traditionally been (almost) monopolized by the flag carrier or the airport operator, to enhance competition in an area of growing consumer dissatisfaction.

Information technology, safety and security

Information technology is also a domain liable to restrictive practices in aviation (Buhalis, 2003). The first computer reservation systems (CRS) suffered from display bias as they favoured the flights of system vendors by design. The latter could also restrict accessibility to carriers willing to participate either explicitly or by raising fees to unjustifiable levels. To address these problems the Council of ICAO approved a Code of Conduct in 1991 and urged its member states to follow it. Partly for this reason and due to the emergence of multiple ownership and partnerships in the area, CRS anti-competitive discrimination is currently reduced. Still, online connections are preferred to interline ones, while carriers can engage in screen padding by overwhelming the display screens with code-shared flights. Advanced technological systems are also vital in ensuring the safety and security of flights. Nonetheless, such protection is expensive and puts substantial cost pressures on the airlines. A possible concern with deregulation, therefore, is that the carriers may decide to compromise safety and security by cutting corners where possible. In the post 9/11 world, however, both passengers and governments have become widely alerted to such issues. The airlines are, in many cases, legally bound to meet high safety and security standards and therefore seek savings from other parts of the production process if possible.

In essence, competition in the airline industry is currently multi-dimensional. One of the major advancements in the deregulation era was the introduction of low cost carriers (LCC), which gave a new momentum and triggered occasional price wars. Such bloodsheds, however, are unsustainable in the longer term. Moreover, network carriers seem to replicate some of the LCC practices in short haul flights. Consolidation seems inevitable across the service quality spectrum at least in the fragmented European market. Whether this rise in concentration will primarily enhance efficiency or lead to an abuse of collective dominance is still an open question.

Case study 8.1 Liberalization in the Cruise Industry

In addition to competition issues in aviation, other modes of transport for tourism should be considered, especially cruising. At present, the world cruising industry is dominated by four large groups, namely Carnival with a global available capacity share of 29 per cent in 2001, Royal Caribbean Cruises Limited (RCCL) with 23 per cent, P&O Princess Cruises (POPC) with 10 per cent and Star/Norwegian Cruise Lines with 12 per cent. Market structure will be further concentrated in the future as the merger between POPC and Carnival has been cleared by the competition authorities. Initially, RCCL was the favourite to merge with POPC but Carnival objected to this deal making its own offer to POPC. Moreover, competition authorities were asked to investigate the investment of RCCL in First Choice Holidays, one of the major tour operators in Britain, because of the fear that the combined entity would have a dominant position in the holiday market. Despite a number of initial concerns, the British authorities concluded ' ...that the proposed merger cannot be expected to operate against the public interest' (Competition Commission, 2002, p.24). Subsequently, both the European Commission and the US Federal Trade Commission approved the Carnival bid for POPC.

Reference
Competition Commission (2002) *P&O Princess Cruises Plc and Royal Caribbean Cruises Ltd – A report on the Proposed Merger*. London: Competition Commission.

Applications of liberalization and deregulation in accommodation

Regulators and competition authorities have so far paid only limited attention to the accommodation sector. With the exception of architectural and environmental regulation, this industry has been left free to operate within a liberal entrepreneurial context. Consequently, the development of corporate affiliations at both national and global levels has been widespread. In addition to the competitive fringe of small independent hoteliers, the accommodation industry comprises integrated chains of owned, franchised or managed hotels (e.g. Hilton). There are also voluntary chains or consortia of independent hotel companies sharing marketing, promotion and reservation systems under a common brand (e.g. Best Western). The main interdependent dimensions of rivalry in the liberal accommodation business are price, quality in terms of facilities and location both at a macro (i.e. actual destination) and micro (i.e. area within destination) level. The latter is of primary importance, especially for hotel chains and their construction conglomerate partners.

Location, location, location

Accommodation is geographically determined and involves substantial sunk (non-recoupable) investment. While transport shapes only modestly the overall tourist experience in most cases, the hotel or other accommodation is an essential part of the 'dream'. Locational advantages and spatial constraints are therefore major issues in corporate rivalry. In fact, although competition problems may arise from network externalities (e.g. loyalty schemes) and IT (i.e. global distribution systems), it is primarily important to consider here the strategic implications of land use. On these grounds, scarcity of good locations may foreclose the market and induce exit. In particular, by purchasing well-located pieces of land, an existing hotelier denies good substitutes to other potential buyers and effectively deters market entry. Similar to patent shelving in other industries (Scherer and Ross, 1990), this strategy might prove expensive, especially if the incremental land is left unused. However, the profit from substantial mark-up pricing and the abuse of dominant spatial position can render it successful. Moreover, such land purchases put pressure on prices; alternative land use (e.g. agriculture) is discouraged and, unless the landowners have the experience and the financial resources to challenge directly the incumbent with their own accommodation establishments, they may decide to sell out; small businesses might follow suit.

The role of hotel chains

The land developer may be more likely to succeed if it is a hotel chain. These are increasingly dominating the world hospitality market. The nine largest companies controlled 2.98 million beds in 2000, while in Britain the turnover of the seven largest hotel corporations amounts to 60 per cent of the total market (Davies, 1999). In particular, a chain may have abundant financial resources to invest in land and properties. Second, a chain can induce the exit of small independent hoteliers or discourage new entrepreneurs by temporarily limiting or even dumping prices. The losses incurred by the chain in the particular location may be cross-subsidized by the rise of its profit margins in other markets where it enjoys a locational advantage. When a large number of hotel chains are present, price competition may be relatively smooth in the fear of a multi-locational war with devastating effects. However, final prices may still be kept at acceptable levels, due to the enhanced cost efficiency of the chain corporations. In fact, the European Commission has shown a rather relaxed attitude in recent hotel mergers cases (e.g. Nomura International – Le Meridien Hotels) arguing that these do not distort competition and are not against the public interest. In the future, though, their stance might change due to increasing concentration in the industry and its business links with the construction sector (Evans, 1999). Moreover, as advantageous locations will become more difficult to find in the future, an 'airport slot phenomenon' may emerge. Competition authorities should, therefore, ensure that the incumbent hotel chains will not abuse their dominant position by restricting market access.

Applications of liberalization and deregulation in travel distribution

The tour operators and the travel agents are the main corporate players in the travel distribution system. The levels of concentration in the industry have recently increased both in Britain (where the four largest travel groups in Britain controlled about 53 per cent of the market in 2001) and on a pan-European basis. Admittedly, the 1997 report of the British Competition Commission found no evidence of market power abuse by the large tour operators. Nonetheless, the danger of anti-competitive behaviour is still valid, stemming mainly from vertical integration practices or other similar contractual agreements. The World of TUI, for example, owns the German charter carrier Hapag Loyd, has a majority share-holding in hotel chains, such as Grecotel in Greece and controls Lunn Poly, the largest British travel agent – one of the main assets of the Thomson Travel Group. In the context of the travel distribution system, the main focus is on downstream relationships between tour operators and travel agents as the latter contact the customer directly and may therefore substantially influence consumer behaviour. Most recently, however, issues related to consumer protection and licensing have become important.

Relations between tour operators and travel agents

Large tour operators can easily foreclose the tourist market to their peers by banning their affiliated travel agents from trading with other tour operators or by signing exclusive dealing agreements of similar content with independent travel retailers. In fact, 80 per cent of the packages sold by Going Places are provided by the parent company, My Travel. The essence of foreclosure derives from the sunk costs of commercial location, business experience, outlet network and customer database building associated with travel agencies. These constitute significant barriers to entry and render the *de novo* establishment of travel agent multiples very expensive. Consequently, the deprived tour operators might decide to exit their business if they do not have substantial financial resources to set up a new network or if they consider direct marketing of their product to be ineffective.

Such explicitly restrictive agreements may be justified by the incumbent tour operators on the grounds of building solid business relationships with travel agents that make investments in training and computer systems (such as the Thomson Online Programme System) worthy (Sinclair and Stabler, 1997). Nonetheless, they can easily prove anti-competitive in an investigation and therefore are rarely used. More implicit foreclosing practices, therefore, occur often associated with Travel Agent Commission Overrides (TACO) – also used by airlines and hospitality companies. In particular, for an extra commission rate, a travel agent agrees to treat the specific tour operator preferentially by directional selling, i.e. encouraging travellers to purchase this operator's products instead of competing ones both verbally and by offering large price discounts. The affiliated travel agencies, which have personal stakes in directional selling of their tour operator products, might go a step further in such 'most favoured customer' practices. They can charge the parent company very low commission rates and rack its brochures in advantageous positions. They might even manipulate the final price of the tour by tying large advertised discounts on specific foreign package holidays with the purchase of compulsory insurance at a high profit margin. This practice may mislead the consumers with the result that they quit their search for better alternatives and obtain less value for money than they otherwise could (Competition Commission, 1997). Finally, affiliated multiple agencies might exercise their retail power and demand *de facto* unacceptable commissions and other contractual benefits from small rival operators. For example, companies wanting to sell through Lunn Poly in 1989 had to agree on rates close to 16 per cent (Yale, 1995).

In addition to competing with their rival peers, the large tour operators can also exercise their bargaining power and brand name to force affiliation of independent travel agents by leaving them market exit as the sole alternative. First, the tour operators might refuse to supply these travel agents with their packages arguing that independence is a threat to effective promotion of their product. Such development might greatly worry a small travel agent, which depends on the sale of popular branded holidays. To guarantee supply, this agent might accept very low commission rates from the particular operator. Nonetheless, this can be a recipe for financial destruction as it is unsustainable in the longer term: affiliation can be the only real choice then. In a milder case, the large tour operator might not refuse supply but price differentiate against the independent retailers. Although the publicized brochure prices act as a form of resale price maintenance by setting a price ceiling, overt and secret price manipulations often render them meaningless. Consequently, a small independent travel agent will not be able to compete effectively with an affiliated one if it cannot match the discounting of the latter on the parent operator packages. If courageous enough, an independent agent can avoid affiliation by playing the large operators against each other, reverting to other companies when it feels pressure. Such strategy is deemed, however, to be pointless if the large operators have already decided to collude tacitly by sharing the retail market and avoiding conflicts. Illustratively, the four largest affiliated British travel agencies accounted for 57 per cent of the holiday market in 1996. This is in sharp contrast to ten years before, when the share of the independent agencies exceeded 72 per cent (Yale, 1995; Competition Commission, 1997).

Consumer protection and licensing

The travel distribution system has been an eminent partner in the emergence of the mass tourism phenomenon. However, the marketplace is highly competitive (especially in the UK) and occasionally results in bankruptcies of even major players, such as the International Leisure Group (ILG) in the early 1990s. To protect consumers against losing their money or being left stranded in unknown destinations, most developed countries have appropriate legal frameworks. In the UK, this takes the form of ABTA (Association of British Travel Agents) bonding and ATOL (Air Travel Organizers' Licensing) licensing. In other words, to participate in business and fly people to other destinations, a tour operator must provide financial guarantees of its robustness; the licence holders contribute to a fund which uses the money for consumer compensation and repatriation in case of bankruptcies. This legal framework, however, does not cover the operations of scheduled airlines. In the past, this was not considered as a major problem given the clear distinction between scheduled and charter-leisure operations. Nonetheless, the march of LCC in the deregulation era and the subsequent emergence of DIY packaging have raised new challenges. Although the LCC may offer low fares, they do not offer customer protection as part of their services – the customer should seek insurance elsewhere, but most customers are unaware of this caveat. Charter carriers argue that the government should address this issue effectively as they currently face an unfair price disadvantage; the occasional failure of LCC and other scheduled airlines (such as Debonair in the past or Duo Airways and Jetmagic more recently) may precipitate state action in the EU in the near future.

Case study 8.2 Collective Dominance in the Tour Operation Sector

Airtours (now called My Travel) and First Choice are two of the major British tour operators. In 1999, their proposal to merge was rejected by the European Commission on grounds of collective dominance in the British short-haul foreign package holiday market. In particular, the Commission stated that the merger would increase further market concentration in the tour operations industry; this would facilitate tacit collusion and marginalize smaller operators or new entrants. Airtours and First Choice appealed to the Court of First Instance, which subsequently annulled the decision of the Commission on the basis of incorrect application of the collective dominance context (Court of First Instance, 2002). Still, the Court raised a number of important issues for future consideration such as capacity planning, demand (growth and volatility), horizontal and vertical integration and relations of tour operators with producers and brokers. My Travel has threatened to sue the Commission for damages. If the threat materializes and My Travel wins the case, a very interesting legal precedent will be set.

Reference
Court of First Instance (2002) *Annulment of Commission's Decision C (1999) 3022.* Luxembourg: European Communities.

Conclusions and the way forward

It seems, therefore, that the deregulation and liberalization process of the tourism industries has created new opportunities and challenges for efficient competition. However, deregulation is not a panacea. Anti-competitive concerns have emerged with potentially detrimental effects for consumer welfare. The possibility of market re-regulation seems unlikely at present but the policy makers should be alert to discover restrictive practices and penalize those in charge. From a corporate perspective, however, firms should compete more effectively to survive. The formation of alliances and consortia by the small airlines and the independent hoteliers and travel distributors can be proactive in overcoming barriers to market entry. By accepting the rules set by the large companies, the humble might be able to take their revenge. Nonetheless, the creation of new robust rivals does not necessarily improve traveller welfare as these firms can collude with previous incumbents to share profits. Public interest, therefore, can only be enhanced if the consumer becomes more active, informed and decisive. Advances in information and telematic fields and especially the wide diffusion of the Internet could perhaps help in this direction by eliminating the need for personal travel consulting and enhancing direct contact links between consumers and tourist producers. Complete disintermediation may not be an inevitable outcome, however, as information overload and time constraints create new opportunities for effective travel managers: liberalization in tourism services may, therefore, transform rather than extinguish players from the marketplace.

9

New Knowledge in Tourism Research

Michael Riley and Edith M Szivas

Introduction: the need for more data

The purpose here is to explore ideas for new areas of knowledge that can advance the topic of tourism as an academic subject. If you ask the same questions you tend to go in a familiar direction even if you ingeniously invent new methodologies. The search for new knowledge requires new questions to be asked. The creation of new questions is, of course, the remit of both theoretical thinking and the analysis of newly minted data. What is being attempted here is essentially a summation of ideas that come from examining unfinished lines of enquiry, old ideas in need of a return visit, obviously important areas unexplored and ideas from other areas of study which might be of interest to tourism. It is not intended as an agenda, but it is essentially a practical perspective written from the 'outside'. The perspective is primarily from an empirical standpoint. This perspective is justified on the rather simple assumption that tourism, in every aspect, needs more primary data! This is in itself contentious because it implies a criticism of pure theoretical and conceptual approaches. No such criticism is intended: they are after all necessary to the production of new questions. The assumption of a need for primary data is merely a reflection of the fact that, while many other areas of knowledge have access to funding that produces a continually advancing body of empirically based knowledge, tourism, on the whole, does not have this luxury. Furthermore, there is the common sense rationale that says that most areas of research could do with more primary data be it qualitative or quantitative. That tourism empirical research in certain areas relies on secondary data, which, to an extent, predetermines the range of questions it can answer, is simply a statement of fact.

Do we need to get more disciplines involved?

Any reasonable review of the history of tourism research would show that it has focused on tourism as a phenomenon: a particular human activity. Research has been pursued mainly, though not exclusively, through the three disciplines: geography with its concern for space and movement, economics for its ability to forecast and measure impact and anthropology for its concern for meaning. This may look like 'three club golfing', but that would deny the undoubted contribution of these disciplines to the establishment of tourism as an academic discipline (Lew et al., 2004). Within these disciplines it is possible to see that there has been an emphasis on a number of major themes, namely:

- Economic impacts and forecasting
- Social and cultural impacts
- Destination and image
- Traveller attributes
- Sustainability and environmental impacts
- Tourism policy

Within this research, the unit of analysis has largely been confined to either the tourist, a defined market segment or a defined destination area. The individual as a consumer, the worker, the workforce, the market, the company or operating unit do not feature widely in the studies. No substantive criticism is implied here, except that it is a narrow base in need of expansion. Unsurprisingly, attributional studies abound but, despite the abundance and good quality of many studies, we still do not know with any authority what determines destination choice, hotel or conference venue choice. Possibly the growing interest in studying processes, particularly decision processes, would be more helpful than continuing to seek the relative salience of known attributes be they of destinations, hotels, restaurants etc. The problem here is that moving towards studying processes would take tourism into disciplines that have, in the past, been used only partially and selectively, namely social and cognitive psychology, social systems and sociology. Although it has practical value in marketing, it would be only slightly unfair to suggest that tourism's use of psychology to categorize types of travellers is both crude and limited. The great advances in social psychology in such areas as identity and cognitive understanding are not being greatly exploited by tourism.

The neglect of structural studies

Even harder to understand is the neglect of structural studies, especially given the fragmented and interdependent structure of tourism and the perennial problems of relationships between centralized authority and the heterogeneous nature of the supply side. Despite the variety of structures and the suboptimal performance of policies, tourism appears reluctant to apply theoretical analysis of social forces, such as power and conflict, to the understanding of the industry and its organizations. Submerged within the fragmented whole are fundamental components of the industry: its meaningful structure and driving forces. Packed with different stakeholders, each with their own interests and agendas, the demands of rational planning have to cope with the entrepreneurial ethos which drives this economic activity. However, when the tourism industry comes under attack from various and numerous unexpected sources, such as terrorism or disease, something strange happens – it becomes visible. Famously difficult to see, the social forces within it suddenly become exposed, not just to outsiders but also to the industry itself. The fundamental components, normally submerged, come to the surface.

Suddenly, the degree of interdependence that exists between these stakeholders becomes raw and visible. Luxury hotels, coach companies and agro-tourism operations make strange bedfellows. When this occurs, a competitive industry looks for consensus, a common solution and normally looks to a super-ordinate authority to provide it. What is important about a crisis is that it acts as a reminder that a human activity such as tourism is an outcome of, not just economic activity, but of many social forces such as power, authority, common consciousness and influence that form both the structure of the industry and its organizing principle. The structure contains many legitimate conflicts, such as those between conservationists and developers. How such conflicts are resolved or accommodated is part of social systems analysis. The central role in understanding these aspects of the industry rightly belongs to economics. However, in truth, economics is more interested in tourism development and impacts than in industrial structure and those disciplines that can help make it clearer make very few appearances in the tourism literature. If we were to ask what is absent from the existing tourism themes it would be social forces, business, management, labour, micro-economics and, in its various forms, organizational behaviour. These missing areas of knowledge represent the absence of disciplines such as sociology, organizational theory, managerial and organizational economics, systems thinking, business strategy and social psychology in the tourism research literature. This is not to say that there are no studies involving these disciplines, but that there are very few and tend to be 'one-off' publications (see for example Townley, 2002). This is to the serious detriment of tourism and needs to be rectified. In other industries these disciplines would automatically be involved. The very diverse nature of tourism makes their absence even harder to explain. Using other disciplines would allow tourism to look again at the forces of divergence and consensus within it and at its fundamental structure and this may be a useful starting point for a fresh view of tourism.

There is a case for stretching some existing ideas a bit further

The planning process naturally assumes a degree of rationality and uses forecasts. It has recently, through the environmental lobby, taken on integrating a degree of consultation and, in some cases, participation by indigenous populations, into the planning process. But the development process is always dependent on the emergence of entrepreneurs and, in most cases, the behaviour of global corporations. Do we know enough about what entrepreneurs have to 'see' before they enter the ring? (Ucbasaran et al., 2003). What are the assumptions made by corporate strategists when they decide to get involved in developing a region? While we have impact studies and forecasting to guide the rational planning process, we know virtually nothing about the social processes, particularly influence processes, that are at work in the planning and development stages of tourism. We need to know about the vested interests of stakeholders. More importantly, we need to know how those interests affect the propensity for cooperation and conflict within the network of interdependences that make up the tourism product. Within the fragmented structure of the industry are processes of influence and balances of power that directly impinge on the planning process. We need to know more about these (see for example Bramwell and Lane, 2000). To put it simply, both development and marketing management are about getting people with contrary interests and priorities to work together. This is the reality that exists beyond blueprint plans and grand strategy documents.

This idea of social forces of cooperation and conflict brings tourism planning and development within the orbit of the study of organizations. The absence of organizational studies is a serious omission in the corpus of knowledge about tourism. Given the enormous changes that have taken place in organizations over the last decade – globalization, the rise of strategic thinking, corporate governance and the emergence of bureaucracy in service industries on the back of information technology – it is remiss of tourism studies to stay so aloof from actual business. Although we know that strategy is important and that many books have been written about it, we still know very little about the process. It really is an area of some urgency so far as research is concerned. Tourism has neglected business and the study of managerial strategy in the industry has fallen between economics and tourism with neither really picking up the baton. We know something about airline strategy; we know something about corporate hotel strategy; but about the interdependence of each – we know almost nothing.

Information technology is not only changing the scope of marketing and opening up reservation channels, but it is also altering the size and structure of the companies that operate these processes. Moreover, power is being redistributed within the structure. Industrial structure is changing, and identifying the changes, their impact and the pressures, which will produce further change, is a clear research agenda. The study of eTourism is not simply a marketing exercise, it is simultaneously the study of industrial structure (Buhalis, 2003).

The study of destinations and products has been concerned with patterns of visitors, image differentiation and marketing and, not unnaturally, it has been influenced by statistics and forecasting. This has, in terms of research, had the effect of emphasizing external tourism over internal tourism – the global over the local. This, in turn, has taken the study of such important subjects as competition into wide arenas to the neglect of the local dimension. Yet so much of the viability of tourism and its quality is determined by local circumstances rather than by the bigger picture. Not enough research exists at the local level that emphasizes both its dependence on the wider picture and independence from it. We know more about the former than the latter.

Tourism is universally put forth as an industry that creates jobs and therefore one which addresses national employment problems. However, the intervening aspect of labour productivity gets little coverage. The problems of measuring productivity in industries which, like tourism, are founded on stochastic demand are well known but not fully explored (Riley, 1999; Riley et al., 2002). All tourism institutions are subject to throughput economics, but the effects of that are not wholly understood, particularly in relation to labour (Brusco et al., 1998). The development of models of service productivity is beginning to make serious progress, but the issue of how they can be incorporated into macro-level productivity studies is still open (Gronroos and Ojasalo, 2004). Even within the political literature on tourism, productivity is not mentioned. It would be difficult to imagine governments not being concerned for productivity in production industries. There is an incomplete argument in the literature about the role of tourism in employment policies. Bringing productivity into the argument qualifies the usual bland assumptions, and evidence on technological substitution or 'reverse employment effects' would advance the employment argument substantially. Of more direct importance to tourism is the need to understand how its rewards are distributed. Despite the techniques for economic impact being well established, the actual distribution of the rewards of tourism and how that impacts on the traditional distribution systems of the indigenous population is under-researched (Onyeiwu and Joners, 2003). This would add further to the general argument that tourism is economically important.

Some established themes need to be revisited

Tourism has for a long time accepted the relationship between leisure and work as laid down by the leisure literature, but that literature has moved on almost without tourism researchers noticing. More importantly, the reality of work life has changed dramatically under the pressure of information and organizational change. In fact, the whole world of work has changed at every level of society. Work has permeated into social life and created a new relationship with consumption. This must mean that the way of both the salience of work and of leisure has changed. Yet tourism research is not clear in this area as it does not pay much attention any more to work. At a pragmatic level, it has not done enough studies on income and hours. Unglamorous it may be, but it is important. More importantly, we do not know enough about how income affects tourism consumption, more particularly how it competes with other consumption. Despite hours of work being a major factor in the decision to consume leisure products, there is a dearth of appropriate research. Theoretically, the world of consumption has moved on to embrace identity and congruity within ranges of consumption.

Although the literature is replete with impact studies, it is worth asking whether there are not still some questions worth pursuing in this area. Do we really know the impact of tourism development on traditional means of wealth distribution? Do we know in any detail how it improves the economic lot of the indigenous population? Often tourism is touted as a cure for employment problems, but the intervention of productivity in that relationship remains unclear.

Some research needs are conspicuous

While tourism is concerned with the identity of tourists and their satisfaction with tourism products, it appears not to be interested in actually what they do. Apart from an interest in extremes such as drunkenness and sexual excess, it has few studies of what might be described as normal behaviour of tourists. Intra-destination patterns of behaviour would have the potential to offer explanations of tourist motivation (Niininen and Riley, 2004). This is particularly important as it seems nobody has noticed that the psychology of motivation has moved on from needs-based theories to embrace social information processing theories, cognitive sense-making processes and identity formation. This brings the experience of making sense of the environment directly into motives and action. Why people travel, why they choose a particular destination and venue goes beyond need theories. If motivation is important to tourism then it needs to explore a greater range of psychological theory and attendant methodologies and to explore why some people do not travel.

Exactly why tourism stays away from business research is hard to explain, particularly in the modern climate of globalization and given the demonstrable fact that tourism is a business. There is overall an emphasis on demand rather than supply. One explanation often given is that tourism does not sit easily within a model of business education. This is to an extent both true and the fault of business education; but both have a shared origin in social science, recognition of which fact by both parties could at least create a rope bridge between them. The obvious problems are that both business and management education are seen as lacking a critical perspective. To make matters worse there is a perceived absence of 'normal science' in the all-important strategy research. In reality both have a critical tradition and strategic studies are becoming more scientific in approach. Business and management are changing and this will force changes not just onto tourism corporations but onto the industry. This will include importing generic ideas and techniques. The hospitality literature has embraced generic management and the friction between the specific context and the generic is bearing interesting material. Economics has examined the industry but rarely from an institutional perspective and even more rarely from a stance that combines organizational economics with business motives. At the heart of it, it is the lack of institutional studies that matters. Tourism marketing is probably the subject area with the closest affinity with generic business ideas but it is not the only relevant discipline. Tourism products are being developed and designed and this process is inhabited by generic techniques taken from the business world.

Service industries in general, including tourism, are not strongly associated with innovation, yet this perspective is to an extent unfair (Gallouj, 2002). There is innovation in service industries such as tourism. Against a background of convergence whereby manufacturing industry is becoming more service orientated and deliberately making itself flexible to short-term demand and service industries are becoming more industrialized through standardization, it is possible to suggest a research agenda that looks at how each can enrich the other. For example, at the moment service tends to borrow techniques first applied in manufacturing believing them to be generic, whereas they are not and this is causing problems. This is another area for research.

True contribution of tourism research

The problem with tourism as an area of research is that there is still a certain degree of fuzziness as to what constitutes its body of knowledge. More established boundaries would not only assist curriculum design, but would also promote reputation and acceptance in the academic community. At the same time, it is necessary to avoid the trap of defining the body of knowledge too narrowly and in a way that allows research to develop only from this narrow base.

It is accepted that tourism research draws heavily on other disciplines bringing in ideas, concepts and methodologies, inevitably enriching tourism knowledge and reinforcing its multidisciplinary nature. One criticism that often arises is that the knowledge that is brought into tourism is superficial. This might be an explanation why the contribution of tourism to other disciplines lags behind its potential. Tourism as a discipline will only be truly on equal footing with other disciplines when its body of knowledge will contribute to other disciplines, in other words, when tourism is not only used as an application but is seen as a source of knowledge for scholars in other disciplines. Many of its strong features could form the context for answering generic questions.

The forces of globalization are inevitable for tourism and the phenomenon is both experienced at a practical level and studied at a theoretical level. Parallel to this, there is an increasing trend for the internationalization of tourism studies and to the casual observer it might seem that tourism knowledge is truly globalized. Not quite so. Geography and language still matter! The Anglo-Saxon approach to tourism research is somewhat different from that taken by German- or Spanish-speaking countries, for example, and certain ideas and philosophies remain inaccessible to scholars on the 'other side'. Bringing together these bodies of knowledge would mean true globalization of tourism knowledge and it would also strengthen tourism's reputation and credibility as a discipline.

Part Two: New Management

10

Organizations and Management in the Future

Colin Hales

Introduction

The accepted wisdom is that organizations and management are undergoing radical transformation and that few industries, including tourism, will be unaffected. Key drivers of this are the pressures to reduce costs and raise quality which stem from increasingly intense competition in an increasingly global marketplace, coupled with growing demands from better educated and informed employees, consumers and other external stakeholders. The major facilitators of this change are rapid developments in technology, particularly those that have increased the volume and speed with which information is stored, accessed, retrieved, processed and distributed.

Three broad, inter-linked transformations are identified: first, a shift away from centralized, process-oriented bureaucracies to more decentralized, performance-driven management structures; secondly, a shift away from fragmented, standardized operating systems to more holistic, integrated forms of working where there is greater employee involvement and empowerment; and, thirdly, a change in the role of managers away from 'command and control' to more loosely-defined cross-boundary leadership and coordination. A key issue, therefore, is: to what extent and how will these changes impact on the tourism industry in the future?

Definitions

Organizations are social entities that bring together people, materials, information and technologies in coordinated activities and relationships in order to pursue specific goals. They may be economic, political or social, public or private, for-profit or not-for-profit, large or small. Tourism encompasses all such organizations.

To achieve their goals, these 'social entities' have to be organized and managed in certain ways. There must be mechanisms in place to plan and decide activities, allocate activities to different individuals and groups, motivate people to do them and coordinate and control what happens. 'Organization', therefore, can be defined as 'the assemblage of institutional mechanisms through which the management of work activity is attempted' (Hales, 2001a, p.48).

Machine bureaucracy

Over the last century, the 'machine bureaucracy' (Mintzberg, 1991), combining bureaucratic management and rationalized operations, has been the predominant organizational form. It has three key characteristics (Hales, 2001a):

1. Specialization. Administrative activities are divided by function into departments, sections and specialist work roles with clearly defined areas of expertise and responsibility. Work operations are subject to systematic analysis to produce a flow-line of fragmented, specialized, de-skilled and mechanized/automated tasks governed by standard methods and times.
2. Centralization. Administration is conducted through a layered hierarchy of power and responsibility where strategy, policy and regulations flow down and constrain lower level decisions and activities, while control information and accountability flow up through vertical reporting relationships. Operations are centrally planned by managers and are monitored and controlled through a combination of close supervision and technology.
3. Regulation. Administrative processes and relationships are governed by formal, impersonal rules designed to produce consistent, standard conduct and outcomes. Operational work is governed by detailed technical procedures, either laid down in production/service manuals or built into hardware and software systems.

Machine bureaucracy in tourism

Many of these features have been evident in large organizations within tourism. Large hospitality and leisure companies, transport organizations, tour operators and central and local government tourism organizations have all, to varying degrees, been centrally managed, functionally organized and regulated, with their operations increasingly rationalized. Where tourism organizations have relatively large-scale operating units, such as up-scale city centre and resort hotels, airports and cruise liners, these, too, have the hallmarks of bureaucratic administration and regulated work processes. However, numerically, large organizations remain the exception in tourism. As will be discussed below, the small and medium-sized enterprises (SMEs) that have predominated in tourism have very different, more loosely-structured forms of organization and informal management systems.

Strengths and weaknesses of the machine bureaucracy

Machine bureaucracy is geared to planning and controlling known, routine, standardized and consistent activities. Its key strengths are that it can produce:

- Consistent, unified strategic decision-making that can take a broad view and over-ride competing interests
- Clearly defined managerial responsibility and accountability and tight managerial control over operations
- Development of individual and departmental specialist expertise at managerial level and proficiency at operative level
- Technically efficient, intensive operating systems, making optimum use of labour, machinery and materials
- Managerial loyalty and employee discipline
- Continuity, consistency and predictability of activities.

These outcomes are highly desirable under stable conditions when markets, technologies and economic, political and social frameworks change slowly and predictably and when the priority for organizations is close monitoring and control of routine processes and production of standard, low-cost products and services.

However, machine bureaucracies are also susceptible to a number of well-documented problems:

- Slowness of decision-making or decisions that are too remote from operational realities
- An expanding and increasingly costly hierarchy
- Routine, unchallenging work at managerial level and repetitive, stressful and dehumanizing work at operative level, each of which has a detrimental effect on motivation and commitment
- Inflexible, imposed work methods and systems that are insensitive to operational realities, make poor use of employee skills and responsibility and are difficult to change
- Poor communication or conflict between functional 'silos' and between management and the workforce
- Over-conformity and a loss of initiative and creativity.

These problems become particularly acute as more intense competition and rapid market, technological, social and economic changes require faster responses, greater flexibility, rapid innovation and fewer standardized, 'mass' products and services. Since tourism is characterized by precisely this kind of volatile, competitive environment, with increasing demand for customer-centric service, the applicability of machine bureaucracy, even to large tourism organizations, is questionable. Any gains in terms of internal operating efficiencies may be offset by a loss of external strategic effectiveness. 'Decentralized' forms of management and 'despecialized' forms of production/service delivery (Hales, 2001a) may match such conditions better (see, for example, Hecksher and Donnellon, 1994; Ashkenas et al., 1995; Quinn et al., 1996; Quinn and Spreitzer, 1997; Pettigrew and Fenton, 2000).

Decentralized management

Although decentralized management takes different forms, depending on the degree of decentralization, there are some common characteristics:

1. Management decision-making and control are no longer concentrated at the centre but are devolved to lower-level managers and professional experts
2. Managers and professional experts are given more autonomy over how they work: controls over processes are replaced by more indirect controls over performance, recruitment and training
3. Expertise is dispersed rather than concentrated, with specialists increasingly working across multi-disciplinary teams
4. Flexible application of expertise, problem solving and learning replaces the rigid application of procedures.

Forms of decentralization: SBU and internal network organizations

Two forms of decentralized management are increasingly in evidence. First, there is the strategic business unit (SBU) organization, divided into market- or product-based profit centres, with their own specialist support, whose managers have considerable autonomy over how the business unit is run and are accountable and rewarded for its financial performance. The centre retains strategic decisions, controls managerial appointments, provides shared services and exploits synergies but, principally, acts as surrogate for the market, redistributing profits to successful units and intervening in or selling off unsuccessful units. An internal market governs the relations among units and the centre, while non-core activities are outsourced to external providers.

More radical decentralization of management is found in the 'adhocracy' or internal network organization. Here, the organization is a loose collection of fluid, temporary teams that are formed for the duration of a specific project and draw, when necessary, on those with relevant expertise. Problem solving based on continuous learning and development of expertise, rather than standard procedures, governs how work is done. Managerial control is replaced by team control and formal authority based on position is replaced by informal leadership based on expertise. Knowledge transfer and organizational learning replace formal coordination (Mintzberg, 1991; Kanter, 2001). Lack of formal structure may reflect an absence of clear organizational boundaries, as in the case of the 'virtual' organization where project teams are linked not by physical proximity but electronic connectivity or the external network organization which centres its core activity (such as marketing or design) on products and services sourced externally.

Decentralized management in tourism

Large tourism organizations are increasingly taking the SBU form, either through the creation of profit centres, in the case of commercial organizations, or through outsourcing to agencies, in the case of public organizations (see Case study 10.1 Sodexho).

Case study 10.1 Sodexho, France

Sodexho is a French-owned company offering a wide range of business and consumer services to different sectors of the tourism industry. These include: catering, vending, maintenance, security and reception, health and safety, staffing, logistics, administration and billing services to public and private sector organizations and management of hotels, food and beverage operations, conferences, exhibitions and hospitality catering for hotel companies, event and tourist venues and leisure attractions. In addition, Sodexho also operates its own commercial restaurants and river cruises. Therefore, it is involved in both the direct provision of tourism services and in servicing other organizations in the tourism industry that have chosen to outsource their non-core business and support services.

Sodexho itself is organized into major divisions focused on types of clients, business sectors or generic services, which are, in turn, divided into corporate and regional accounts. Specific client accounts (such as event catering venues like Ascot or Henley) or operated services (such as Bateaux London cruises) function as profit centres whose managers are accountable for financial performance. Managers have to focus as much on managing client relationships, matching services to needs and promoting the full range of services, as managing internal operations. Sodexho is also a good example of the limits to decentralization. Profit centres are not stand-alone mini-companies operating autonomously but are governed by brand standards and controlled through a hierarchy of regional and sector managers. Individual units are organized functionally and hierarchically.

www.sodexho.com

Tour operators such as TUI are probably one of the best examples of network organizations, bringing together and marketing all the elements – transport, accommodation, tours – comprising the 'package' holiday. Equally, many tourism organizations are outsourcing non-core activities such as payroll, training, catering and security. Adhocracy continues to be evident among smaller tourism organizations, such as single-unit hospitality establishments, travel agencies and attractions, particularly those that are family-owned and run, and operate fluidly on the basis of close inter-personal relationships. However, large organizations, where safety and reliability are paramount, such as airlines, or where there is a distinct branded offering, such as chain hotels and restaurants, could not operate in this way.

Decentralized organization: strengths and weaknesses

Decentralized management has a number of advantages over bureaucracy:

- Decisions are taken more quickly and closer to operations and, therefore, the organization is more flexible in its response to external threats and opportunities. With unit managers/team leaders having greater autonomy and accountability for performance, the role of and need for middle managers is reduced and the resulting 'delayering' brings reductions in management overheads
- Managerial and professional work becomes more challenging and this, coupled with greater autonomy, can instil greater motivation and commitment
- Managerial autonomy over operations coupled with sharper accountability for performance means that organizational units must become more outward-facing and customer-driven.

However, decentralization can bring problems:

- Business units or project teams concentrate on their own short-term objectives or work to local rationalities to the detriment of the longer-term interests of the organization as a whole. The pressure to do so is particularly acute when units/teams are judged and rewarded on achievement of performance targets
- Scale economies are lost if there is duplication of effort across units/teams or failure to identify and exploit areas of cooperation and synergy
- Managerial/leader roles are broader and more loosely defined and therefore there is greater reliance on high calibre, generalist managers/leaders able to combine a range of business and technical skills and who can be trusted to take decisions in the interests of the organization as a whole as well as their own
- There is some loss of centralized control over operating standards and procedures that can lead to inconsistency, loss of the cost efficiencies that come from standardization, excessive risk-taking and a loss of corporate identity and coherence. The organization can fragment into a collection of separate mini-organizations that are locally effective but corporately inefficient.

Despecialized operations

The desire to improve the quality of working life, increase operational flexibility or improve the quality of processes and products will continue to prompt attempts to move away from fragmented, regulated organization of operational work. Although these take different forms, they share some common themes:

1. Replacing imposed, fixed methods of work by more flexible methods that take account of worker choice and their sociopsychological needs
2. Reducing specialization by re-combining tasks to create jobs with greater variety, skill demands and significance and by creating cross-functional teams
3. Reducing the rigid division between management and operations by giving employees more involvement in planning, monitoring and controlling their own work or more say in organizational decision-making

4. Treating employees as a key resource in which to invest through training and development, rather than a cost to be minimized.

Forms of despecialization: job redesign, team-working and empowerment

In practice, 'despecialization' covers a variety of changes to operational work (Pettigrew and Fenton, 2000; Hales, 2001a):

- Rotating employees among different jobs, according to levels of work activity
- Creating broader multi-task jobs, with employees responsible for a whole work process rather than part of it
- Empowering employees to plan and organize their work and use their initiative and judgement to solve problems or introduce improvements
- Creating self-managing teams with collective responsibility for scheduling, allocating, coordinating and monitoring their work without direct supervision
- Creating cross-functional project teams.

Despecialization in tourism

Examples of work redesign, employee involvement and empowerment in tourism include:

- Job rotation and flexible deployment of multi-skilled 'shift' staff in hospitality operations and visitor attractions
- 'Host' employees designated to look after all the needs of specific customers
- Clerical or service jobs expanded to include selling
- Empowering sales/reservation staff to use their discretion to secure a sale or empowering customer service staff to choose how to handle customer requests or complaints
- Team-working among front-of-house or restaurant staff in hospitality organizations or among airline crew.

These forms of working have always been and will continue to be common in SMEs in tourism, not because of formal work redesign programmes but because organizations with a limited staff complement require flexible working. However, in larger organizations, as in other industries, despecialization remains limited in extent and depth – confined to a few experiments or programmes in selected areas of operation, rather than applied across the board and often amounting to less in practice than is claimed in the corporate rhetoric. For example, 'empowerment' programmes can amount to little more than giving front-line service employees very limited and carefully monitored discretion over how they respond to customer requests and complaints or running training courses about 'responsibility' and 'taking ownership' that are not matched by any greater say in how work is organized (Hales, 2000) (see Case study 10.2 Southwest Airlines).

Case study 10.2 Southwest Airlines, USA

One celebrated exponent of team-working is Southwest Airlines, the no-frills American regional airline offering a low cost, convenience and 'fun' service. A key element of this offering is rapid turnaround between flights (Southwest aim for 17 minutes) which permits tighter scheduling, a need for fewer aircraft and lower fuel and maintenance costs. To this end, flight attendants, customer service representatives, check-in and ramp staff, mechanics and pilots work with a minimum of job demarcation, as cross-functional teams, or 'crew', with pilots as team leaders. Flight attendants help clean the cabin, ground staff assist pilots and pilots have been known to load baggage. Focus on completing the task is sharpened by emphasis on open communication and problem solving, rather than hierarchical decisions and rules.

Southwest also points up the conditions and limitations of 'empowerment' and 'team-working'. The main characteristic of teams is not autonomy but flexibility: crews do not so much control their work as have to find ways of doing it quickly. Teams are embedded in a broader corporate culture where the emphasis is on loyalty, 'spirit', hard work and friendly, entertaining service and where 'fun' is an obligation. To reinforce this culture, Southwest's recruitment is highly selective (1 interviewee in 50 succeeds) and based on having the 'right' attitudes, rather than skills. There is a six-month programme of intensive induction, mentoring and training, focused as much on indoctrination as on acquiring skills, much of which is carried out in employees' own time. Those who do not 'fit' the culture leave early (about a third during the first six months); those who do work long hours under pressure while maintaining a show of good humour.

www.iflyswa.com

Despecialized operations: strengths and weaknesses

Despecialized operations have a number of potential advantages over earlier methods:

- More flexible and efficient deployment of human resources and better use of employee skills
- More challenging and satisfying work and, consequently, higher morale and lower absenteeism and labour turnover
- Employees exercise more responsibility, initiative and problem solving, particularly over quality or process improvements
- Employees have a greater sense of ownership of and commitment to decisions.

However, despecialized operations also carry a number of potential problems:

- There is a need for more selective recruitment and extensive training, both of which are costly
- Work becomes more intensive and this, coupled with team pressure, can increase employee stress

- The work system as a whole becomes less efficient as employees move between tasks or spend time in planning and decision-making
- The loss of managerial control may result in inconsistencies in methods and standards
- 'Team working' and 'empowerment' may simply be forms of rhetoric that are not matched by any substantive changes.

Management and organization structures in tourism: future trends

It is dangerous to assume that there is a clear, inevitable linear 'trend' to greater decentralization or despecialization in tourism organizations. Four counterpoints should be noted. First, any trend towards greater decentralization may be reversed as organizations re-establish centralized controls and bring activities back in-house in order to maintain standards and control costs. For example, in the wake of 9/11, airport security, which had been outsourced to external contractors, has been brought back under internal control in order to monitor procedures more closely.

Secondly, changes in many large bureaucratic organizations are not always as radical as is claimed and for good reason (Hilmer and Donaldson, 1996). The number of management levels may be reduced and the emphasis may shift from processes to performance and from human and paper systems to electronic systems, but there is still centralized control (albeit exercised differently) of individual managerial responsibility and accountability (albeit to more senior managers and in different ways). The result is not a loose network organization but 'bureaucracy-lite' (Hales, 2001b). Rather than becoming facilitators, coaches, leaders or internal entrepreneurs, managers continue to focus on the traditional functions of command and control.

Thirdly, the trend in large tourism organizations, as in services generally, is still towards greater rationalization or 'McDonaldization' (Ritzer, 1998) of operations, focused on efficiency, quantification, predictability and control. As well as the minutely-controlled production-line processes of fast food and budget hotels, there are the mechanization and self-service (where the free labour of customers is enlisted) of internet reservations and automated ticketing systems, the stripped down operations of 'no-frills' budget airlines and the tightly regulated work tasks, 'guest management' techniques and scripted service encounters in some theme parks and attractions.

Finally, given the high proportion of SMEs in the tourism industry, large machine bureaucracies have always been relatively few in number and of limited significance for employment. The small independent hotel, guest house or restaurant, specialist travel agent or tour operator and small-scale attraction or resort service have informal, simple structures. There is a fluid division of labour and flexible work methods, driven more by what needs to be done and who can do it than rigid job demarcations and by custom and practice rather than formal rules. Decision-making is vested in the owner-manager and coordination and control are based more on inter-personal relationships and face-to-face communication than on formal systems. This is often coupled with a 'family' culture based on informality, mutual obligation and loyalty (Goffee and Scase, 1995). If these businesses are successful and grow it can be difficult for them to avoid creeping 'bureaucratization' and rationalization. Increasing scale and complexity of operations requires more complex and formal division of work, formal systems of planning, decision-making, coordination and control and more rules. However, through choice or circumstances, many small organizations in tourism stay small and informally organized.

Conclusion: future forms of management and organization in tourism – clear trends or subtle blends?

There is no simple answer to the question posed at the beginning of this chapter. Other things being equal, more turbulent, competitive environments will demand greater strategic adaptability, operational flexibility and service customization and these, in turn, are more effectively delivered by decentralized, performance-driven organizations. However, any significant 'trend' to decentralization or despecialization in tourism will depend on the extent to which environments continue to be deregulated, the extent to which organizations are shaped by, rather than are able to influence, their environments and the extent to which organizational decision-makers are prepared to risk adopting new organizational forms. Consequently, decentralization may be modest rather than radical and reversed by a swing back to centralization, particularly if organizations come to regard control as more important than flexibility. Similarly, employee empowerment or team-working may be limited in scope, modest in substance and offset by continuing rationalization of operations.

Because any benefits of such changes are always benefits on balance and linked to particular circumstances, it would be dangerous to over-generalize, especially since tourism encompasses such a wide diversity of activities, organizations and cultural contexts. Modest, localized and multi-directional change is the most probable, if less exciting (or threatening), future prospect. What is most likely is that tourism organizations will attempt, pragmatically, to combine elements of bureaucracy to ensure consistency and control, a business unit structure to capture local rationalities, networks to foster cooperation and knowledge-sharing and empowerment to encourage creativity and commitment. How many will get the blend right is an open question but the future success stories will be those that do.

11

Innovation, Creativity and Competitiveness

Peter M Burns

Introduction

As with most business and social enterprises, innovation cannot be separated from the economic and cultural milieu from which it springs. For this reason, the chapter starts by rehearsing some of the arguments that frame the geopolitics of tourism and the impact of terrorism as well as changing attitudes towards consumption and consumerism. This is followed by a brief historic overview of tourism sufficient to act as a reminder of the stages that tourism, tourists and destinations have come through to arrive at the present era. The chapter finishes with some speculation leading to a future vision for tourism. Within the text, three brief case studies are included as being topical and representative of different aspects of tourism. In the past, examples of innovation in tourism would have included customer loyalty schemes, computerized check-out systems for hotels (and check-in systems for airlines), efficient and reliable long-haul airliners, employee empowerment, all-inclusive resorts and, as we should not forget, the very concept of the packaged tour as well as the introduction of traveller's cheques.

The geopolitics of tourism

At the cusp of the twentieth and twenty-first centuries, the world and thus tourism was undergoing mixed fortunes. On the one hand there was unprecedented growth fuelled by a potent mixture of technology, deregulation and economic buoyancy, while on the other, global confidence had been knocked by a series of natural and political disasters (for example, strange weather patterns, terrorism, SARS). Against this background, global and regional geopolitics were rapidly changing with the old Soviet empire having collapsed along with its communist ideologies (a period that Francis Fukuyama famously called 'the end of history' 1992). As a consequence, the remaining single superpower (perhaps suprapower?) was in search of a role to reflect its ideological and political victory: following 9/11, it turned out to be as unilateralist, *de facto* global policeman pursuing a war against terrorism. For Europe, with the new emerging markets physically located upon its doorstep, the ensuing freedoms for former Eastern bloc countries to pursue independent political paths led inevitably to an enlarged Europe and a host of new opportunities.

In the immediate aftermath of 9/11, world tourism was severely shaken but, having faltered momentarily, it did not implode. International tourist arrivals for the year ending 2001 were down by only 0.5 per cent (WTO, 2003). In 2002, tourism showed its resilience, even in the face of the Bali bombing and general tension in the Middle East, by increasing international visitor arrivals to an unprecedented 715 million (up 3.1 per cent on the previous year) (WTO, 2003). On the other hand, the sudden spread of SARS showed a new side to the global airline industry: its role in spreading diseases. Canada's tourism, along with many destinations in the Far East such as Hong Kong, China, Malaysia etc., had their international tourism, inbound and outbound, severely disrupted. Thus, the beginning of the twenty-first century has given destinations, companies and consumers the most chaotic, confusing and yet exciting times ever known in the history of modern tourism.

The consequences of all these paradoxical activities have been multiple and include:

- Acceleration of structural changes to the airline industry including the collapse of weaker, traditional network carriers in the face of global competition and the rise of short-haul low-cost airlines. Since 2000, budget airlines worldwide 'expanded capacity by 44 per cent [and] low cost carriers currently have orders for 400 new planes, whereas the old network carriers have only 150 planes on order' (*The Economist*, 2004, p.67)
- Further changes to tour operating and airline owning patterns with bankruptcies/near bankruptcies (Alitalia, Lufthansa, United Airlines, US Airways) and acquisitions and mergers (Air France-KLM, possibly Qantas-Air New Zealand)
- Confirmation that 'global' tourism is mostly regional and that while data from the World Tourism Organization (WTO) and World Travel and Tourism Council (WTTC) show global growth, they can hide huge national and regional differences (Table 11.1)
- The desire for international travel is deeply ingrained in post-industrial cultures and has changed from an aspiration to the expectation of an 'experience economy' (Pine and Gilmore, 1999)
- Markets are more volatile (Table 11.1) with more demanding consumers.

Table 11.1 International tourist arrivals showing percentage change for selected destinations

	2000	2001	2002	2003*
Britain	−0.7	−9.4	4.8	0.9
France	3.5	1.2	2.0	−4.1**
Indonesia	7.1	1.8	−2.3	−34.6
Israel	4.5	−50.5	−27.9	−15.1
Kenya	4.3	−6.5	−0.4	na
Mexico	8.4	−4.0	−0.7	−14.8
South Africa	−0.4	−1.5	10.9	5.0**
Spain	2.4	3.4	3.3	3.2
Turkey	39.1	12.5	18.5	−11.2
USA	5.0	−10.7	−6.7	−7.6**

* January–April; ** January–March.
Source: WTO data, from an idea by *The Economist* (2003)

In summary then, the rapidly changing geopolitical situation has provided a vivid background for innovation, creativity and competitiveness in tourism which has, in recent years, been driven by a sense of adventure and willingness on the part of consumers (demand-led expansion), the low cost airlines putting out cheap fares to new (sometimes obscure) destinations (supply-led expansion) and (in Europe), by regional authorities who were willing to make flexible arrangements (including subsidies) with budget carriers (regulatory freedom-led expansion). All these developments have led to increased mobility and according to some (Stallard, 2004) a democratization of air travel.

The examples illustrated in Table 11.1 show the sort of extreme visitor arrivals fluctuations that make forecasting, predicting, planning and investment problematic. In a sense, this emphasizes the need for creativity and innovation in tourism.

Historic overview

As an integral part of history, culture and economics for all regions of the world, tourism has influenced social mobility, identity and business milieu in developed and less developed areas, in both sending and receiving nations. Cultural attitudes towards travel have gone from the early feelings of wonderment and acceptance (for example the first generation of outbound European mass tourists in the 1960s) to litigious and demanding tourists of all generations who have high expectations and somehow 'know-what-they want and how-to-get-it' so to speak. Table 11.2 gives a snapshot of early tourism (the 'artisan' stage in a term coined by Fayos-Sola, 2004) along with other periods of tourism that will be referred to later.

Tables 11.1 and 11.2 illustrate certain paradoxes for tourism and it should be remembered that predictions made in the 1950s about leisured society with an abundance of time on their hands were overly optimistic.

Innovation, creativity and competitiveness in the early days of tourism were focused around the destination and transport and capitalizing upon the novelty of paid holidays and sufficient discretionary income to fund a vacation (which would most likely take place at a seaside resort), then the novelty of 'abroad' with

Table 11.2 Ages and stages of post-war tourism (supply-demand factors)

	Supply	*Demand*	*Business organization*	*Destination systems*
Artisan age of tourism (inter-war years to 1950s)	Local/fragmented/ unimaginative/ static	Individual/ basic/limited/ wary	Limited to chambers of commerce and professional associations	Poorly developed/ uncoordinated/ unsophisticated
Fordian mode of production (1960s–1980s)	Homogeneous/ price-competitive/ low cost labour	Mass/ standard 5Ss/ price not quality driven	Vertical/ horizontal integration	Sophisticated, coordinated
'Modern' age of tourism (metanarrative of consumption) (1980s–2000s)	Recognition of 'ageing' resorts and attractions	Growing demand for ethical/ sustainable products	Ruthless competition, mergers and acquisitions	Re-engineering airports, smoothing cross-border entry requirements
Postmodern tourism (the metanarrative of mobility) (2000s–Future)	Hyperniche/ super-segmentation and quality driven	Experienced consumers, technophiles, price and quality conscious	Diagonal' 'coopetition' (strategic alliances)	Sustainable, re-engineered, coordinated, increased security

Source: from ideas by Fayos-Sola (2004) and author

the post-war opening up and development of the new Mediterranean 'triple S' resorts (in Spain, followed by the likes of Greece, Portugal, Morocco, and Tunisia). This was followed in the 1980s and 1990s by the product development in long-haul destinations such as the USA (in effect, Florida) for Europe and South-East Asia for the USA and Europe. Visitors to these destinations were unlikely to be first time or 'novice' travellers, so they demanded (and often got) good hotels and services at relatively cheap prices.

Tourism 1980s–2000

The past two decades of tourism up until the present time could be described as 'transitional' in that there is a heightened sensitivity that consumption, through various forms of mobility (in the sense of mobile populations engaging with tourism), is largely unsustainable. At the same time, awareness existed that innovation, creativity and competitiveness were not really beginning to produce answers (Sundbo et al., 2003a, b). For example, restructuring technologies for the travel industry and increased efficiency for the airline sector led to growing attention towards the concept of knowledge management being an integral part of how companies innovate. But these business paradigms take place within political and social structures that both help and hinder tourism's progress. Political instability and uncertainty in many parts of the world is undermining gains made through the new liberalism of deregulation and denationalization. Affluence in the form of disposable income in advanced economies (loosely called the West or the North, according to which literature is being read), a prerequisite for leisure travel, is part of the global shifting social conditions that include a widening gap between rich and poor. Moreover, the globalization of cultures and food both stifle and encourage social innovation in response to tourism. For example, where powerful destination influencers encourage the 'freezing' of cultural characteristics and manifestations in order to show tourists lifestyles and culture as a visitor attraction, then technology and innovation are used to reinforce images of the past, in effect, museumizing place, space and people for the sake of tourism.

However, on the other hand tourist interest in local culture may reassert or reawaken local interest leading to cultural pride and revival (see Case study 11.1).

Case study 11.1 Destination Innovation through Culture and Religion

The area of Eichsfeld in Germany is an area that was split by the old division of East and West and was thus off the tourist map during the Cold War period. With the reunification of Germany in 1990 local authorities looked to tourism as one of a number of economic options. The attraction of the region was historical, cultural and religious (the area has a largely Roman Catholic population in a mostly Protestant region). Several local villages capitalized on this by marketing and developing special events such as an annual passion play that eventually enabled the funding of restoration works to religious buildings. The creativity was in using existing assets at a time of economic and political turmoil (albeit with a positive outlook) to create spiritual sustainability and cohesion in an area undergoing rapid transition. More can be seen on http://www.natureparktravel.com/nature-park/nature-park.htm

This fits in with the idea that visitors may be shifting their consumption paradigm from passive fun to active learning. The sensitivities derived from careful interpretation of local cultures may help create awareness about social impacts in the same way that knowledge of environmental impacts has grown and developed over the last decade.

Emerging trends, approaches, models and paradigms beyond the millennium

In the unstable, unstoppable world of tourism, predicting trends is problematic. Different sectors have differently paced developments. Aviation, driven by low-cost business models is changing the way it operates and we can expect to see more mergers with the three main global loyalty partnerships, One World, Star Alliance and Skyteam coming even closer together in new forms of 'coopetition' (Quinion, 1998). However, the fact that no tax is charged on aviation fuel is coming under the spotlight and the jury is out as to whether the powerful airline lobbies can maintain this particular status quo. The hotels sector is still trying to resolve the paradox of what makes a great hotel even greater and for them cost cutting is difficult unless it is in the non-public areas that remain unobserved by the tourist (an exception here is the semi-automation of budget hotels where

Table 11.3 Ages of tourism in review (economic and social factors)

Epoch/era	Factors
'Fin-de siecle' (1890–1914) cultures of consumption (Walton, 2001)	■ Working class demand for full-scale holidays as well as day trips (paid holidays) ■ Industrialization of mobility (trains, coaches) ■ Spatially captive ■ Health-giving properties of the seaside (sea air, sea bathing) ■ Childish innocence (buckets and spades, sandcastles, nature: starfish, rock-pools, gulls) ■ Informality/democratization of food mobile cross-class 'take-aways' opposite from stifling formality of 'home' (ice cream, fish and chips) ■ Suspension of 'normality' (awakening sexuality, play as opposite to work)
Artisan age (inter-war years to 1950s) (Fayos-Sola, 2004)	■ Basic technologies (mechanical, slow) ■ Harsh social conditions for many ■ Economies characterized by rural/industrial schism ■ Naive, uncritical, uncertain consumers with low expectations framed by their own utilitarian standards of living
The Fordist years (1960s–1980s) (Fayos-Sola, 2004)	■ Technologies for productivity (cost cutting, consumer irrelevant) ■ Crumbling welfare state ■ Increasing disposable income ■ Politically stable regions ■ Increased educational, cultural and political awareness in an emergent consumer society
'Modern' (1980–2000)	■ The 'grand narrative' of mass tourism as being the dominant model with last-ditch efforts by likes of WTTC and WTO to hold on to traditions and 'talk down' impacts and problems. Technology developments and science will make problems go away ■ Emergent eco-movements challenge existing order focusing on environment, culture and representational aspects within late-capitalism
New age of tourism and the 'Experience economy'	■ Goods were commoditized by the service economy, services are being commoditized by the experience economy ■ The business becomes theatre through which to offer memorable experiences ■ Ultimate aim of business is to build relations with consumers by making their lives better ■ Mobilization of ideas, knowledge and expectations ■ Fragmenting customer loyalty ■ Ennui (post-modernism) driving continued experience-seeking and the 'shock of the new' for consumers

Source: Pine and Gilmore, 1999; author's own reflections

customers accept lower levels of personal service as an acceptable trade-off against much lower prices). There is, however, still much room for innovation in design and décor as many hotels continue to look and feel as though they are operating in the middle of the twentieth century instead of the beginning of the twenty-first. Boutique and other specialist hotels (such as those designed by the likes of Philippe Starck, and Ian Schrager's group of avant-garde hotels including the St Martins Lane Hotel in London) are obvious fashion innovations, but have neither critical marketing mass nor capacity to cope with the increasing numbers of people on the move to influence the entire sector.

Interestingly, railways (especially in Europe and Japan) are continuing to provide reliable levels of long-distance international service and rail companies are now trying to position themselves as 'citycentre to citycentre' service providers for trips that total less than four hours door to door, reminding air passengers that while the flight time may be short, getting to the final venue takes (sometimes) unacceptably long times (*The Economist*, 1998). Consumers themselves, as mentioned elsewhere in this chapter, have become adept at using the Internet at the same time that various travel industry sectors have realized the potential for using it as a vast clearing-house in the form of a strategic distribution resource. Many sources cite tourism as the world's largest e-sector, 'American consumers [in 2003] spending more than $27 billion on travel online ... [perhaps] 30 per cent of all travel business will be booked online by 2005' (*The Economist*, 2003).

One analytical approach to thinking about twenty-first century innovation in business (especially services) is the idea of the 'experience economy', as shown in Table 11.3, which shows how the tourism and travel mobilities fit with Pine and Gilmore's (1999) notions for service companies in the future. Tables 11.2 and 11.3 also illustrate (among other things) how tourism as a business paradigm and social concept is seen in various stages including the present time. Business organization and distribution are being dominated by strategic alliances, some in the form of 'coopetition' (Quinion, 1998) in which competition is tempered with collaborative networks and partnerships and social capital is nurtured to help expand the market share for all players (see Case study 11.2).

Case study 11.2 Local Tourism Clustering

Business clustering is a well-established approach to creating critical mass among small companies within a given geographic location. The advantages come through the strategic alliance provided by the cluster grouping and through the innovation that arises from producers and suppliers meeting regularly to discuss and brainstorm ideas. The Centre for Tourism Policy Studies (CENTOPS) University of Brighton, funded by the South East England Development Agency, developed such a cluster based around the English seaside town of Eastbourne. The cluster brought together about 50 businesses related to tourism ranging from hotels to specialist regional food producers. The theme of the cluster was 'healthy lifestyle' and during the first nine months businesses reported fresh energy and ideas in the way in which they ran, marketed and thought about their businesses. The cluster went on to sponsor the Beachy Head Marathon (Eastbourne, England) in October 2004. Details can be seen at www.hltcluster.co.uk.

Experienced consumers, who know how to get the best out of technology, are both price and quality conscious with issues of quality spilling out into the domain of environmental and social quality.

Vision for the future of the tourism industry

Tourism in the future is likely to be even fuzzier than it is now and dominated by an experience economy (Pine and Gilmore, 1999). They make the important point that 'memorable experiences' are not simply about entertaining people in a service setting, but about capturing their imagination and meeting a combination of four needs: entertainment, education, escapism and aesthetics (one could add individualism). This somewhat post-modern model fits with the place that tourism finds itself at present and the ways in which a globalized political economy, with all the accompanying mobilities, is working. For example, in the UK (which is certainly no exception in the general political economy of the post-industrial world):

> Developments in the labour market have led to a new categorization of British society. There is a bottom 30% of unemployed and economically inactive who are marginalized. Another 30%, who, while in work, are in forms of employment that are structurally insecure. And there are only 40% who can count themselves as holding tenured jobs that allow them to regard their income prospects with any security. The 30/30/40 society is a proxy for the growth of a new inequality and the new risks about the predictability and certainty of income that have spread across all occupations and all classes.
>
> (Hutton 1995)

So, in the experience economy, we can imagine the richest 40 per cent seeking to have their senses engaged while the insecure middle 30 per cent who will fill the low-paid jobs that enable the experience economy companies to operate, being observed by the bottom 30 per cent who have little chance to engage with the process as consumers or providers. How long the resultant myth of mutual engagement with the view to enhancing the consumer's life will last is open to discussion, but as the 'post tourist' knows (Urry, 1990), it's all a game where both sides of the consumption equation understand (and generally play by) the rules. Twenty-first century resorts, destinations and businesses based on knowledge and experience of the new consumer are paradoxes that can only be understood and analysed at the levels of:

- Culture and power (where innovation has to be framed by cultural sensitivities and an understanding of power relations between producers, consumers and local citizens)
- Class image (furthering Hutton's (1995) point about the 'new' class structures and the fact that they are being reflected at a global level so that far more nuanced and subtle class divisions are hindering mobility and access to tourism)
- Global shifts in consumer patterns (at the levels of demographics whereby the baby-boomers represent an enormously important market and new patterns of consumption)
- Social, economic and cultural practices of physical and virtual mobility (wherein the world has, for many, become smaller and has lost its mystery).

The tendency for market makers and planners in tourism to cling on to out-moded means of production and planning such as making changes to marketing or tinkering with product development simply won't do (for a small example of thinking outside the box, see Case study 11.3).

Case study 11.3 Low Cost Airline 'Bans' Hold Luggage

Ryanair is one of the leading innovators in air transport through its policies of cheap fares with a 'no frills' business model. The latest attempt at innovation and creative thinking (July 2004) is a proposal to charge passengers £50 fee for hand-ling checked-in baggage. The idea is that Ryanair could negotiate lower ground handling fees at airports if there was no hold-baggage to handle. The business model would be to allow passengers a reasonably large bag that fits into the overhead locker along with electronic purchase of tickets and check in. This type of thinking the unthinkable or 'outside the box' in ways that might not appeal to all is the trademark characteristic of a risk-taking, entrepreneurial company in a free market environment. Developments on this can be seen on www.ryanair.com

The future shape of tourism is, as mentioned before, notoriously difficult to pre-dict. However, Figure 11.1 captures the spirit of the future by emphasizing the way

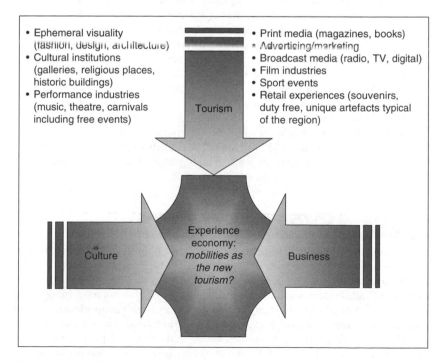

Figure 11.1 Future shape of tourism?

in which different parts of a destination's economy not normally associated with tourism will be drawn into its web as consumers continuously seek new experiences.

Figure 11.1 shows an image whereby culture, tourism and business come together to form a highly mobile 'experience economy' as the emerging model of tourism. At the juncture of tourism and culture (Figure 11.1, left) a range of phenomena blend together, starting with 'ephemeral visuality' meaning the unintended bonuses of tourism such as cityscapes, old and new architecture including street architecture, signs, billboards etc. which all add a frisson to individual and collective experience. On the right-hand side, a variety of commercial media, events and experiences contribute to the emerging paradigm showing the growing complexity of the relationship between the visitors and the visited in the light of globalizing cultures and communication. The tourist in the above model is no longer central to a simplistic service economy but an integral part of the cultural system at the destination akin to Walter Benjamin's concept of allegorical commodity which, 'with its emphasis on exchange and exhibition-value ... is devoid of substance. Its fate within the cycle of production and the contingencies of fashion is to become out of date, old-fashioned, obsolete' (Gilloch, 1996, p.136).

The ephemeral, disposable, obsolete nature of both resorts (in the sense that they become outdated unless continuously reinvented) and tourists (who seemingly are on the lookout for novelty in and through an 'age of mechanical reproduction' Benjamin, 1935) are only 'saved' for prosperity (and later analysis in a different historical context) by Benjamin's 'modern hero' the flaneur, who strolls through the paradoxes of everyday life slowly observing and thinking about seemingly trivial transactions, and the 'rag picker' who collects and gives meaning to the detritus and ephemera of industrial society whereby, 'All such cultural phcnomena ... aie broken down by history – not into *narratives*, as expressed through the fictions of conventional history writing, but into *images* that the dialectical gaze needs to read in order to decipher their true significance' (Pausch, p.1). Just a little effort can trace the roots of the seemingly post-modern view of Pine and Gilmore's (1999) experience economy to the émigré critical essayist, Walter Benjamin who saw townscapes (in particular) as giant collections of sounds, images, bustle: whimsical space and time to be experienced at a truly profound level. These speculative ideas match emerging trends in familiar global markets where the potential visitor of the future is likely to be older, more affluent, thoughtful and discriminating, as well as increasingly wishing to stimulate and enhance their knowledge through experiences.

Conclusions: future innovations in tourism

This chapter has attempted to bring together a number of disparate ideas concerning innovation, creativity and competitiveness for an industry that struggles to innovate, create and compete on anything but the most basic, unimaginative level. The English seaside is a case in point, as it was left to languish for decades failing, for the most part, to deal with competition from cheap Mediterranean vacations and, indeed, a change in expectations and attitudes in consumers. In an age of furniture innovation, design and house make-over TV programmes, very few customers under the age of 40, one might venture, would feel comfortable in resort or seaside hotels which seem rooted in the dusty past rather than in the uncluttered modernism of polished beech floors, black and chrome leather sofas and minimalist white walls!

These new consumer attitudes are impacting destinations, which are increasingly likely to offer low impact tourism facilities, consistent with consumer demand for environmental values and the desire not to contribute to negative impacts. It could be suggested that suppliers are becoming more sophisticated and using technology-driven consumer profiles to develop highly personalized and targeted messages ('ultra-info'). This process could be termed 'hyper-niche', 'super-differentiation', or 'super-segmentation' (Saayman and Slabert, 2004).

There is no doubt that tourism will continue to provide massive injections of cash into economies at various stages of development and a mix of good governance and imagination will ensure it stays one of the world's biggest industries.

12

Chaos Theory and Managerial Approaches

Roslyn A Russell

Introduction

Chaos theory has emerged as a useful framework that provides a greater insight into phenomena that are complex, unpredictable and uncertain. It is often referred to as the 'science of change' (Briggs and Peat, 1999) and can therefore add value to the study of any field that involves humans. Any system that is characterized by elements that dynamically interact is naturally prone to a chaotic state. Over the last ten years, chaos theory has emerged in the management literature providing a far more realistic framework for today and the future than previous management models based on stability, predictability and control. Organizations can be seen as complex adaptive systems and most are, more than ever before, experiencing edge-of-chaos states, making them sensitive to initial conditions where small impacts can have large consequences that cannot be predicted (Thietart and Forgues, 1995).

What is chaos theory?

Chaos theory is a descriptive device in the form of a major metaphor – chaos, with a number of metaphorical appendages. There is, however, a distinction between the common connotation of 'chaos' as unrestrained disorder, confusion and disarray and its scientific usage signifying behaviour in a system, such as a hotel, a car or family life. Impinging upon these systems are pressures, usually unpredictable, that induce or, more often, force a response that seems inconsistent with what was before. Chaos theory proposes that everything exists in a state of flux, that any appearance of a steady-state, in the usual sense, is illusory and that catalysts pop up to dislodge the system from its quasi-rest. Depending on whether the catalyst is negative or positive the response may be immediately disadvantageous or profitable. Sometimes the system may respond positively from what is perceived as a negative impact.

There are degrees of susceptibility. An enterprise tottering on the brink of the abyss does not need much of a nudge to topple into a more dynamically chaotic state where the survival struggle is intensified. On the other hand, successful organizations can profit from external catalysts; for example, a hotel with high occupancy rates, buoyant profits and enterprising management may be resilient enough to be advantaged by the opportunities suddenly offered by the abrupt downturn at foreign destinations due to terrorism fear.

All areas of human interaction – the stock market, or politics for example, but none more than tourism – are sensitive to shocks. Physical sciences deal with areas usually more stable – eclipses, tides and sunrises can be predicted with unerring accuracy and apples that detach themselves from trees still fall downwards. Hence, the principles of Newtonian science that deals very well with more stable phenomena are less than adequate in helping us to understand incidents, events or areas of our lives that are not so predictable or stable.

Where has chaos theory come from?

Newton crystallized thinking about the material world. He perceived tangible realities as being like giant clocks utterly dependable, ticking away with mechanical precision, all components performing their individual functions in coordination – springs transferring energy through cogs and levers to hands. God-given rules governed all aspects of the physical world and the scientist's task was to fathom and verbalize those rules. This could be done by reductionism, dismantling the whole to examine its parts in isolation to determine their functions in order to conjecture about the resynthesized whole.

Laws permitted no exceptions. What did not fit the rigid pattern was dismissed as 'noise', rare and freakish aberrations. The University of Vienna went so far as to throw out a collection of meteorites because no niches could be found for them in the concept of the ordered universe. Such was the unwillingness of the scientific fraternity to recognize abnormal or unique occurrences. Scientists did not know how to account for externalities so therefore it was better if they did not exist.

But as science became more exacting, the tools of trade more sophisticated and scientists more sceptical, the exceptions became more numerous and obvious. As

Table 12.1 Contrasting principles of traditional science and chaos theory

Traditional science	*Chaos theory*
Based on 19th century Newtonian physics	Based on biological model of living systems
Systems seen as simple and characterized by linearity	Systems seen as inherently complex, non-linear
Systems viewed as being in equilibrium	Systems viewed as unstable, turbulent
Externalities that cause differences or instability in the system are seen as abnormal or 'noise'	Externalities, internal or external, are seen as 'normal' and can be significant in shaping the system

Source: adapted from Toohey (1994, p.286) and Waldrop (1992, pp.37–38)

new specialities like quantum physics probed more deeply than Newtonians had been able to or dared to, exceptions multiplied. An alternative to Newton's linear, mechanical, stable model was needed.

Henri Poincare, a French mathematician had, in the late nineteenth century, done the groundwork to support such a framework. It was proposed that the natural world of living things provided a better model of a complex world than a clock. Reality functioned more like a forest of individual trees interacting with their total environment than a congregation of machines. Chaos theory reflects the change-proneness, the dynamism and the self-healing properties of living organisms. The work of Ilya Prigogine and Isabelle Stengers (1985), Fritjof Capra (1982), James Gleick (1987) and Mitchell Waldrop (1992) has further developed the concepts of chaos theory and complexity and they are considered to be the most significant authors of chaos theory work. Table 12.1 shows the contrasting principles of traditional science and chaos theory.

What or where is the edge-of-chaos?

Edge-of-chaos is a condition of extreme readiness for radical change. It may be visualized as a table heaped with sand to the limit of its capacity. The pile has been built by trickling down sand a grain at a time until the limit of tolerance is reached and the only cohesion is provided by the moisture and friction between the grains. When critical instability is reached, there is a bifurcation point leading to a dramatic phase-shift into dynamic instability in the form of an avalanche as friction enables sliding grains to drag others after themselves. Alternatively, the pile of sand can readjust itself and form a new shape (probably quite different from the original pile) so that it can better cope with the added complexity (Mathews et al., 1999). In chaos theory, emphasis is on provocations and responses that are unforeseeable. Nor can the configuration of the heap replenished by more grains of sand be precisely known but it should be noted that the heap, like living organisms, has the capacity to self-heal.

What is a chaos butterfly?

The ultimate grain of sand was a butterfly. The straw that broke the camel's back was a butterfly. The term was coined by Edward Lorenz (1963), a meteorologist who, in 1960, was seeking pattern and predictability in weather systems. He had graphed the relationship between several variables that affected the dynamics of moving fluids. The line connecting the intersect points traced out a pattern similar to the opened wings of a butterfly. However, when repeating the experiment, a minute change in the input occurred due to a rounding error at the millionth position. When the computer ran the data again completely different outcomes were observed. Weather patterns are extremely capricious and sensitive to minute changes in any of the variables. The butterfly, it was theorized, aptly symbolized this tentativeness and capacity of small triggers to cause responses out of proportion to their size. The fluttering of a butterfly's wings in the Amazon could initiate a ripple that would magnify to a dust storm in Texas.

The underlying premise of chaos theory is the acknowledgement that tiny deviations can produce large outcomes. Some changes in our environment, for example, interest rate rises or changes in government powers, are probably more manageable. Small changes come suddenly and sometimes with catastrophic results. At the personal level, the alarm clock did not ring, the traveller missed the plane and so lived to tell about it after the plane subsequently crashed mid-ocean (a positive outcome surely). At the corporate level, the impact of a single rogue trader in one of the world's largest financial institutions can bring the organization to its knees. At the national level, a fumble in vote counting in Florida may have sent the wrong man to the White House. The failure of a small 'O' ring worth a few cents caused a tragedy that shook a nation and jeopardized the whole NASA operation. At the international level, a single, well-aimed bullet assassinated an obscure Austrian prince launching nations primed for conflict into the multiple catastrophes of World War I. Could the intervention of quality management have averted or moderated any of these outcomes?

Loops? Tenuous equilibrium?

Unlike the linear model, the organic paradigm traces progress with a line that oscillates, meanders and loops. A loop represents a critical episode of development triggered by some unplanned-for circumstance. Sudden decline may be followed by a slower recovery as coping mechanisms are set in place and conditions improve. The loop is thus completed but the compensatory influences may not be adequate enough to lift the system to its former path. Or it may rise above that path because the fall itself can be a powerful engine to drive attainment. A terrorists' bomb devastates an island resort frequented by foreign tourists, plunging the café in the next block into the financial disaster zone. But some innovative planning, venturesomeness and physical effort make the building more attractive and the menu more extensive. Recuperation occurs as services are fully restored and the streets are repopulated, at first by the re-builders and bravely curious and eventually by an increased flow of tourists attracted by reassuring advertising and special deals. What initially was disruptive was ultimately beneficial.

A more positive loop may be an unexpected or accidental breakthrough in R&D that enables a revolutionary medical device to be presented to a hungry world market. The looping back towards the former path may ensure that, when the market is saturated, the product is displaced by a superior one from a rival firm or when the exclusive patent rights lapse. The lesson here for organizations is to be alert to 'accidental' opportunities that can change the direction of the loop. Managers should not be so attached to their strategic maps that they cannot see other opportunistic paths that lie before them (Stacey, 1992). Staff at all levels have the capacity to stumble upon unexpected breakthroughs that could produce or improve a service or product (Briggs and Peat, 1999). By unleashing latent creativity in all staff, the rate of converting 'accidents' into profit will be higher.

When climactic looping is absent, when agitation is minimal and business-as-usual seems to prevail, stability is tenuous and, because subtle undercurrents persist, may be illusory. Nor are the loops that punctuate this qualified equilibrium equal in size or spaced at regular intervals. Unlike the recurring seasons or the chiming of Big Ben, they are spasmodic, or 'aperiodic' and irregular in size. They come, like the arrival of the health inspector at the kitchen door or an earth tremor in Turkey, unheralded.

How can an attractor be strange?

A pendulum ball is energized by the initial push. This is dissipated in an orderly way as gravity exerts braking force. The path is straight back and forth and the slowing rate is calculable. The pendulum is 'attracted' to its normal state which is rest, in much the same way as a toy car energized by winding exhausts its means of propulsion and stops. All systems, including people and businesses are subject to entropy, according to the second Law of Thermodynamics, until their energy is consumed. Some systems, however, can be revitalized by a new energy input.

But the pattern and vigour of the pendulum's swing may be modified by a new force, a puff of breeze, or a bump. A new pattern of movement emerges in sympathy with the direction and vigour of the supplementary force. The pendulum has been strangely attracted to this new behaviour. The new behaviour is the strange attractor – strange, because it is a departure from the norms for pendulums, one that would be difficult to duplicate.

Innovation constantly seeks to disturb patterns of consumption. Radical innovation is discontinuous, a disruptive force that destabilizes. Innovation exerts forces that draw us (the pendulums) into new and perhaps erratic responses. In chaos theory perceptions, it is relatively easy to veer away from the routine as status quo is a fragile condition. Uncertainty, flexibility and change are the constants. Future success of an organization will depend upon its ability to innovate the best and the most often and hence its ability to function effectively in an environment of uncertainty and instability.

Lock-in, irreversibility and sensitivity to initial conditions

An enterprise that is so embedded in a modus operandi that it has routinely practised, while enjoying the good luck not to be seriously challenged, may be said to be 'locked-in'. The mind-set that holds onto the belief that what worked ten years ago will be equally successful in a decade's time is difficult to dislodge. It may not sabotage some niches like handcrafting violins but, in the turbulent world of vigorous competition, it is a disaster formula. Again, entrepreneurial agility is the survival essential.

Time cannot be reversed. We still cannot swim the same river twice. Things cannot be replicated with precision. What emerges from a change loop is more than a restoration of the former state. It will be refurbished, replenished, revitalized and redirected according to the magnitude and nature of the unsettling stimulus and the curative agency.

But nor will it lose all resemblance to its former self. There is sensitivity to the original state. The DNA that gave shape, texture and colour to the leaves that fell in autumn will determine what sprouts in spring. Living things are, after all, the chaos models. The regenerated business may reflect the old as the new tree reflects the former without replicating it. It is worth noting that regeneration comes from within the tree. The organization in chaos terms is self-healing, a process that comes from within and proceeds upward. Bali is being built again, mainly through a bottom-up process. It will never be the same as it was before – but that might not be a bad thing.

Implications for tourism resort management

A resort's image and profitability is shaped by a number of factors such as its location, market match, management and ultimately the degree to which it delivers what it promised. These factors in turn, are determined by the degree to which many spheres and tiers can achieve a symbiosis. They are as multiple and varied as the government funding for infrastructure, the promotions by the local tourism council, the activity of the events committee, the frequency of sand or snow grooming, safety strategies in the fun parks, the coordination of operations in the large hotels as well as reliability and value in ancillary services – tour and commodity provision and banking. Chaos theory tells us that understanding and managing the relationship between these elements is just as significant as an understanding of the elements themselves. It is the dynamic interaction of these elements that can push a system into a chaotic state.

Market acceptability is influenced by human responses as diverse as the cheerfulness of the service staff, the promptness of the cook at the fish and chips shop, the alertness of a CEO and the imagination of the publicity officer. The frown of a single waitress would not alone mar the image but the aggregation of many frowning waitresses would. Reputation is based not so much on the trees as the forest, but each tree gives to or takes from the quality of the forest. Tourism is a complex forest where the application of chaos theory is highly appropriate (McKercher, 1999).

Entrepreneurs – a chaotic factor

Resorts attract entrepreneurs. Entrepreneurs tend to act independently. Entrepreneurs introduce innovation to the system, often destroying the status quo and causing instability (Russell and Faulkner, 1999). The organic model is accommodating enough to contain both the buzz of contention between rivals and the cooperation and cohesion when resourceful people decide to act together on matters of common interest. Organizations such as Chambers of Commerce and Tourism Councils usually evolve from the grass roots. They exemplify the self-healing bottom-up properties of chaos theory. They emerge to shape, protect and project an appealing image and are more intensely active in times of greater stress.

Managing chaotic triggers

Tourism is bombarded with a multiplicity of chaos catalysts to which it is highly sensitive. A prolonged blackout stems the inflow of kitchen provisions; a baggage handlers' dispute diverts most back-packers; a major client defaults his payment to a struggling bus company; the dollar soars but so does the oil price; the engineer overseeing the multi-million dollar extension quits. Nature can also be dramatically disruptive. After years of immunity, an island resort is suddenly devastated by a cyclone; a weather quirk gives an alpine resort its thickest powder snow in decades. Technology keeps the status quo unsettled – computers have revolutionized booking systems, but failure to check the clip that secured a pin on the wild ride of an itinerant theme park caused disaster.

How can dissonances so numerous in an industry so shock sensitive be managed? It needs to be accepted that tourism, and resort health generally, are volatile and constantly likely to be bombarded with perturbations. Change is always imminent; some impacts are positive and even negatives can create strength through challenge. The challenge to management is to do more than hang on hoping somewhere beyond the edge-of-chaos. Rather it is about exploiting the favourable and finding opportunity in the apparently unfavourable. 'Management' connotes the ability to use circumstances, whenever they may suddenly come, to achieve the goals of the enterprise. Since in the organic model, the enterprise is analogous to a living entity, management in these terms touches and involves every part. This implies a consultative openness involving communications mechanisms that involve the coalface without weighing the system down in micro-management baggage. Responses to crises must not be delayed but general ownership of decisions should be maximized within the constraints of available time.

Collapse into irreversible complexity is a product of poor management. When top management refuses to recognize that crisis demands change, if they are 'locked-in' to redundant patterns, their 'management' becomes a pretence and they become statues posing as conquerors. Besides recognizing the problem and limiting its destructiveness, management must create the means of recovery and maximize possible benefits. In chaos philosophy, forward planning is difficult in the short term and near impossible in the long term. A manager may entertain hopes but cannot predict where his system will be in five years' time. Scenario planning, having exigency plans A, B and C, having a broad view of possibilities, is commendable but the ability to be adaptable, to move quickly to opportunity is even more important. Damming the tide is not a viable option. It magnifies the need to change and erodes the capacity to respond profitably. An extra dose of 'what is not working' is unlikely to cure. Chaos theory holds out the possibility of exploiting the loop's momentum to return to tenuous equilibrium. Successful adaptability depends on:

- The extent of pervasive resilience
- The insight to discern problems and possibility
- The foresight to make changes that are prompt, appropriate but not impulsive

- A willingness to detach from the redundant (i.e. overcoming lock-in)
- An organizational culture of change orientation
- Acceptance that a degree of staff liquidity is a contemporary norm and is an indicator of motivated people with professional integrity
- Encouragement of diversity, mild turbulence to enhance creativity
- An alertness to the power of 'little things'
- A confidence in operating at the edge-of-chaos.

It is not suggested that these attributes displace all of the traditional aspects of good management. Of course, it is not only the little interceptors that are to be managed any more than it would make sense to overlook the large predictable impacts. It is not that chaos theory introduces techniques that are startlingly new, but it does put some of the more recent practices into a more graphic, more urgent, more compelling setting.

Conclusion: a framework for change

Chaos theory postulates that organizing systems are, like organic systems, constantly agitated, pushed and pulled by forces of stability and instability that they may not discern. Change can be rapid and totally destructive, positively stimulating or highly beneficial. The tide of change runs rapidly because industry and capital are being globalized, competition is fierce, technological, social and cultural changes are more rapid and provocations of various kinds are proliferating. Equilibrium has never been so shaken. Chaos theory seems to fit usefully in that kind of milieu.

For managing organizations, chaos theory helps to make sense of the current environment and provides a framework for the future. Once strategies are implemented that are congruent with uncertainty, unpredictability and complexity, the butterflies, loops and strange attractors can be exploited.

13

SMEs in Tourism

Dimitrios Buhalis and Mike Peters

Introduction

Small and medium-sized enterprises (SMEs) prevail in the tourism sector. European tourism is a 'fragmented industry' as it consists of many SMEs producing and selling undifferentiated products or services in a highly competitive marketplace. Fragmentation is far stronger in leisure tourism, as compared to business tourism. It is also less of an issue in under-developed economies where tourism arrived late and with the helping hand of multinational enterprises. This chapter discusses the importance of SMEs in the tourism industry, presents their strategic strengths and challenges while exploring strategies for their future evolution.

Definitions and contribution of SMEs

Micro, small and medium-sized enterprises are socially and economically important. The European Commission defines as SMEs, all organizations with less than 250 employees, less than €50 m turnover or total balance sheet of less than €43 m (Table 13.1).

The Observatory of European SMEs (2003) demonstrated that 93 per cent of all enterprises have less than 10 employees (Table 13.2). There are 20.5 million enterprises in the European Economic Area (EEA) and Switzerland, providing employment for

Table 13.1 EU definition of SMEs

Enterprise category	Personnel headcount	Turnover	or	Balance sheet total
Medium-sized	<250	=€50 million		=€43 million
Small	<50	=€10 million		=€10 million
Micro	<10	=€2 million		=€2 million

Source: European Commission, 2004

Table 13.2 Basic facts about SMEs and large enterprises in Europe (2000)

		SME	Large	Total
Number of enterprises	(1000)	20 415	40	20 455
Employment	(1000)	80 790	40 960	121 750
Occupied people per enterprise		4	1020	6
Turnover per enterprise	€Million	0.6	255.0	1.1
Share of exports in turnover	%	13	21	17
Value added per occupied person	(1000)	65	115	80
Share of labour costs in value added	%	63	49	56

Source: The 2002 Observatory of European SMEs (Europe-19)

122 million people. Some 93 per cent of these enterprises are micro (0–9 employees), 6 per cent are small (10–49), less than 1 per cent are medium sized (50–249) and only 0.2 per cent are large enterprises (250+). Two-thirds of all jobs are in SMEs. Employment differs between countries, as the share of micro enterprises in total employment is 48 per cent in Italy, 57 per cent in Greece, while large enterprises account for over 45 per cent in Iceland and the UK. The average European enterprise employs 6 people. This also varies between countries as, on average, an enterprise employs 2 persons in Greece and 3 in Italy and Liechtenstein, against 10 in Ireland, Luxembourg and the Netherlands. The average age of new entrepreneurs is about 35 years and more than 29 per cent are women. The decision to found one's own business is frequently taken some years after completing education and acquisition of some specific know-how as employee and/or manager.

SMEs are gaining strength in the political agenda for support from the EU. A number of socio-political and economic reasons are frequently given, including:

- Small business and entrepreneurship fuel regional development
- SMEs propel innovation and growth by providing a continued stream of new ideas, concepts, products and resources
- SMEs employ flexible specialization strategies to enhance competitiveness
- SMEs offer the social and economic laboratory where entrepreneurs can be best trained
- SMEs are more sensitive and responsive to market changes than large firms due to flat hierarchies. Hence they can adapt and change faster
- Self-employment can reduce unemployment, particularly for under privileged social groups (e.g. ethnic minorities, young people with little education, redundant

managers in mid career, unemployed woman re-entering the workforce after childbirth)
- SMEs create clusters of value creation at the region and support multiplier effects
- Most of the economic benefits generated remain in the region rather than being exported
- SMEs often preserve local culture and character by using local resources
- Owners/managers are self-motivated to survive, thus possessing superior incentives towards working 'hard' and 'smart'.

After stressing the importance of SMEs in general we will have a closer look at the relevance of small businesses in the tourism industry.

SMEs in European tourism

Tourism SMEs (SMTEs) are responsible for a considerable proportion of the economic production as well as providing employment to a large percentage of the local population, especially in peripheral and insular regions. SMTEs often provide superior services, deeply rooted to the local culture and resources (Thomas, 2004). Because of their small size, owners/managers have the ability to develop special and personal relationships with customers/tourists (Morrison, 1994; Morrison et al., 1999). What they lack in standardization and quality control, they make up in flexibility, niche production, personalized services as well local character and charm. In addition, they have the ability to use local networks of contacts and information to produce and distribute integrated services/products sought by individual customers. The product can therefore be personalized 'on the fly', according to customer requirement, providing a unique and customized experience for each individual. For example, the combination of health or sports services with food and accommodation or the integration of local agricultural products and culture with an active holiday can offer unique experiences. Traditionally, low entry barriers exist in the tourism industry in terms of technology, capital or specialized know-how. Thus, SMTEs provide an ideal starting or testing ground for concepts and product ideas as well as for self-employment and entrepreneurship.

About 95 per cent of the accommodation and food sector is classified as small business, employing nine employees or less. The big companies with more than 250 employees cover over 17 per cent of all employees. SMEs are prevalent in the hospitality industry: in Europe, SMEs employ about 83 per cent of all hospitality workers, while across all industries SMEs provide employment for 66 per cent of the labour force. The average size of hotels was 48 beds in 2001 (Eurostat, 2003). The trend towards fewer hotels with higher bed capacities and towards higher levels of concentration is confirmed in the hospitality industry all over Europe, but differences in hotel firm size and net utilization rates (EU average = 45.2 per cent) exist from nation to nation (Table 13.3). SMTEs contribute to individual countries' GDP, as 6.5 per cent of the total turnover generated by SMEs in Europe is sustained by tourism SMEs (European Commission, 2004). A similar experience can be observed worldwide.

Table 13.3 Indicators for hotels and similar enterprises, 2001 (in thousands)

Country	Number of hotels (and similar enterprises) (000)	Number of beds (000)	Average number of beds per hotel (and similar enterprises)	Average net utilization (%)
Austria	15.3	587.3	38.4	38.1
Belgium	2.0	65.0	32.5	34.6
Denmark	0.5	64.0	128.0	40.0
Finland	1.0	118.5	118.5	37.1
France	19.3	1201.0	62.2	59.9
Germany	38.5	1603.0	41.6	34.5
Greece	8.3	607.6	73.2	56.4
Ireland	5.2	139.6	26.8	48.5
Italy	33.4	1891.3	56.6	41.6
Luxembourg	0.3	14.3	47.6	26.5
Netherlands	2.9	174.3	60.1	45.9
Portugal	1.8	228.7	127.0	79.7
Spain	16.4	1333.4	81.3	58.5
Sweden	2.0	194.8	97.4	34.3
United Kingdom	50.5	1190.6	23.6	41.8

Source: Eurostat, 2003

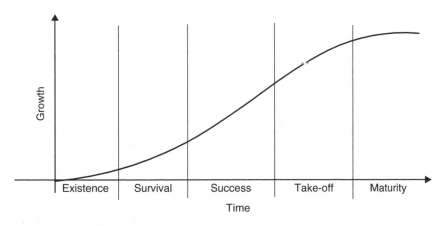

Figure 13.1 Enterprise growth phases.

Management of growth processes and entrepreneurship

The management of small businesses is closely linked with management of growth processes and entrepreneurship. An ideal enterprise development is presented in Figure 13.1, based on the life-cycle concept. The different phases of existence, survival, success, take-off and maturity and the managerial challenges arising are discussed in social sciences literature (Churchill and Lewis, 1983; Finley, 1990; Flamholtz, 1990).

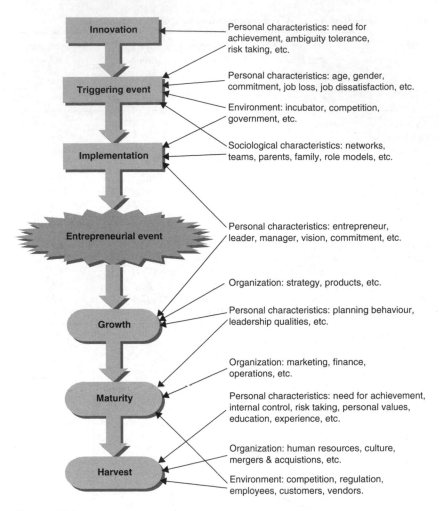

Figure 13.2 A model of the entrepreneurship and small business management process. (Source: Hatten, 1997, p.18)

The model of entrepreneurship and small business management process (Figure 13.2) explains all the facets of small business growth, starting with an innovation and ending with harvesting the profits. The personal characteristics of the founder or owner play a very important role for enterprise success or failure. The entrepreneur's skills and abilities have to change from phase to phase and a main hurdle to growth can be the inability of entrepreneurs to learn how to delegate tasks and functions. Often the business is growing too fast to be managed by the founder, while the entrepreneur often tries to control all processes rather than concentrate on the strategic issues (Kirby, 2003). Harvesting is often associated with the sale of the SME to a larger organization or the flotation on the stock exchange. This is something that many entrepreneurs find difficult to do as they feel by selling their business they betray their child (business) as well as all the employees and partners that contributed to their success. In reality, by being too involved in their original idea, entrepreneurs often feel that it is difficult to let go and to generate alternative ideas that can be developed and harvested. In addition, many entrepreneurs, particularly in tourism, build their business as a lifestyle option and are not motivated by rational growth and profitability criteria. Their prime concern is to generate just sufficient profits to finance the lifestyle they have chosen either by decision or by default.

- The small business management process starts with the so-called entrepreneurial event. The implementation of an innovative idea, together with the knowledge of how to establish a new venture, are prerequisites for small business growth (Figure 13.2). Many variables influence small business management processes. Today, many environmental changes challenge the tourism entrepreneur or manager: higher competition in the banking industry and regulations force small businesses to formulate clearly their business and growth strategies. Raising capital requires long-term orientation and the ability to write business plans which may convince financiers or risk capitalists. Future areas of entrepreneurial qualification in SMTEs are market research based on customer segmentation strategies, the conceptualization of service management processes, the development of new products and services as well as cost/benefit analyses.
- In the future, tourism businesses will have shorter life cycles. Tourism owner managers must find opportunities for products and services that satisfy few needs instead of focusing on the lengthening of the enterprise life cycle. Tourists force small businesses to concentrate on product and service life cycles which naturally form the basis for enterprise growth. Small business owner managers often adhere to maintain ownership and thus are not open for cooperations or strategic alliances. In addition, they often miss the opportunity to sell their business at the most profitable time.

To learn more about the problems of SMTEs we examine the changes in their competitive environment and derive future opportunities.

The competitive environment and strategic challenges for SMTEs

Competitive forces constantly change the structure and functioning of the tourism industry. Two forces shape the patterns of growth and development in any industry:

1. the quantity and quality of entrepreneurs forming new tourism businesses and sustaining and developing existing ones
2. the existence and development of competitive forces shaping the competitiveness of entire regions and/or industries.

In the build-up of mass tourism (1955–1980s) many resource owners in the primary economic sectors, such as fishing and agriculture, converted their resources into tourism properties and became owners/managers of hotels, restaurants and other tourism related businesses. Among them only a small proportion were true entrepreneurs in the Schumpeterian sense, who transformed fishing villages or sleepy alpine farming communities into destinations. The majority of entrepreneurs entered tourism in the 1960s and 1970s, at a time when a sellers' market existed in Europe. This facilitated low entry barriers in terms of physical, financial or human capital, technology and management know-how. Many tourism 'lifestyle entrepreneurs' enjoyed local monopolies and could afford to pursue satisfying lifestyles, instead of concentrating on optimizing their production and maximizing their yields (Williams et al., 1989). Non-economically motivated entrepreneurs constrain the growth of their business as well as the development of destinations (Shaw and Williams, 1990, 1998, 2004; Ateljevic and Doorne, 2000; Burns, 2001). Strategic management is absent and will remain so as long as business performance is acceptable. Market shifts are not realized by the owner-manager, or are interpreted incorrectly. The opposite are firms which are set up by an entrepreneur in the traditional Schumpeterian sense, to grow and to raise profit (Schumpeter, 1961). Schumpeter saw in the entrepreneur an exceptional individual, capable of developing new product combinations, attributes or innovations. Entrepreneurs had to be far-sighted in order to come up with a realistically calculated risk for future market opportunities, based on past experiences and the transformation of uncertainty into profitable outcome (Legohérel et al., 2004).

Weiermair (2001) suggests that both types of entrepreneurs can be found in the development of Europe's mass tourism. In Alpine tourism, those who took over SMTEs from their parents or who entered tourism from agriculture/forestry and who obtained most of their external financing through land collaterals frequently fall into the category of lifestyle and/or part-time entrepreneur. Many one and two star inns, guest houses, bed and breakfast places and local restaurants fit these criteria. Many, notably in the food and accommodation industry, who survived their incubation period, are today facing very serious strategic gap problems and often threats of bankruptcy. Innovative Schumpeterian type of entrepreneurs showed vision with the construction of new alpine ski lifts and cable ways, the creation of larger incoming travel agencies or the construction of luxury-type hotels. Not surprisingly some of these old pioneers and entrepreneurs and/or their descendants have also been the first owners to sort out strategic challenges through innovation, reorganization, new technologies, new products and/or new markets. Facilitated by the first generation of tourism pioneers who had prepared the infrastructures, most entrants in the 1970s and 1980s found it easy to enter into an industry with low entry barriers, in terms of required qualifications or previous career experience, technology and/or capital requirements. They did so in large numbers, choosing similar and often imitated forms of incubator organizations which were close to their place of birth and family holdings, employing largely local networks and local/regional personnel and consulting.

In the 1980s, tourism markets went through dramatic changes, with the expansion of the industry and the transformation to a buyers' market. This required that lifestyle entrepreneurs had to reorient themselves strategically towards these new market conditions. Many SMTEs were unable or unwilling to change and found themselves facing significant competitive disadvantages (Peters et al., 2004). Once again the Schumpeterian innovative entrepreneur is called upon to help restructure and realign the industry. To succeed in the future SMTEs need to adjust their businesses and to restructure internal management processes (Table 13.4).

However, these competitive challenges do not affect all SMTEs and a number of enterprises emerge to demonstrate best practices. The following sections give an insight into the advantages and disadvantages of SMTEs.

Table 13.4 Sources of competitive challenges for traditional SMEs in tourism

Due to firm external developments	*Due to firm internal developments*
Unpredictable market development in sending countries (economic situation, exchange rate/price level, leisure trends, changing preferences)	Inefficient and ineffective management Insufficient adjustment of entrepreneurial capacities and behaviour Problems related to firm succession
Technological development	Problems related to quality management
Altering competitive situations in old and new tourism destinations	Insufficient adjustment towards leadership styles (e.g. employee guidance and coaching)
Development of the domestic economy (highly improved productivity in other industries – cost pressures)	Missed market opportunities (in terms of new competitive strategies, new positioning, internationalization, etc.)
Development of tourism related industries (such as agriculture, transportation, architecture, trade, leisure industry, etc.)	Incorrect investment planning (wrong investment focus, abandoned investments)
Consumer requirements growth	Deficiencies in product development
Necessity for business adjustment	Necessity for restructuring and/or reorganization of internal processes

Source: adapted from Weiermair, 2001

trategic advantages and disadvantages in tourism SMEs

A number of advantages and disadvantages will be affecting the SMTEs' competitiveness, growth and profitability. Advantages often relate to the small size and independence that allows entrepreneurs the flexibility that larger organizations often lack (Table 13.5).

Many of the disadvantages of SMTEs occur due to their lack of economies of scale and scope, resulting in high fixed costs and relatively high costs per unit. Globalization and concentration of power in a few corporations will be jeopardizing their future. SMTEs find it difficult to achieve overall cost leadership, which requires efficient-scale facilities, tight cost and overhead control. Economies of scope can be generated by internalizing and sharing services and products which cannot be produced by the market at the same price or quality level. SMTEs can raise economies of scope when they are willing and able to cooperate with other tourism industry partners. Beside these basic size disadvantages, small businesses also face a number of typical problems or growth hurdles (Table 13.6).

With these advantages and disadvantages in mind we explore the future competitive situation of SMTEs.

Future challenges and strategies for SMTEs

SMTEs are often resource oriented. Effective resource exploitation leads to high performance levels and forces SMTEs to develop organizational capabilities.

Table 13.5 Strategic advantages of SMTEs

Entrepreneur's motivation	Determination to succeed, backed by hard work and personal, family, social sacrifices
Market niche advantages	Market niches often ignored by large enterprises, offer growth chances for small businesses. Small businesses identify customers' wishes and produce tailor-made niche products for specific segments through customization
Personal relationship with enterprise stakeholders	Personal relationships with customers, suppliers, distributors and employees can be a main source of competitive advantage as favourable terms and conditions may be negotiated and support is offered at difficult times
Family involvement	Family involvement ensures human resources are used flexibly to meet demand variations while ensuring commitment and trust
Flexibility and reaction	SMTEs are flexible to respond to client requirements and changes to the external environment. Due to a generally flat hierarchy they can decide quickly and react immediately to market changes
Continuity	The continuity of family businesses ensures strong social values

Table 13.6 Strategic disadvantages of SMTEs

Lack of economies of scale	High overheads and costs per unit make SMEs unable to compete on price and lack the benefits of mass production
Informal management	Most SMTEs lack a strategic long-term plan and very rarely formalize strategic business plans. This leads them continuously to fire-fight and to neglect strategic developments
Traditional approaches/reluctance to change	Although in theory SMTEs should be innovative and flexible, they often adopt traditional lifestyle-driven approaches and are reluctant to change
Knowledge and qualification hurdle	Strategy development, quality management and technology adoption are often deficit areas of SMTEs due to knowledge gaps, lack of education and qualifications. Attracting and financing qualified personnel is difficult. Education of entrepreneurs and key employees can support small business growth (Johnson et al., 1999)
Delegation and leadership hurdle	When small businesses become more formalized the founder has to find ways to plan, organize and delegate main tasks. Entrepreneurs are often reluctant to give up control and to delegate while they often lack leadership skills to motivate others
Finance hurdle	SMTEs find it difficult to attract start-up capital and raise capital for expansion as they have small assets. At the development or survival phases cash-flow problems arise when expansion expenditure exceeds cash flows
Personal relationships	Personal relationships can also be a burden if incapable family members play an active role or when uncompetitive suppliers are used

Table 13.6 (*Continued*)

Family involvement	While large enterprises act anonymously and autonomously, SMTE owners often interpret their enterprise as heritage for following generations. SMTEs are closed to investors and potential shareholders as family businesses display different growth strategies. Family values, systems and situation as well family unity often prevail in SMTE business decisions. For example, family members cannot easily be made redundant. Nevertheless, family business success is heavily dependent upon the support structure within the family.

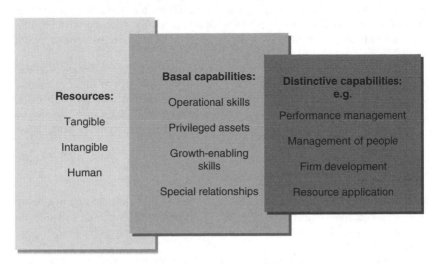

Figure 13.3 How to build capability platforms.
(Source: Augustyn, 2004)

These core competencies have to be unique, not imitable and should create additional customer value which should differentiate products/services towards enhancing competitiveness (Hamel and Prahalad, 1994). Augustyn (2004) proposes a three stage framework to build core competencies and expand distinctive capabilities for SMTEs (Figure 13.3). Tangible resources, intangible and human resources form the starting point for the development of enterprise core competencies. In the 'basic capabilities' stage SMTEs should develop operational capabilities, quality management and control processes. SMEs rarely follow quality management principles and often refuse to employ quality process optimization procedures. However, special relationships, direct customer contact and feedback and flexibility should empower SMTEs to compensate for problems and to produce satisfying personalized/customized products and services 'on the fly'. Advanced SMEs can use service delivery overview instruments, such as blueprints or flowcharts to track and improve internal activities. Brainstorming, writing, process and system design and testing and marketing tests can facilitate new ideas development.

Innovative and creative SMEs can benefit from differentiation advantage based on customization and personalization strategies. Differentiation and niche strategies can benefit from unique and privileged assets which are hard to imitate.

Family SMTEs benefit from the loyalty associated with the family itself and personal relationships with all stakeholders as well as the intimate knowledge of local resources, culture and networks. Active communications with all employees and stakeholders should lead the innovation circle and a systematic service/product development approach which is both proactive and reactive can support SMTE growth. Another distinctive capability of SMTEs is the creation of assets to maintain the firm's development capability. The growth-oriented entrepreneur is able to adjust firm resources and market demands throughout the various enterprise growth phases. Entrepreneurs, however, need to allocate time for strategic planning, rather than focus solely on operational management. SMTEs should also exploit the opportunities emerging from the Internet and technology to expand their customer reach, develop relationships with global partners and improve their internal efficiency. SMTEs can develop their virtual size by expanding and specializing their value chain (Buhalis, 1999).

SMTEs can benefit from cooperation with complementary businesses as well as with competitors at the destination (coopetition) in order to support regional competitiveness and achieve economies of scope. Consumer-oriented networks can reduce production costs and attract professional assistance by sharing resources. Recent developments in tourism destinations focus on regional cooperation and the development of collective competence.

SMTEs have a number of opportunities in the future which underline the strengths of small businesses and organizations:

- Instead of focusing on resource allocation they should optimize resource leverage: as creative small but flexible organizations SMTEs should focus on the continual search for new, less resource intensive means to achieve their goals (Augustyn, 2004)
- SMTEs need to collaborate in order to initiate training and education. External know-how providers (such as universities or tourism colleges) can offer courses to improve manpower qualifications and skills
- Cooperation among SMTEs will focus on the optimization of the destination input, e.g. resources such as manpower, nature or infrastructure
- Basel II will force SMTEs to concentrate on their skills and competencies and to promote them to potential financiers. Weak SMTEs will fall out of the market while those who display a sufficient equity ratio will face more qualitative or quantitative growth options.

The main challenges which lie ahead for SMEs in tourism are the dynamic interaction with the marketplace; optimization of cooperation management; balancing operational management and strategic planning; and quality management and control. SMEs' lack of market orientation and their reliance on resource capabilities lead to an unbalanced management behaviour, where own strengths or weaknesses cannot be assessed properly because market needs are unknown. Information asymmetry still plays a remarkable role for small businesses in tourism and constrains their business growth. Entrepreneurial skills and education/training are critical for building sustainable competitive advantages for SMTEs. Policy makers should therefore focus on growth-oriented entrepreneurs and support them through professional advice, incentives and training on critical business aspects and leadership qualities in order to support the long-term competitiveness.

Case study 13.1 Hotel Segas, Loutraki, Greece

Following the termination of an 18-year exclusive contract with an International Tour Operator only a few months before the summer season was about to start, Hotel Segas found itself in a very difficult situation. Having only 24 rooms and a fairly undifferentiated product apart from the superb personal attention, the hotel had no resources and only little strength to approach prospective customers. Having over-relied on the tour operator for many years they had abandoned all other markets and could not easily attract new customers at such short notice. Given the limitation of the destination, the lack of funds for marketing activities and the insufficient marketing expertise internally the hotel trusted a willing close relative to develop and maintain a web page promoting the hotel. There was no budget for the development of the site and as a result the hotel could only be registered a free server.

The web design and text developed were significantly different from normal hotel web pages. A much more personal and informal approach was adopted, giving a life story and introducing members of the host family. Also emphasis was given to the destination and the practicalities. The web page went live in September 2000 and was gradually registered with most search engines by March 2001. The lack of funds delayed the registration as multiple submissions through free submit engines were made. The cost of developing and maintaining the web page was only the volunteering time of the helpful relative demonstrating clearly that the Internet can enable even tiny, but innovative organizations to maximize their potential. Personalized answers to all e-mails and booking requests were adopted, engaging with prospective travellers and assisting with all their travel planning rather than the reservation with the hotel. In 4 years of operation the web pages have generated about 24 000 viewings from remote areas such as Japan, Nicaragua and Canada. Bookings included an equally diverse background of bookers. A total of €6000 worth of incremental turnover or about 220 bed-nights was generated in 2004 contributing about 12 per cent of the hotel annual turnover.

For more information see http://www.hotelsegas.com

Case study 13.2 lastminute.com: growth of SMEs

lastminute.com seeks to differentiate itself by generating some of the lowest prices for many travel and entertainment deals and by packaging and delivering products and services, such as restaurant reservations, entertainment tickets and gifts, in convenient, novel and distinctive ways. They positioned their business as a lifestyle portal offering a wide range of products and services to people who impulse purchase. The site aims to inspire its customers to try something different. Although tourism products dominate the site, several additional products are available including meals delivered at home, gifts including electronics and underwear and insurance. lastminute.com was founded by Brent Hoberman and Martha Lane Fox in 1998. Their web site was launched in the UK in October 1998. lastminute.com aims to create the one-stop shop for all last minute needs. Using the Internet they match suppliers' distressed inventory with consumer last-minute demand at short notice.

lastminute.com works with a range of suppliers in the travel, entertainment and gift industries and is dedicated to bringing its customers attractive products and services. lastminute.com has relationships with over 9300 suppliers, including international scheduled airlines, hotels, package tour operators, theatre, sports and entertainment promoters, restaurants, speciality service providers, gift suppliers and car hire, both in the UK and internationally. Supplier relationships include Lufthansa, Air France, Alitalia, British Midland, United Airlines, Virgin Atlantic Airways, Starwood Hotels and Resorts Worldwide, The Savoy Group, Sol Melia, Kempinski Hotels, English National Ballet, The Royal Albert Hall and Conran Restaurants.

lastminute.com aims to be the global marketplace for all last-minute services and transactions. Following the success of the UK site, localized versions of the website have since been launched in France, Germany, Sweden, Italy, Spain, The Netherlands, Australia, New Zealand and South Africa. lastminute.com is Europe's most visited travel and leisure website. By September 2003 the company had:

- 9.8 m unique users per month across Europe (source: Digimine, September 2003)
- 100 m page impressions per month (Digimine, September 2003)
- 7.5 m newsletter subscribers – Europe (source: lastminute.com, September 2003).

This growing multinational presence was further boosted by the acquisition of a number of complementary companies, as demonstrated in Figure 13.4, which enabled lastminute.com rapidly to expand its business.

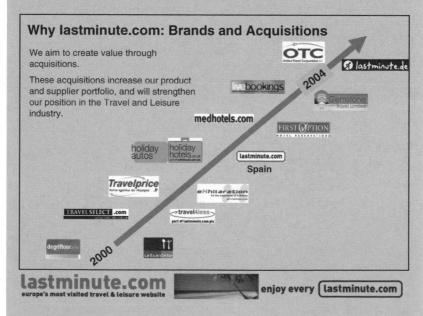

Figure 13.4 lastminute.com acquisitions.

For the future, lastminute.com aims to be the global marketplace for all last-minute services and transactions. lastminute.com seeks to differentiate itself by generating some of the lowest prices for many travel and entertainment deals and by packaging and delivering products and services, such as restaurant reservations, entertainment tickets and gifts, in convenient, novel and distinctive ways. It also aims to inspire its customers to try something different and to maximize penetration of the lifestyle solutions market.

In May 2005, lastminute.com was acquired by the SABRE/Travelocity group for £577 million. This will support SABRE/Travelocity to strengthen their position in Europe, and it will also enable Lastminute to distribute inventory to the US and global markets served by SABRE.

For more information see www.lastminute.com

14

The Future of Work and Employment in Tourism

Tom Baum

Introduction

This chapter addresses issues relating to one of the key themes within contemporary international tourism, namely the changing role of people in the delivery of service through a discussion of work and employment within the sector. The chapter demonstrates how tourism work and employment are likely to develop in the future, although tourism and labour market behaviours are both particularly difficult to predict with real accuracy.

It is a much overplayed truism to describe tourism as a 'people industry'. What does a cliché such as this mean in the context of contemporary tourism? To what extent can such a clichéed descriptor remain a label within tourism in the twenty-first century and will it retain its significance in the sector in future years? The major change environment which tourism, worldwide, constantly experiences in terms of its products, marketing and operations is generally seen to be driven by the external political and economic environment as well as by evolving consumer demand, the pressure of competitive forces and by technological innovation. To what extent does the work and employment environment within which tourism operates drive change within the sector rather than playing what is generally seen as a reactive role?

Notwithstanding the challenges imposed by major diversity within the international tourism industry and, indeed, contradictions in the area of work and employment, it is possible to identify a number of underpinning themes with respect to work and employment in international tourism. These themes have emerged as important beyond traditional approaches to the management of people within tourism and impose challenges. They have implications beyond traditional HR departments and create wider challenges for marketing, quality, product development, finance and operations. The purpose of this chapter is to address a number of key contemporary themes in the management of human resources within international tourism and to consider how the sector is responding to the pressures, challenges and opportunities afforded by them.

The nature of tourism work

Tourism work (and thus the skills that are demanded in its delivery) also exhibits diversity in both horizontal and vertical terms. In a horizontal sense, it includes a very wide range of jobs, the extent depending upon the definition of the sector that is employed. The traditional research focus on tourism work concentrates on areas that are located with the hospitality sub-sector of tourism and, largely, focus on food and beverage and, to a lesser extent, accommodation. Research into wider areas of tourism work, particularly those that have emerged with the expansion of services and functions in the area (front desk, leisure, entertainment, reservation call centres) is much more poorly served. This chapter draws on a limited range of work in these areas. The 'newer' areas include functions and tasks that exhibit considerable crossover with work that falls outwith normal definitions of tourism in food and drink manufacture – office administration, IT systems management and specialist areas of sports and leisure. The characteristics and the organization of the tourism industry are subject to on-going restructuring and evolutionary change. There are major labour market and skills implications of such change, as businesses re-shape the range of services they offer or respond to fashion and trend imperatives in the consumer marketplace.

Vertical diversity in tourism work is represented by a more traditional classification that ranges from unskilled through semi-skilled and skilled to supervisory and management. This 'traditional' perspective of work and, therefore, skills in tourism is partly described by Riley (1996) in terms that suggest that the sector is dominated by semi-skilled and unskilled employees (64 per cent) and that knowledge-based positions account for as few as 14 per cent of the total workforce. This simplification masks major business organizational diversity in tourism, reflecting the size, location and ownership of tourism businesses. The actual job and skills content of work in tourism is predicated upon these factors, so that common job titles (e.g. restaurant manager, sous-chef) almost certainly mask a very different range of responsibilities, tasks and skills within jobs in different establishments.

The skills profile of tourism, in turn, is influenced by the labour market that is available to it, both in direct terms and via educational and training establishments. The weak internal labour market characteristics in themselves impose downward pressures on the skills expectations that employers have of their staff and this, in turn, influences the nature and level of training which the educational system delivers. There is an evident cycle of down-skilling, not so much in response to the actual demands of tourism work or of consumer expectations of what it can deliver, but as a result of the perceptions of potential employees and the expectations that employers have of them.

There is a strong case to argue for the social and cultural construction of what we understand to be work and employment in tourism. This argument is built upon recognition of the changing nature of work across services in general that has seen a move of emphasis from technical to generic skills considerations. This discussion is part of the growing interest in the nature of service work and recognition of its complexity and variety (Korczynski, 2002) and, indeed, status as suggested in Nickson and Warhurst's (2003) reference to the changing nature of work hierarchies through consideration of aesthetic labour's contribution to a 'new labour aristocracy'. A move away from technical-driven definitions of work in tourism adds concepts such as emotional labour (Hochschild, 1983; Seymour, 2000; Morris, 2003) and aesthetic labour (Warhurst et al., 2000). The context in which these attributes feature and the combination of skills that they demand, generate work attributes that are context specific. Therefore, debate about work issues, in the context of tourism, is informed by wider, generic consideration about the nature of work in the context of changing employment, technology and vocational education, within both developed and developing economies. The major gap in understanding is the extent to which work which is perceived to be 'low skills' in the western, developed context, can be described in this way in other contexts because of differing cultural, communications, linguistic and relationship assumptions which underpin such work in developing countries. Work in tourism varies greatly in both the skills base it requires and in its social status according to its location in either a developed or developing world context.

The impact of globalization on tourism work and employment

The impact of globalization on the management of people in tourism is primarily driven by three factors: technological, political and economic. Globalization makes distance a relatively insignificant factor in the establishment of long-distance economic, commercial, political and sociocultural relations. It is more than simply a way of doing business, or running financial markets – it is an on-going process. The modern communication systems make the process easier. For example, the British and American service sectors are increasingly dealing with their customers through outsourced call-centres in India. Another major manifestation of globalization is the increasing power of global business corporations, which follow a strategy of global expansion.

Globalization has definite influences on work and employment in tourism. Changing labour markets make low-paid jobs for the low educated scarcer, simultaneously making the amount of low-paid jobs for the higher educated grow. These trends create a mismatch between available labour and labour for which a demand exists. Job seekers with a lack of vocational training get more and more excluded from job opportunities. At the same time, because of globalization, the supply of labour from less developed countries affects the market position of all of those who have no scarce skills to offer. This results in a position where only the most competitive can retain their relative position in the labour marketplace.

The globalization of business firms has a number of implications for human resource management. Knowledge and skilled workers will increasingly become mobile so that the recruitment will be from a global pool rather than a national or local pool. Employers who are unable to provide competitive packages will be confronted with an increasing 'flight' of these types of workers and an accompanying shortage.

In recruiting new employees from a global pool, employers will have to use global media rather than local or national media. The information technology capacity and the extent to which workers who possess knowledge and skills to be competitive in a global sense will be connected to new media will enhance their recruitment. Selection procedures will also increasingly be based on media using electronic information technology. Face-to-face testing and interviewing will be used less, due to long distance and possible cost factors and will be replaced by electronically mediated selection procedures. The ability to operate in a global environment will be one of the key selection criteria. Appointments will be made on the basis of internationally acceptable contract laws and agreements and at remuneration and benefits levels, which increasingly become standardized across national boundaries.

A major consequence of globalization in tourism is the issue of matching employee skills with changing industry requirements. The traditional practice of employees learning the majority of the skills on the job and gradually progressing to senior positions is threatened by the rapid technological changes and the need to respond to the changing service requirements. Employees at the operational and managerial levels are now required to be more flexible and adaptive to constant change. Globalization has major implications for work and employment in tourism and these include (Becherel and Cooper, 2002):

- The need for different skills and competencies in the employees to be able to deal with the widespread use of technology, especially the Internet
- Dealing with employment-related consequences of mergers and strategic alliances
- Issues of relocation of employees and social and cultural sensitivities of those working away from home
- New forms of tourism utilizing natural and cultural environments create a demand for indigenous employees, who could deliver better quality and original products and services
- Meeting the needs of 'high-skilled tourists', who are more experienced and demand higher quality products and service.

These pressures of globalization in tourism have significant implications for work and employment, especially for human resource development and dealing with the cultural aspects.

The de-skilling of tourism work

The extensive debate that surrounds the issue of 'McDonaldization' as introduced by Ritzer (1993) has suggested that de-skilling is an inevitable consequence of growing standardization or routinization across the service sector. There is evidence to support this process in tourism and tourism in the form of a growing fast food sector, within budget accommodation and through the growth of no-frills airlines. The growth of these sectors points to a simplification of tasks in the workplace, aided in part by technology substitution but also by changes in consumer demands and expectations. It is also arguable that these sectors have grown in response to new consumer demand as opposed to displacement of demand for traditional services. Therefore, while their growth may have had the global effect of 'dumbing down' average skills levels in tourism and hospitality, it is difficult to argue that they have eliminated demand for higher order skills within other sectors of the industry.

The argument that tourism is moving towards increasingly multi-skilled models of training and work has been aired since the early 1980s (Baum, 1987). The focus of this argument has been targeted towards meeting employer needs, particularly in smaller businesses where the notion of flexible rotation between different hotel departments in a way to suit the demand cycle is presented as a logical business solution. In reality, such work represents multi-tasking because the level and nature of the work in question (food service, bar service, portering, housekeeping) offers little by way of enhancing the actual skills of employees other than extending the operational context within which they are exercised (Baum, 1995). The specialist educational programme described by Baum (1987) represents the accumulation of complementary but not progressive skills in various hotel departments.

Creating the opportunity to develop a wider range of skills within the workplace is frequently included within models of job enrichment. Multi-skilling or multi-tasking across departments, as generally practised within the tourism sector, does not offer much to employees that can be described as 'enriching'. Of probably greater value to employees is the breakdown of job demarcation within tourism departments, such as the virtual elimination of the traditional partie system within kitchens in Britain and the merging of front office functions (cashier, reception, concierge) in many hotels (Odgers and Baum, 2001).

Technology – why bother with people at all?

There is little doubt that technologies across a wide range of tourism work, including production, operations and communications technologies, have impacted greatly upon tourism work. The routinization of work in many areas of tourism (food preparation, airport handling, reservations) is all due to the introduction of technologies which allow a wide range of tasks to be performed both more efficiently and, frequently, more effectively with less or, indeed, no human input. Low-cost airlines have demonstrated clearly how the introduction of technological systems and the use of creative operational approaches can significantly reduce labour costs in tourism and, indeed, impact on employment across the wider sector (for example, on travel agencies). It is conceivable (but unlikely) that technology substitution for labour will eliminate a wide range of work within tourism except within highly standardized, low-cost areas of activity.

Labour intensity is a widely attributed feature of the tourism sector, although changes with respect to product, service expectations and technology have altered this picture to some degree in recent years (Baum and Odgers, 2001). With the development of various forms of support technology, the operational systems in tourism have been improved towards the development of more efficient and cost-saving practices. For example, central reservation systems in airlines and hotels, employing effective yield management, benefit the industry in terms of forecasting sales, arranging essential 'raw material' and managing good customer relationship marketing and after-sales service. Moreover, the introduction of labour-saving technology provides the industry with opportunities to improve the quality of much soul-destroying work so accurately described by writers from Orwell (1933) through to Gabriel (1988). All these new technologies make the hotel sector more efficient and responsive to customers' expectations.

However, there are some functions which cannot be replaced by technology, such as room cleaning, table serving, door greeting and other personal services. The new technology brings out better 'tools' for the operations to manage, but not for them to replace entirely routine work. In a people-oriented or labour-intensive industry, labour still plays an important part in production procedures. However, as Guerrier and Adib (2001) point out, the duty of the many tourism workers is still to manage the 'dirty' and to keep it away from the guest as far as is possible. To a certain extent, tourism staff have much in common with nurses, sharing similar working conditions, in terms of difficulty, relatively poor pay, low-status, shift work and feminized activity.

Employment matters as drivers of change in tourism

Traditionally, the area of employment (and human resources management in general) has been seen as an area that is reactive to changes and the demands of the wider business environment. Thus, there is a widely accepted assumption that the role of people within organizations is required to change and develop in response to developments in markets, products and technology. Most large tourism companies operate on the basis of this assumption and this permeates into the manner in which they organize work and support human resource functions, such as training and development. This model is only valid in so far as the external labour market permits employers the luxury of thinking in this way.

In situations where quality, 'contemporary' labour, skilled in emotional, aesthetic and information management skills, is scarce and in high demand, tourism companies may need to re-engineer the way in which work is packaged for existing and potential employees. This will require new approaches to flexibility in the workplace (traditionally seen as flexibility by the employee to the benefit of the employer) (Lai and Baum, 2005) so that the focus is on accommodating the lifestyle requirements of workers and facilitating work-life balance for all employees. This is already happening. Underlying the practice of many organizations in tourism, recognized as excellent in terms of their approach to work and employment, is appreciation by such companies of the need to respond to work-life balance issues within the workforce. Effective people management is designed to move out of traditional employment paradigms (40 hour week, fixed shifts) and to tailor the work environment so as to meet the needs of both employers and employees. The consequences of this approach include the creation of fluid workplaces, characterized by diversity in terms of who works there, what their motivation for work is, when they work and what they do. Organizations that fail to respond to the need for flexibility in its broadest interpretation are likely to suffer in terms of recruitment, retention, commitment and productivity. This fluidity has significant implications for training and development policy and practice, both within organizations and in the context of external training providers.

A consequence of a focus on employee work-life balance needs at a micro level, manifest at a company-wide level, is that recognition of these needs can become important drivers of an organization's approach to its markets, its products and its use of technology. Creating flexibility in the workplace in a way that suits both partners to the employment contract probably requires compromise and adjustment on the part of both parties. It also requires a sophisticated understanding of the labour market at a local, national and, in parts of the world such as Europe, at international level as well. This understanding can then drive the shaping of the products and services that a tourism company is able to offer and will also help to identify the investment costs (in terms of training and development) that are likely to be required in order to meet the human resource demands of such decisions.

Conclusions

A number of themes and issues are currently impacting upon the nature of work and employment in international tourism. In experiencing change across a wide spectrum of areas relating to work, tourism is by no means unique and a similar analysis could readily be constructed for areas such as retailing or office administration. However, the visibility of tourism work to the consumer, combined with our exposure, as customers, to the execution of tourism work in both developed and developing countries, does make this sector significantly different from most other parts of the service economy.

Predicting the future from an analysis of the present is hazardous but a reasonable assessment is that mega trends such as globalization, de-skilling and technology impact will continue to play major roles in shaping the tourism workplace for the foreseeable future. Less predictable in their potential impact on work are changes in consumer expectations and taste with respect to both product and service in tourism. These both have the potential to influence greatly the manner in which work is carried out in all sub-sectors of the industry. The notion of work-life balance and its impact on tourism is also an area where prediction is hazardous. Evidence points to increasing recognition, by both employers and employees in developed countries, of the value in meeting the wider life aspirations of tourism workers through flexibility in employment arrangements. At the same time, there is little evidence of such approaches in the developing world where exploitation of the vulnerable within the tourism workforce (child labour or sex workers as examples) remains a major challenge. There is also evidence that employers within the developed world are looking to circumvent their moral obligations with respect to work-life balance by looking beyond their traditional, local labour pools to more vulnerable, less demanding migrant labour sources. If this continues to be the case on a large scale into the future, the prognosis for tourism work remains relatively bleak and does not point to real progress from the time of Orwell in the 1930s.

15

Managing Globalization

Frank Go and Erik van't Klooster

Introduction: globalization drivers

Globalization – defined by Webster's dictionary as a process that renders various activities and aspirations 'worldwide in scope or application' – has been underway for many centuries. People, ideas and goods have travelled the globe since ancient times, in pursuit of conquest (soldiers and sailors), prosperity (traders), religion (preachers and pilgrims), curiosity and wanderlust (adventurers and travellers) (Diamond, 1998). The few who crossed borders and connected the world for various purposes, gave way to the industrialization era, transnational trade and mass-tourism on an unprecedented scale.

The rise and spread of global supply chains cause markets and production of corporations, countries and communities to grow increasingly interdependent. It implies that decisions and actions taken thousands of miles away affect the lives of people everywhere (Held et al., 2000). Subsequently, the diffusion of technologies, particularly the speed of information and communication technology (ICT) has led to an 'information revolution' and, in its wake, the annihilation of space by time, which is one of the hallmarks of global capitalism (Castells, 2001). ICT has had several major effects. Developments such as satellite television, the Internet and mobile phones have resulted in instantaneous global communication. They enable consumers to undergo poly-inclusive experiences or the simultaneous inclusion in both virtual and physical encounters (Go and Fenema, 2003).

Increasing cultural interaction through the developments in mass media as well as travel and tourism enables people to encounter and consume new ideas and experiences from a wide range of cross-cultural sources in fields ranging from music, fashion, literature, film, food and sports. In turn, such cultural interaction encourages the permeability of national borders and alters perceptions of the concepts of 'time' and 'place'. The material and the digital worlds have traditionally struggled against each other, each working to overcome the constraints or mimic the advantages of the other. As a consequence of pervasive technologies a cybernomadic landscape, comprised of 'global cultural flows' is emerging. It causes fundamental disjunctures (Appadurai, 1996, p.33) and raises critical issues ranging from 'outsourcing', environmental pollution as a consequence of increased mobility and other common problems, including the spread of worldwide health problems such as SARS, refugees and international terrorism.

Held et al. (2000, p.2) distinguish three theoretical perspectives on globalization:

■ First, the hyper globalists believe that the global process defines a new era with consequences for the way people and organizations operate around the world. They opine that nation states and local cultures are being eroded by a homogeneous global culture and economy. Hyper globalists suggest that globalization will eventually lead to tolerant and responsible world citizens.
■ Second, the 'sceptics' regard globalization as a myth or at best exaggerated. They argue that the international economy is divided in three major regional blocs in which national governments remain powerful.
■ Third, the 'transformationalists' occupy a middle ground between the former categories. They argue that globalization should be understood as 'a complex set of interconnecting relationships' with power, for the most part exercised indirectly. The 'transformationalist' view suggests that the globe is experiencing a profound process of change and uncertainty which implies a need to link research and development to the practicalities of managing in an increasingly globalized environment.

Globalization in the tourism context

Globalization in relation to tourism is pervasive in that it involves demand, supply and mediation aspects. Tourism in the twenty-first century needs organizations and managers who understand how to operate on a global stage. It implies managers who open their minds and coordinate processes to overcome local differences and forge a global operational management standard, in which ICT provides flexible responses and orchestrated guidelines for sustainable, high quality results. It raises the issue whether tourism industry practitioners are aware of blurring geographical, industry, organizational and ethical boundaries (Tulder, 1999) and competent to manage the globalization process.

First, from an *economic geographical boundary* perspective, an issue is whether the proclaimed trend of globalization can be observed. The tourism sector still has a continental rather than global character. The tourism sector in Europe has historically been made up of small and medium-sized enterprises (SMEs). During the 1980s the growth process was primarily organic in nature and mid-size groups began to evolve. In the 1990s consolidation intensified and larger groups began to enter the equities market to fund continued expansion. At the same time, the investment community started to take control from traditional operators. This resulted in the formation of multinational groups, such as Travel Union International (TUI) and Thomas Cook, both pan-European players, represented by local (national) brands. When considering trends such as shifts in the value constellation, outsourcing and technology, the USA is ahead of the EU and Japanese firms in terms of vertical integration (Tulder, 1999, p.3).

Second, an issue from an *industry boundary* perspective is whether under conditions of 'information capitalism' the traditional 'inside-out' view of tourism operator is tenable. Some argue that an 'outside-in' view (e.g. investment community, media community) might lead to better performance. Perhaps such debate is meaningless from a 'distributed cognition' viewpoint, as ICT enables the coordination and interaction of knowledge and competencies transfer within social networks.

Third, an *organizational boundary* perspective raises the issue whether the 'boundaryless' organization, including alliances and outsourcing, leads to better performance. For instance, Jack Welch's General Electric used the image of a house to explain the difficulty of understanding the all-encompassing idea of 'boundarylessness'. This helps to overcome barriers in three dimensions:

- 'The horizontal barriers are the walls – such as function, product line, or geographic location – that divide groups of peers into isolated compartments.
- The vertical barriers are the layers – the floors and ceilings – that come with hierarchy.
- The external barriers are the outside walls of the company itself. Beyond them are found many groups with whom close relationships are essential, such as customers, suppliers and venture partners.' (Tichy and Sherman, 1993, p.287).

Welch credited 'boundaryless' thinking and acting as the key to General Electric's unequalled value-adding performance.

Finally, from an *ethical boundary* perspective, an issue is whether business ethics represent a burden or asset for the tourism sector. The global tourism industry may be perceived as 'footloose'. Transnational corporations based in the West sell standard commodities linked to a brand, which is controlled by 'foreign' boardrooms, as opposed to the host community culture which they purport to represent. In times of crisis or given more lucrative opportunities elsewhere they may be quick to pull out. Due to resource scarcity and the rapid expansion of mass tourism, the negative effects of the interaction between the global and the local have become more prevalent. Simultaneously, the awareness has grown that within the complex global environment a more structured stakeholder dialogue is needed to enhance decision-making processes.

Managing globalization practice

In the following section we examine two cases concerning stakeholders whose success depends on the ability to manage globalization competently. In particular we explore tour operators' practice on a global stage and their performance. Next, we discuss how the city of Amsterdam is trying to come to terms with the process of managing globalization, i.e. inter-urban economic competition and simultaneously the shaping and governance practice of a new tourist destination brand.

Tour operating in the globalization era

Tour operators represent an influential stakeholder in transnational tourism. Among European tour operators only Kuoni and Airtours/Mytravel boast a global representation. By contrast, Europe's other major tour operators are mainly represented in Europe, which limits their interaction patterns with buyers on a global scale. Preussag offers a broad selection of 'travel experiences' and allows for tailored packaging. In addition, it offers clients additional value-added advisory services, which result in higher margins. Airtours/Mytravel and Thomas Cook have much in common. Both offer a limited selection of tour packages, which are standardized in nature. Both compete on price in a low margin business. Airtours/Mytravel, Preussag and Thomas Cook all seem to have best responded to the challenge of implementing an effective international e-marketing strategy. All three apply an integrated multi-channel and dynamic pricing strategy to optimize yield and forward and backward integration to control margins. Furthermore, they provide a direct market channel, i.e. a chain of electronic links which enables potential buyers actively to compare products and prices. While Kuoni compares favourably with its rivals it lacks backward integration in the channel.

Globalizing destination marketing

On a tourist destination level, the issue of managing globalization has also become increasingly relevant. During the 1980s and 1990s cities across Europe became occupied with cultural industries and tourism to fill the gap left by industry and create an urban image to attract mobile investment and mobile professionals. It implied more intense competition between European cities with some performing better than others.

Case study 15.1 Globalizing Amsterdam Tourism

Amsterdam, for example, perceived its competitive position in the world cities' ranking to be under pressure and concluded that this would have serious economic consequences. The competitive edge of cities appears increasingly synonymous with the marketing of 'the city' and the ability to draw residents, investments and tourists. Recent statistics indicate that Amsterdam hosted fewer tourists (7.2 million), which put Dublin (8 million), in fourth place, after London (44 million), Paris (23 million) and Rome (10 million) (Berenschot, 2004, p.21).

Amsterdam dropped from fifth to eleventh position in terms of the number of hosted conferences. Recent research indicates that Amsterdam's opportunities for the mid-term 2005–2010 reside in developing its image as a business city, knowledge city, residential city, linked to excellence and intellect (Berenschot, 2004, p.25). It does not mean that Amsterdam should abandon its traditional strengths, including 'dimensions such as cultural city, and city of canals'. But it implies that city policy will be driven by a personalized approach to sharing the qualities that reside in the hearts of Amsterdam's citizens with the world. This approach is coined I-amsterdam, 'the personal proud flag on the ship [...] I Amsterdam expresses the diversity, cohesion and individualism of all the people of Amsterdam. Together we build the city we love' (Berenschot, 2004, p.6).

How should Amsterdam deal with the responsibilities of decision-making and duties associated with managing the transformation process of location in relation to mobile investment, mobile professionals and tourists and ensure satisfaction not only of the former but also the locals? The research findings indicated that the host community culture, including its cultural disruptions, offers opportunities for a new brand that would play a key role to stressing the unique, thereby enhancing Amsterdam's competitiveness, instead of emphasizing generic qualities through a 'commodity-oriented' brand advertising campaign. Given its focus on 'knowledge', 'business' and 'liveability', the I-Amsterdam initiative may be perceived as a framework of opportunity for visitors for whom image creation and utility is a vital part of their personal success.

Marketing a city involves a myriad of stakeholders including users (tourists), commercial marketing, multinational interests, public planning and professional practitioners (consultants), fields with different backgrounds and interests. It therefore, 'is neither a centrally controlled system nor a democratic process. It is teamwork in which a large number of actors play on a large number of stages and must be able to work independently within their specialized fields of expertise and networks, yet with a broadly agreed script. Too much central control in such a diverse field leads to the system failing to function. It is about all the actors working on a cooperative basis with the same toolkit.' (Berenschot, 2004, p.28).

Particularly in the international tourism context, the different uses of local space by host and guests, indigenous and migrant populations has become a cause of cultural misunderstanding and confrontation instead of fostering cross-cultural understanding. It exacerbates the existing contradictions between the interests of business, tourist and government. It raises the risk of conflict, thus turning many a tourist destination into 'contested space' (Figure 15.1).

In essence, the success of any destination management initiative depends on stakeholders who are able to balance the 'importance' of destination positioning (priorities) with the 'performance' of the stakeholders (results). In the context of global competition and scarce resources, the efforts should be based on understanding what different tourist profiles expect, how they each perceive the destination and how the destination meets those expectations by rendering the support for the co-creation of a desired experience.

There is a body of thought (Prahalad and Ramaswamy, 2000), which suggests that the co-creation of a narrative between the host and the potential tourist is extremely important. It posits that only through searching for and activation of this co-creation process can the needs of both host and guest be appropriately met.

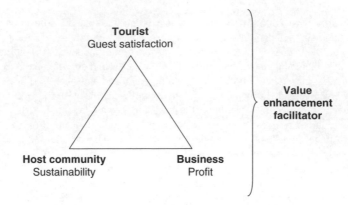

Figure 15.1 Tourist destination as a contested space.

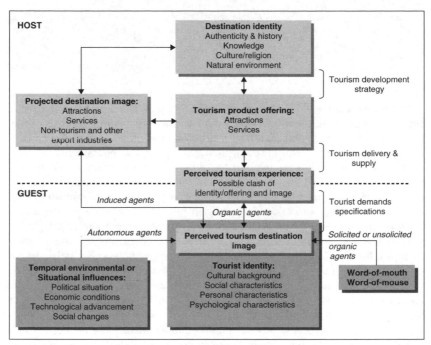

Figure 15.2 The 3-gap tourism destination image formation model. (Source: Govers and Go, 2004)

For the co-creation process to take shape in a coherent experience, it is necessary to bridge three primary gaps between host and guest (Figure 15.2). The first gap concerns a discrepancy between the 'true' destination identity, i.e. one grounded in local heritage and 'authentic' local stories and the image projected by the destination. The second gap occurs when the perceived image is not in tune with the projected image, due to a lack of alignment between stakeholders, i.e. different image formation agents (Gartner, 1993; Govers and Go, 2004). The third gap concerns any discrepancies between the actual on-site tourism experience and the tourist's perceived expectations. Globalized tourism makes all those interactions complex due to the diverse cultural backgrounds of all stakeholders.

Co-creation in tourist brand community

From a performance perspective, destination marketing needs a regime of coordination which supports teamwork among a wide range of stakeholders. The use of ICT is essential in this regard as it enables dispersed stakeholders to bridge time and spatial differences and reduce transaction costs. The process can be supported in two ways: directly or indirectly. Directly, through a content management system which enables tourists to become co-creators of their own travel experiences (Prahalad and Ramaswamy, 2000). Indirectly, through tourist-online user community interaction, (e.g. www.virtualtourist.com). The online co-creative process enables elicitation of consumer preferences, in terms of script, monetary and time expenditures.

With networking on the rise, the opportunity exists to cultivate a new ethos of connectivity, socialization and trust between the tourism stakeholders, but such a collaborative or network culture would need to be fostered (Braun, 2002). Destination brands needs to be aware of the need to facilitate connectivity and build trust among stakeholders. ICT can enable connectivity but needs the support of regular face-to-face meetings to build trust in the community, especially in its initial phases (Wenger et al., 2002). Destination brand communities should focus specifically on teamwork in order to 'stretch' resources and share knowledge to ensure a consistent profiling of the destination.

Information and communication technology is typically viewed as contributing to innovation. However, recent research underpins the former's shortcomings. For instance, Brown and Duguid (2000) indicate that trust, tacit knowledge and social capital are critical success factors to achieve innovation within social networks. Therefore, the model for localized value enhancement facilitation (Go et al., 2003, p.66) 'seeks to capitalize on the existing cultural networks, promote their growth and creative potential, and connects them to whole regions and geopolitical contexts, working as an incubator that enlarges their own virtual communities. In this way, a technological link is established between heritage and a sustainable tourism economy based on the cultural richness of places'.

Conclusions: tourism in the era of globalization

This chapter has examined managing globalization, particularly how the blurring of boundaries has resulted in the need for value-adding 'boundaryless' thinking and acting. It advocates that the creation of sustainable, high-quality tourism on a global scale requires cooperative innovation of stakeholders, including the active involvement of tourists in the experience innovation process.

The issue of managing globalization is paradoxical, but relevant to tourism practice. On the one hand, the *interdependencies* between organizations within global supply chains have increased dramatically in recent decennia. On the other hand, the globalization process implies the emergence of tourism as a contemporary *footloose industry*, characterized by a strong convergence in tourism quality concepts. It sells standard commodities linked to a brand, which is controlled by 'foreign' boardrooms as opposed to the host community culture, which it purports to represent. This has significant economic and regional development implications which are often referred to as Neocolonization (Britton, 1990).

Globalization or boundaryless thinking and acting is as much an expression of values as a description of corporate structure, a matter of cooperation across all the artificial barriers that separate people with a common interest (Tichy and Sherman, 1993, p. 285). With this change in the marketplace, the traditional communications programmes that corporations and tourist destination organizations have used, become increasingly irrelevant. The need is for an innovative, people-driven approach to experiential marketing communications. Furthermore, the traditional function-based division of organizations of the past is no longer effective. The need is for integrated, coordinated, cohesive delivery and communication systems which inform, serve and support tourists and prospects on a global basis. This new focus demands an innovative method of developing tourist experiences in an effective and efficient manner. This process focuses on what individuals and prospects want or need to know about products and services, not just what marketers want to tell them. It must be interactive. But, most of all, it must be effective in the eyes of the client. Within this context of innovation tourism is offered a unique opportunity for global face-to-face (F2F) communication and experiential marketing in contrast to other media, as well as the measurement of effect in terms of client satisfaction. An integrated, coordinated decision system and collaboration platform should inform, assist and support customers' experiences. In order to succeed in the future, destination managers need to interpret 'the new game rules' and re-define 'efficiency' ('doing things right'), 'equity' ('doing the right things') and 'effectiveness' ('doing the right things right') on a global scale.

16

Resource Management: Social, Cultural, Physical Environment and the Optimization of Impacts

David J Telfer and Atsuko Hashimoto

Introduction: resource management for tourism

An important part of the decision-making process to visit a particular destination is a favourable perception of the environment at the other end of the journey. It is the physical and cultural attributes of a destination's environment that provide the resources for wealth creation through tourism (Holden, 2002). Whether tourists select a destination by a specific landscape or cultural festival, these resources are interrelated and how they are managed not only impacts tourists but also the residents and local flora and fauna. Managing social, cultural and physical resources in destinations for tourism is as manifold and complex as are the resources themselves.

Environmental and resource problems have been characterized by terms such as 'wicked', 'messes' or 'metaproblems' (Mitchell, 1997). In examining the historical evolution of environmentalism, Macnaughten and Urry (1998, p.73) note the controversies of the meaning of the term 'nature', which have come to include the idea of 'nature as a landscape, as the object of scientific study, as threatened and in need of protection, as providing resources and life support essential for human survival, as a source of spiritual renewal and communion, and most generally as "the environment" '. Allaby (1998) defines the term environment in a very holistic manner as the 'complete range of external conditions, physical and biological, in which an organism lives. Environment includes social, cultural, and (for humans) economic and political considerations, as well as the more usually understood features such as soil, climate, and food supply'. These resources can be tangible and intangible and they can be renewable or non-renewable. Zimmermann (1951, p.15) argues that neither the environment nor parts of the environment are resources until they are considered capable of satisfying human needs, thus 'resources are not, they become'. Resources are subjective, relative and functional and Mitchell (1989) stresses that what is a natural resource in one culture may be 'neutral stuff' in another culture.

As the tourism product base continues to evolve worldwide, more and more varied resources (social, cultural and environment) are being drawn into the tourism domain, both in developed and developing destinations and the view on tourism impacts has changed over time. A focus on the negative environmental impacts of tourism has given way to examining a way forward in terms of how resources can be managed for future generations. Ritchie and Crouch (2003) categorize core resources and attractors that motivate travel as well as enhance destination appeal as physiography of the destination and, in particular, the landscape, scenery and climate, culture and history, range and mix of activities available, special events, components of the destination superstructure, types of entertainment and strength of market ties. These are supported by infrastructure, accessibility, financial capital, resident attitudes, enterprise and political will.

The focus of this chapter is to explore how the resources in destination areas can be managed to optimize impacts of tourism and hence promote development. In summary, Mitchell (1989, p.2) suggests 'natural resources are defined by human perception and attitudes, wants, technological skills, legal, financial and institutional arrangements as well as by political customs'. Therefore the management decisions on the sociocultural and physical environment as tourism resources depend on how the government or controlling bodies perceive the economic values of the 'resources'. The concept of competing ideologies in resource use will be explored in the following section.

Destination resource development ideology

Resource management has been defined as 'the actual decisions concerning policy or practice regarding how resources are allocated and under what conditions or arrangements resources may be developed' (Mitchell, 1989, p.3). Recent resource management concepts can be traced in part through the English environmental movement.

The contemporary English environmental movement has an intricate history influenced by a diversity of factors. Some of the key factors Macnaughten and Urry (1998) identify are tradition of preservationism; critique of post-war modernization; scientific critique of unlimited growth; expansion of expertise in ecology and nature conservation; the counter-cultural movement; and mediations of social life. Along with these factors, Macnaughten and Urry (1998, p.73) also highlight recent trends that environmental NGOs (non-governmental organizations) have been working within the 'new political space afforded by the shared language of sustainability' following the Rio summit. They have often had to work with the state and industry in consensus-seeking round tables trying to influence policy incrementally.

Figure 16.1 suggests that development of a destination's resources is governed by an ideology influenced by a variety of actors in a given political environment. The ideology may be very pro-development or very anti-development. Holden (2002) suggests that there are two main ideological approaches to the environment: technocentrism and ecocentrism. Technocentrism is characterized by beliefs that environmental problems can be solved by technical solutions through the application of science focusing on quantifiable solutions; the physical environment should be viewed as a resource that can be exploited by humans as they see fit and the position favours centralized control rather than local decision-making. At the other end of the spectrum is ecocentrism, which is linked to romantic transcendentalists with a belief in the wonderment of nature. Ecocentrics advocate alternative technologies as they have a lack of faith in modern technology and technical bureaucratic elites. This position has also been equated to deep ecology, recognizing the rights of nature independent of humans and favours local decision-making.

Figure 16.1 Integrating destination resource base towards optimization of impacts.

Between these two positions, a range of contrasting positions can be taken on sustainable development (Holden, 2002).

Figure 16.1 includes a partial list of varying actors and stakeholders who either have the power to set policy on resource management or are trying to influence decisions on policy. Robbins (2001) refers to firms with a traditional corporate culture centred primarily on generating wealth; firms with a social-environmental culture focus not only on wealth but also being socially-environmentally active. There has been an increasing interest in ethical standards for businesses since the 1980s, which has resulted in pressure for firms to be more socially and environ-mentally active, a reflection of the growth in environmental ethics. Some firms are attempting to be genuinely more 'green' while others are using the title as a mar-keting ploy. Within the tourism industry, companies such as Grecotel, the largest hotel company in Greece and the German-based tour group TUI have taken steps to integrate environmental management in their operating procedures (Holden, 2002). These contrasting positions are, however, similar to possible approaches taken by governments following either a Tourism First approach focus-ing on the industry or a Development First approach where planning is framed by broader national development needs (Burns, 1999).

Whoever has power in decision-making should be aware of the importance of interpreting national strategies and policies which are implemented through legal, administrative and direct government operations mechanisms (Austin, 1990). However, technocentrists tend to be politically influential and the dominant world view they hold is linked to capitalism, free trade and the global economy and tourism is firmly entrenched as a global phenomenon with countries competing for tourism dollars (O'Riordan, 1981 in Holden, 2002). In the technocentric realm, tourists are consumers and their taste for landscapes and 'exotic cultures' changes like a fashion vogue (Holden, 2002). It is 'illogical and naïve' (Sharpley, 2002, p.317) to expect even ecotourists to modify their behaviour to be more environmentally friendly.

Although it has not seen noticeable changes for the better yet, the tourists and the tourism industry can set the tone of what type of holidays are offered and thereby influence resource use. NGOs such as Tourism Concern and local residents can also influence decisions on resource use for tourism. Case study 16.1 illustrates the efforts of local residents to stop a potentially environmentally threatening tourist development. Other supranational organizations including the World Tourism Organization have published manuals on sustainability and UNESCO has designated World Heritage Sites for protection. Recognizing the complexity of the range of issues and actors at work on the social, cultural and physical resources for tourism, the following section will attempt to highlight selected potential management strategies that will result in the optimization of impacts.

Case study 16.1 Niagara Falls, Canada Tourism Development

There has been a rapid expansion in tourism construction projects in Niagara Falls, raising debates over what types of development should be approved near the Falls. The $1 billion CDN Niagara Fallsview Casino Resort Complex opened in June of 2004, the largest casino complex in Canada with a 30-storey hotel overlooking the Falls. The 1998 Niagara Tourist Area Development Strategy (Urban Strategies, 1998) cautioned against the adverse effects of over-development of high-rise buildings suggesting a 30-storey limit; however, hotels of 58 stories have already been proposed.

A study is underway investigating if the high-rise hotels along the top of the Niagara escarpment have caused changes in wind currents increasing the num-ber of days where mist from the Falls lands on the tourist viewing area (Draper, 2004). The latest proposal by the Niagara Parks Commission (NPC) to create a $23 million CDN gondola near the Canadian Horseshoe Falls sparked intense debate. The twelve-minute ride would extend from Table Rock, the main viewing area at the brink of the Falls down into the gorge to the loading area for the Maid of the Mist boat tour that runs to the base of the Falls. Forty gondolas holding up to eight people would be suspended on eight towers, six of them in the gorge.

The NPC claimed that it would provide needed revenues, while others called it over-commercialization and asserted it would destroy what the agency was established to protect. The city voted against it but the NPC, an independent provincial agency with jurisdiction over the Falls, obtained permission to borrow the necessary funds. Opposition petitions were circulated in the community and one on the Internet asked the question, would you put cable cars over the Pyramids (Hume, 2004)? Given the extent of the controversy raised over the project, the NPC decided to cancel the project.

Selection and implementation of management strategies

Discussion around the strategies

The relationship between tourism and environmental conservation can range from conflict to coexistence to symbiosis (Budowski, 1976). Mercer (2004, p.466) suggests that 'arguably biodiversity decline is the most serious global environmental problem and is representative of an emerging set of new problems in tourism management that is the subject of ongoing, and at times acrimonious debate'. Weaver and Oppermann (2000) identify three key elements in terms of the man-agement implications of sociocultural and environmental impacts of tourism. The first is that all tourism-related activity causes a certain amount of stress and the critical issue is whether proactive management strategies can be used to reduce the level of stress to acceptable levels. Acceptability is influenced by the percep-tions of the benefits received from tourism. The second point is that stress is linked to carrying capacity, which varies from site to site and, in some cases, can be manipulated through adaptive measures. However, ecosystems, societies and cultures all have different levels of resiliency and adaptability. Their third key point is that carrying capacities are difficult to measure as stress and its impacts are incremental and long term.

The selection and implementation of proactive resource management strategies in tourism is not without difficulty as no one management strategy can be applied universally, nor can it be done in isolation from other sectors of the economy or from local political realities. Resources created for tourism are also used by locals and many other resources are shared in common with local people in everyday life (Briassoulis, 2002). There are broad goals and specific strategies that can be or have been adapted to tourism. 'Think Global, Act Local' is a broad motto put forward by the environmental movement (Macnaughten and Urry, 1998). At a minimum the motto means that there are many transnational environmental problems at the local or regional level, requiring cooperation between states and secondly, there are large-scale problems that require local solutions based on the decentralized actions of many. Tourists cross international borders on airplanes and cruise ships generating pollutants and cause individual impacts at natural, historic and cultural sites after they arrive.

Resource management approaches and techniques

There has been a paradigm shift in the development debate to a focus on sustainability, which includes not only the biophysical sphere but also the sociocultural sphere (Sofield, 2003) and tourism is no exception. The roots of the term can be traced to the conservation movements in the mid-nineteenth century and gained popularity after the publication of the Bruntland Report in 1987 (Holden, 2002). Defined in that report as 'development that meets the needs of the present without compromising the ability of future generations to meet their own needs' (World Commission on Environment and Development, 1987), it is a term not without controversy. There has been great debate over definition and measurement (Telfer, 2002) with some arguing it is a way to perpetuate the Western capitalist system (Mitchell, 1997). Agenda 21 with its focus on sustainable development from the United Nations Conference on Environment and Development in Rio de Janeiro is now over a decade old. Lobbying organizations criticize the 2002 Rio plus Ten Summit as being shifted to the well-being of businesses rather than the well-being of the environment and local population. In fact, some argue that sustainable development is actually a barrier to development, while others are looking for more concrete ways to implement and monitor sustainable development through the use of a variety of tools such as sustainability indicators (Weaver and Oppermann, 2000).

Despite criticism, sustainable development is often held up as a vision or an end for resource and environmental management. Various approaches/frameworks have been developed to try to move towards sustainable development (Mitchell, 1997) and which are adaptable to tourism and a few are outlined in Table 16.1. All of these selected approaches have their supporters and detractors and the complex issues of definition, implementation, measurement and monitoring surround all of these approaches.

One aspect of sustainability is empowerment (Sofield, 2003) and within this framework there is an increasing need to consult local people and understand local knowledge systems through partnerships as illustrated in Case study 16.2. Murphy (1985) argued for a *community approach* based on an ecological model of tourism planning. Until recently, little concern was given to the protection and preservation of the sociocultural environment. Fear over the loss of sociocultural diversity, in part accelerated by tourism activities, raised concerns that appropriate management techniques need to be implemented. Tourism development can bring

Table 16.1 Management approaches/frameworks on the path to sustainable development

Approach	Characteristics
Sustainability criteria and indicators	Factors used to measure ecological, social, cultural and economic sustainability
Ecosystems management	Integrating scientific knowledge of ecological relationships within sociopolitical and values framework
Adaptive management	Resource and environmental systems contain surprises; change and adjustment are necessary
Precautionary principle	Rather than waiting for complete understanding, managers should anticipate potential harmful environmental impacts and make decisions to avoid such harm
Benefit-cost analysis	Identify all benefits and costs over the lifetime of a project emphasizing economic efficiency
Impact assessment (environmental, social)	Identify ways of improving projects environmentally and/or socially through preventing, minimizing, mitigating or compensating
Cumulative effects assessment	Sum of ecological changes on resources as a result of incremental impacts
Life cycle assessment	Holistic approach to evaluate environmental effects across the lifespan of a project or activity
Carrying capacity	Maximum sustainable population in a given area; idea has been expanded to social, physical, ecological resources
Limits of acceptable change	Specifies acceptable resource and social environmental conditions and guides management techniques to direct development
Co-operative management	Sharing rights and responsibilities between the government and civil society. Associated with partnerships, collaboration and co-management
Visitor impact management	Assesses impacts of visitors on a resource and recreation experience
Visitor experience and resource protection	Used in parks to look at desired ecological and social conditions rather than measures of maximum sustainable use
Tourism stewardship council	Emphasizes the need of holistic and collaborative efforts in management among the tourism stakeholders
Recreation opportunity spectrum (ROS)	Rational comprehensive planning approach to define user opportunities for different classes of recreational experiences within land use management categories (primitive-urban)
Tourism opportunity spectrum (TOS)	Adoption of ROS to tourism (ecotourism to urban tourism)
Ecotourism opportunity spectrum (ECOS)	Adoption of ROS to ecotourism

After Grumbine, 1994; Mitchell, 1997; Wight, 1998; Dawson, 2001; Ritchie and Crouch, 2003; Plummer and FitzGibbon, 2004 commoditization. However, if handled correctly it can lead to the protection and enhancement of traditions, customs and heritage, which would otherwise disappear (Hashimoto, 2002). The first step is to create inventories and indices to identify the sociocultural resources that need to be managed. These resources are of immense value to the cultural groups that own them, of fragile nature, easily irreversibly damaged or consumed, or have potential economic values. Understanding and controlling the tourist types the destination attracts helps minimize the damages to the social cultural resources. *Tourist typologies* by Plog (1977), Cohen (1972) and Smith (1977) often emphasize the numbers and adaptability of tourists to the local culture, so that the magnitude of sociocultural impacts can be estimated. From another perspective, the residents' view and well-being through tourism development need to be investigated. *Doxey's Index of Irritation* (1976) measures the local residents' feelings and acceptance as tourism develops. For intangible and symbolic resources, there have been precedents of national and supranational initiatives to designate intellectual property rights on living practitioners and cultural groups, especially among the indigenous people. *Living Human Treasure* or *National Treasure designations* have been developed in order to protect and manage them.

Case study 16.2 New Zealand, Opportunities for Mäori Tourism, Te Puni Kökiri

In 2001, the Office of Tourism and Sport and Te Puni Kökiri (the government's principal advisor on Mäori issues) undertook a major study to identify issues in Mäori Tourism and made recommendations. This study revealed the employment conditions of the Mäori in the tourism sector, felt barriers in performance in the tourism industry, perceived economic impacts, needs of tailored marketing research, etc. From this study recommendations came out such as the implementation of market research programmes for Mäori tourism; facilitation of access to more tightly defined business skills and tourism training courses; protection of intellectual and cultural property by legislation, by the 'Mark of Authenticity' designation and by monitoring the use of intellectual and cultural property in tourism promotion, to just name a few.

New Zealand Tourism recognizes the significance of Mäori tourism and has initiated efforts to provide needed education and training, access to resources and business opportunities, employment opportunities and more autonomy in tourism development which will enhance Mäori participation in tourism and hospitality and as a consequence empowerment of indigenous Mäori people in New Zealand.

Sustainability criteria and indicators

The first item in Table 16.1, where the future of resource management seems to be heading, is sustainability criteria and indicators. Mowforth and Munt (1998) identified criteria often used for sustainability in tourism as ecological, social, cultural and economic sustainability along with an education element and local participation. They also outlined a list of the *tools of sustainability* under eight headings. Area protection involves creating categories of land with protected status, such as biosphere reserves or national parks. Industry regulation involves not only governments but also works through industry association and voluntary regulations. Visitor management techniques include zoning, restricted entry and differential pricing structures. Environmental impact assessment covers a range of approaches such as overlays, matrices, cost-benefit analysis and environmental auditing. There are a variety of approaches to carrying capacity ranging from social to environmental. Consultation or participation techniques cover meetings, surveys and contingent valuations methods. Codes of conduct have been suggested for tourists, the industry, hosts and governments. The final technique identified by Mowforth and Munt (1998) is *sustainability indicators* which cover a wide diversity of factors from pollution to freedom from violence and oppression.

Weaver and Oppermann (2000) suggest that once a suitable definition of sustainable tourism is established, criteria need to be set to determine if there is sustainable tourism present. A first step is to identify appropriate *indicators* and they have established a candidate list under five headings. Under management, indicators include: recycling and fuel efficiency performance of tourism accommodation, attractions and transportation; presence of EIA procedures for tourism-related businesses; and a number of codes of ethics and good practice put in place. Cultural indicators include extent of cultural commoditization and conformity of tourism architecture to local vernacular. Environmental factors include resource consumption of tourism (water, fossil fuels, metals, food, forest products, agglomerate); wildlife or habitat deterioration, hazardous waste production; and density of tourism activities and facilities. Economic indicators focus on profitability, but also on what happens to the profit. Indicators include revenue earned directly from tourism, economic leakage, backward economic linkages and percentage of jobs held by foreigners or non-locals. The final category are the social indicators and a few examples include resident attitude towards tourism that can be examined with an Irridex, ratio of residents to tourists, destination image of the destination, seasonality and amount of tourism-related crime. Weaver and Oppermann (2000) note, however, that while some of these indicators are easy to measure, others are very difficult due to expense and gaps of knowledge in the field. Research on sustainable tourism indicators is relatively new and political realities also play a role in what can be accomplished. The other key questions are who is responsible for implementing these indicators and how are they monitored?

Towards optimization of impacts: future dimension

Tourism businesses and tourists are sharing sociocultural and physical resources with host communities. These resources have some kind of economic value to all parties; thus careful management is required in order to ensure good quality and quantities are available to all stakeholders now and in the future. Management issues are no longer a simple matter in today's world. Sustainable development concepts that encourage respect to multi-culturalism de-emphasize a universal method of resource management.

Management strategies vary from one destination to another as no two destinations share resources of the same kind and sensitivity. The level of socioeconomic development in the destination is one component. A highly developed and built-up environment with a western-culture base may have the advantage of infrastructure and social constructs, which can easily accommodate technology-led management methods. On the other hand, developing nations of non-western culture may not function well with western style management, which encourages modernization (or westernization) of host nations.

The key is how management decisions are implemented and how conflicts are resolved if resources are to be used in an optimum fashion. Mitchell (1997, p.243) identifies nine obstacles to implementation of such management which include: 'tractability of the problem; lack of clarity of goals; commitment of those responsible for implementation; resource (means) available to achieve goals (ends); inadequate access to information; inappropriate assumptions about cause-effect relationships; the dynamics of enforcement; conditions specific to developing countries; and different styles due to cultural variations'.

There is an increased awareness of environmental issues by some members of society and, as the tourism product continues to diversify, more remote areas are being opened up (Holden, 2002). As Mercer (2004) suggests, the future of research in resource management in tourism will surround the issues of monitoring and analysis, ethical and power-sharing issues as well as scale and boundaries. It is becoming increasingly important that all resources (social, cultural and physical) are managed appropriately in a sustainable manner for possible optimum utilization.

17

Actors, Networks and Tourism Policies

Bill Bramwell

Introduction

Public policy is a vitally important aspect of tourism matters because of its role in regulating the tourism industry and its related activities. Policy-making is a political activity that is embedded within the economic and social characteristics of society. As such it reflects society's values and ideologies, distribution of power, institutions and decision-making processes (Hall and Jenkins, 2004). An understanding of the public policy processes in relation to tourism depends on our conceptual or theoretical frameworks. These frameworks serve as the basis for explaining policy processes and for identifying the links between people, activities and policies. Different theoretical perspectives will conceptualize the policy process and its implications in distinct ways.

This chapter provides an introduction to network frameworks for the study of public policy processes related to tourism. These network approaches are likely to become increasingly important in the future. One reason for this is because public policies are increasingly influenced not just by government but also by a range of other actors who interact with each other within various networks. A network is taken to be a system in which actors are linked by a set of relationships, such as the transfer of resources, overlapping membership or friendships. The discussion explores the application of network ideas to evaluations of tourism policy processes and contexts, including the potential future use of ideas from actor-network theory and actor-oriented perspectives on networks.

Networks and tourism policies

Network perspectives usually rest on the assumption that the relationships that link social actors together possess a certain constancy in the form of recurring patterns of relationships. These patterns are known as networks. In tourism there may be some consistency in the patterns of relationships between, for example, hoteliers in a destination and external tour operators, or between a hotel developer and local environmental groups. Networks provide a relational focus, yet one that recognizes the importance of individuals within the system. In this way networks bridge macro and micro systems. Policy networks are a specific type of network that represents 'the social infrastructure of policy formulation and implementation' (Marin and Mayntz, 1991, p.15). Public policies are made and implemented by interdependent actors within policy networks. According to Kickert et al. (1997, p.1), the concept of policy network 'connects public policies with their strategic and institutional context: the network of public, semi-public, and private actors participating in certain policy fields'.

The network perspective in policy research actually comprises many different approaches, but all direct attention to the ways and means by which actors formulate goals and seek to achieve them in relation to others, often through various forms of association. It also highlights the relative power of actors and organizations as they interact and come into conflict over policies. It has been suggested that the occurrence of 'power' in relation to policies depends on the actions of others, notably on others attributing power to someone (Murdoch and Marsden, 1995, p.372). From this perspective the analysis of power becomes the study of collective interactions. Thus the success of actors in achieving their policy objectives has to be fought for in interactions with others.

One advantage of the use of network concepts in policy research is that these concepts help to integrate local and non-local actors, i.e. they bring together the local and the global. Relations between the global and the local are particularly significant for tourism due to the often long-distance movement of tourists and also the potential flows of investment and returns to capital in the industry between tourist destinations and metropolitan centres of capital. Policy issues in tourism are rarely resolved within a locality; rather they implicate networks of actors that extend from the local to the national and international, and back again. Local actors are tied into sets of relations both with other local actors and those located elsewhere. The idea of networks can assist in uncovering what Massey (1991) calls the 'power geometry' of the relationships between local and non-local actors.

A central element in the study of tourism policy networks is the identification and evaluation of relevant individuals and groups of actors. These actors are active participants who process information and use their own strategies in their dealings with other actors and institutions. Within limits imposed by outside forces and local conditions, the individual actors process the social experience and devise ways of responding and adapting. As well as single individuals, there

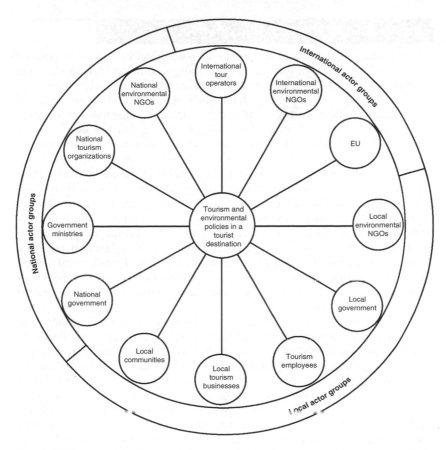

Figure 17.1 Examples of potential actor groups related to tourism and environmental policies in a tourist destination.

are also groups of actors who can respond collectively or at least share some similar interests, values, discursive forms or power relations. Figure 17.1 identifies selected examples of actor groups from among the many that may be directly or indirectly involved in policies related to tourism and to tourism's impacts on the environment in a tourist destination. Bramwell's (2004) study of policies affecting tourism and the environment in the coastal areas of southern Europe identifies a number of groups of actors related to these policies. These groups of actors are depicted as operating in the context of capitalist development, but are also seen as active participants. They include commercial tour operators, residents in tourist areas, environmental groups, government organizations and the European Union. While they are found at international, national and local geographical scales, it is argued that they can be conceived as interacting in local 'multi-actor fields'. Within these fields the different actors 'have their own specific interests, can espouse certain views, and have varying degrees of influence on the policy process and on the resulting policy direction' (p.32).

The emerging interest in tourism policy networks

Recent studies of the public policy process by political scientists have recognized that a complex set of institutions and actors drawn from within, but also beyond, government are involved in the process of policy formulation and implementation. There is a blurring of the boundaries and responsibilities between state and non-state actors and it is argued that this blurring has become more prevalent in many countries over recent decades. Analysts of the policy process have thus begun to adopt a multi-agency and multi-actor perspective in order to uncover how the various policy actors coordinate their actions and also compete with one another. This has led to a growing interest in policy networks in political science. A feature of these networks that is often highlighted is the development of multi-actor advocacy coalitions, which compete to influence policy in line with the policy beliefs which bind each coalition together. Another feature that is given prominence is the character of multilevel governance, i.e. the way policies tie together the different tiers of the state. Thus, modern political systems are depicted as fragmented, with networks and coalitions that are composed of state and non-state actors that are bound together through either shared beliefs or resource dependencies and with the varied parties competing to influence the policy processes and outcomes.

While researchers in other disciplinary fields have constructed typologies of economic, social and policy networks, these ideas have made relatively little impact in the tourism literature. One exception is Pavlovich's (2003a) account of the network system involved in the tourism industry in an icon tourist destination, the Waitomo caves in the North Island of New Zealand. In the social sciences, different network systems have long been characterized by certain properties. Some of the most common properties used to describe social networks are size, density, cliques, clustering, centrality, multiplexity, strength, multidimensionality, link reciprocity and heterogeneity (Smith, 1999, p.640). Pavlovich describes two characteristics of the Waitomo caves tourism network: its relational centrality and its density. Here, centrality reveals how critical an actor or organization is within the network structure and it also refers to 'an actor's power obtained through the network structure, rather than through individual attributes' (Pavlovich, 2003b, p.42). Density describes the overall structure of the network and, in particular, 'the number of ties that link network actors together' (p.42). Densely tied networks tend both to produce strong constraints on a focal organization and to act as a catalyst for knowledge building. By contrast, in networks with less relational density, a focal organization may have more discretion over its actions but the fragmented nature of ties in the network may result in fewer information exchanges. Pavlovich's use of the network approach in the case of Waitomo shows how a group of small firms has become self-governing within an interdependent network and also how this process has assisted the destination in building the knowledge needed for competitive advantage.

A rare explicit use of network concepts to examine tourism policy processes is provided in a study by Tyler and Dinan (2001). They use these concepts in an assessment of relationships between tourism interest groups and government in tourism policy-making in England. Part of their analysis uses the concepts of 'policy communities' and 'issue networks'. This draws on the work of Marsh and

Table 17.1 Some characteristics of policy communities and issue networks

Policy network dimension	Policy community	Issue network
Openness of membership	More closed	More open
Diversity of interests	Often economic and professional interests	Range of affected interests
Frequency of interaction	More frequent	Less regular
Stability of membership	More stable	More fluctuating
Consensus	Often shared values	Often lower levels of agreement
Power	A balance of power. One group may dominate, but all see themselves as gaining	Unequal power

Source: Adapted from Marsh and Rhodes, 1992

Rhodes (1992), who identify 'policy communities' and 'issue networks' as two ideal types at opposite ends of a continuum of policy networks, with various hybrid networks existing between these extreme poles. The characteristics of these two types of policy networks are shown in Table 17.1.

The 'policy community' has a more closed and stable membership, sometimes involving a government ministry or agency and a handful of privileged economic or producer groups, who regularly interact and share a consensus of values and predispositions, almost a shared ideology, about that policy sector that sets that community apart from outsider groups. The cement that joins the members of the policy community is said to be their mutual resource dependency: each has resources that can be exchanged or bargained with so that a balance of power prevails, allowing every member to benefit. While there is a balance of power, it is not necessarily one in which all benefit equally, but one in which all members feel that they gain. Through their ability to control the policy agenda, the members can produce continuity and stability in policy outcomes that transcend changes in the political complexion of government and can largely be immune from the gaze and control of either democratically elected politicians or the public. Here the power and interests of producer groups and the fragmented administrative structure can become mutually reinforcing; both producers and the state may want to maintain this cosy situation as it reduces policy conflict and enables them to determine policy outcomes more easily. In contrast to the policy community, the more open 'issue network' often has many competing groups that reflect a range of affected interests and that have unequal powers. This more diverse network involves a more fluctuating membership and less regular interactions. The government tends to consult rather than bargain with members of this more varied network and, as a result, the policy outcomes are far less stable and predictable.

Tyler and Dinan (2001) use the two concepts of policy communities and issue networks to evaluate tourism policy processes in England. They conclude that 'at present, the English tourism policy network can be characterized as an "issue network"', but also that one 'may begin to see a network dominated by the well-resourced interest groups ... gaining direct access to senior departmental civil servants and ministers' (p.249).

The future use of actor-network theory

Actor-network theory or the 'sociology of translation' was developed by researchers studying the sociology of science, notably Michel Callon, Bruno Latour and John Law. It is a framework for analysis that allows for the investigation of a diversity of actors and of the interactions and relations between them. It has developed over a period of over twenty years. This framework has become an influential approach in the social sciences for the study of economic, social and political change, so it is very likely to influence future research on tourism policy.

The central tenet of actor-network theory is that, in order to achieve their intended outcomes, actors have to enrol other actors into their own 'projects'. If other actors are successfully enrolled in an actor's network, then that actor is able to borrow their force and speak and act on their behalf or with their support. This process means that the actor becomes both the network and a point within it. The methods by which an actor enrols others are described by Callon et al. (1986, p.xviii) as a process of 'translation'. This process includes defining and distributing roles, devising a strategy through which actors are made indispensable to others and placing others within an actor's own itinerary (Murdoch, 1998). Another key notion in actor-network theory is that power is not invested in the actors but instead it emerges from the associations or relations that are made. Thus power only exists when it is exercised or actively performed through interactions with other entities in the network (Morris, 2004, p.179).

In actor-network theory the potential actors are not limited to humans, as they may include non-human agents, such as organizations, machines and technologies. Distinctions are not made between the inanimate or natural and the social in this approach. The process of achieving a 'project' can therefore involve the use of human and non-human resources, with these social and non-human entities depicted as coming into being as a result of the complex relations or networks that link the human and non-human resources together.

In future research actor-network theory could be applied to understanding tourism policy-making processes and the conflicts in tourism policy arenas. Thus, attention might be directed to how a tourism policy idea or dispute is developed by an actor and how the actor attempts to enrol others to its 'project', with or without resistance. One attraction of actor-network theory is that it focuses attention on how power arises from the construction of networks, which allows an outcome to be achieved by the actors. These tactics of translation or 'enrolment' adopted by actors and the tactics of the opponents who respond with alternative 'projects', could provide a framework for understanding how tourism policy coalitions are constructed and challenged.

Figure 17.2 illustrates the application of an actor-network perspective to a hypothetical case of conflict between actors over a development proposal for a tourist hotel in a pristine rural area. In this fictional instance a hotel developer has a 'project' to build a hotel and the developer manages to 'enrol' local government to support its scheme. Together these actors form a pro-development network, which is opposed by a network of actors against the initiative. Among

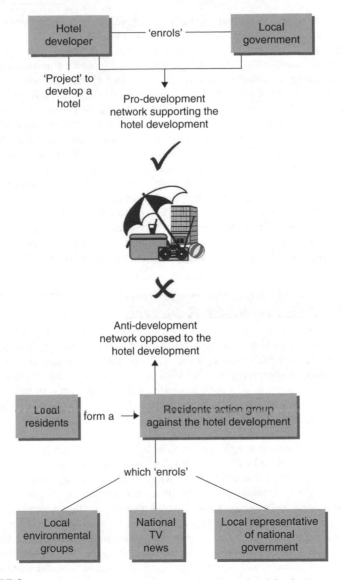

Figure 17.2 Hypothetical network of action for and against a hotel development.

the latter actors, the local residents form an action group united in a shared concern about the development. In another 'translation' process the action group then connects with a national government representative, environmental interests and the national media in order to campaign against the hotel. The outcome of this type of conflict would depend on which set of associations remained strongest and which meanings became dominant (Murdoch and Marsden, 1995). The future use of actor-network theory in ways such as this could provide helpful analytical tools for conceptualizing the people involved in tourism policy-making and policy applications and also the relations between them.

But it would be a mistake for tourism researchers to adopt uncritically the ideas contained in actor-network theory, especially as some recent commentators have expressed concerns about the approach (Law and Hassard, 1999). Significant reservations have been noted by John Law, one of the leading early exponents of the approach (Hetherington and Law, 2000). He suggests that it has become a 'grand narrative' around the notion of 'enrolment', with everything seen as capable of being absorbed into the networks being studied. Law is concerned that this allows for little space outside – thereby excluding 'otherness' outside the network – and he argues that this fails to recognize the importance of features that are external to the network. He also suggests that research using actor-network theory usually focuses on cases where actors successfully enrol others to their 'projects' and it concerns him that this can divert attention from studies of failure or of marginal or alternative views. This latter point has been noted in particular by feminist theorists. One might also object to an approach that treats non-human objects, such as technologies and landscapes, as equal to human actors (Woods, 1997).

The future use of actor perspectives

Future research on tourism policy networks might also draw on other social science approaches, notably various actor-oriented perspectives. Actor perspectives can help to counter the tendency for social or political networks to be treated in some research as structures from which one can 'read off' the interests, beliefs and actions of individuals. Policy network research that follows this tendency stresses how networks limit participation in the policy process; decide which issues will be included and excluded from the policy agenda; shape the behaviour of actors through the rules of the game; and privilege certain interests. By contrast, actor perspectives emphasize that the beliefs and actions of individuals are not wholly determined by their position within various networks. Actor perspectives tend to focus on 'human agency', while often also recognizing the importance of structures, including social and political networks.

Advocates of actor perspectives vary, however, in their interpretations of human agency. The notion of agency attributes to the individual actor the capacity to process social experience and to devise ways of coping with life, even under the most extreme forms of coercion. It depends on the idea that all actors exercise some kind of 'power', with leverage or room for manoeuvre, even for those in subordinate positions. Yet, while actors actively engage in the construction of their own social context and experiences, they encounter circumstances that are not simply of their own making. Advocates of actor perspectives can hold differing conceptualizations of the balance and relationships between 'internal' human agency and the 'external' structural conditions in society. One valuable conceptualization of these processes is by the Dutch development sociologist, Norman Long (2001), who stresses the interplay and mutual determination of the internal and external factors and relationships. Rather than conceiving of structures as stable features, he sees them as emergent properties that are the product of the interlocking of specific actors' projects and practices. Through this process certain possibilities are excluded and others are made possible or are realized.

Policy network research from actor perspectives is likely to stress issues such as the ways in which social actors engage in or are locked into struggles over the attribution of meaning to particular policy debates and how particular individuals and groups attempt to make space for themselves to pursue their own projects that ran parallel to, or perhaps challenge, government policies or the interests of other parties.

In an unusual direct application of an actor perspective in research on tourism policy processes, Verbole (2000) explores the complex social relations involved in rural tourism policies and development in Pišece, a small rural community in south-eastern Slovenia. She argues that 'local people are not passive recipients of the consequences of rural tourism development policy, but are instead capable of making the most out of a given situation' (p.480). Based on that premise, it is contended that an 'actor-oriented approach allows us to conceptualize rural tourism development as a dynamic, on-going process that is shaped and reshaped by social actors' (p.480). Her study of this rural community in Pišece embraces an evaluation of the interests of the social actors, their organizing practices and strategies, their power relations and their different discourses in relation to the development of tourism. An ethnographic methodology is used because 'using an actor-oriented approach, it was important to identify the problems and concepts as perceived and presented by the social actors themselves, and to look for similarities and/or differences in their social interpretations and to investigate the types and content of the social relationships among them' (p.481). One of Verbole's findings is that kinship-based family clans as well as various networks and cliques, based on religion, politics and links to influential actors, were very important in obtaining and controlling access to the decision-making processes related to tourism development in the community.

Conclusion: network perspectives on tourism public policy processes

Future studies of tourism policies need to pay more attention to how policies are influenced by diverse actors and by actor networks. This will enhance our understanding of the policy process and also it can help in strengthening the practical arrangements for tourism policy making and policy implementation. This chapter has provided a brief introduction to network perspectives on the study of public policy processes for the tourism industry. It has outlined some network approaches that have emerged in other disciplinary areas of the social sciences and it has considered their potential future use in order to understand tourism policies. The approaches include the notions of policy communities and issue networks, as developed by political scientists, and also actor-network theory, a theoretical approach that emerged from studies of the sociology of science. Another potential direction for future research on tourism policy processes was also indicated, this being the use of actor-oriented perspectives on policy networks. These approaches have yet to make a substantial impact on tourism policy research and the discussion indicated their potential strengths and drawbacks for future work.

18

Collaborative Networks and Partnerships for Integrated Destination Management

Tazim Jamal and Ute Jamrozy

Introduction

Destinations face increasing challenges in an international marketplace where multiple stakeholders with diverse values and often divergent needs compete for scarce or unique resources. Rapid population growth combined with the global mobility of labour, capital, technology and people means that places now have to compete on an international and highly multicultural stage for capital and goods. The growing populations of travellers and inhabitants increasingly impact on natural and social environments, and success in the twenty-first century marketplace depends on the ability of firms and destinations to engage in sustainable use and conservation of vital resources. On this mobile world stage, social equity and cultural diversity emerge as crucial development-related items. Environmental

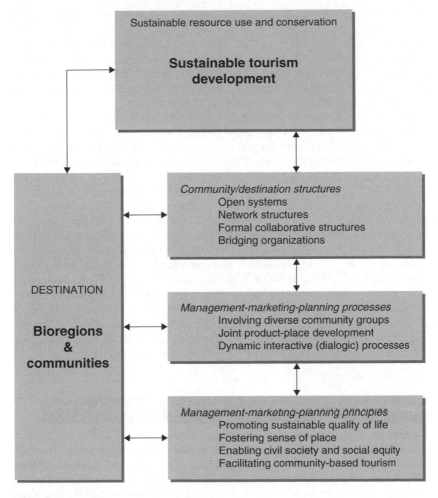

Figure 18.1 Integrated destination management: structures, processes and principles.

and social justice issues (related, for example, to gender, sexuality, ethnicity) have to be addressed from both the supply and demand side of the tourism system.

Sustaining the natural and cultural resources on which tourism depends has therefore been taken up as a key initiative in tourism, e.g. *Local Agenda 21 for Travel & Tourism*. Heritage institutions like English Heritage reveal a major shift in heritage and cultural resource management, from physical preservation and visitor management to developing sense of place and identity through the inclusion of diverse cultural voices (English Heritage, 2002). But planning and managing tourism in such a complex domain requires new tools and methods. Close interaction between the public sector (e.g. city planners, transportation department), the destination's tourism marketing organization, the private sector and the local residents in planning is a key tenet of sustainable tourism and *Local*

Agenda 21 (Hall, 2000b). Yet, the processes and structures by which a destination's stakeholders can work most effectively together to manage the local-global influences on their natural and cultural resources are not well understood empirically or theoretically. Effective destination management is possibly the most problematic issue facing tourism managers in the twenty-first century. Developing an integrated management approach to deal with interconnected impacts in the local-global domain is the main focus of this chapter.

The chapter presents a framework for integrated destination management (IDM) based on sustainability and collaborative principles. It adopts a systems view where the ecological-physical-social spaces are linked by various types of networks and institutional structures. The new framework extends beyond the 1990s sustainability paradigm that was based on balancing economy and environment (WCED, 1997), to encompass social equity and cultural diversity as integral to quality of life, sense of place and healthy living environments (see Figure 18.1). A theoretical overview and two case examples illustrate this framework: (i) community-based tourism in Palacios, Texas and (ii) sustainable tourism planning in Hawaii. The framework moves tourism management into a new future characterized by the *integration* of marketing and planning in a diverse destination system that facilitates social, economic and cultural equity. By integrating management with diversity, the new sustainability paradigm addresses the political nature of planning and development far more effectively than the old modernist paradigm where scientific knowledge and measurement were privileged over local and indigenous knowledge and participation, and decision-making was authoritative and top-down rather than holistic and participatory.

Perspectives and objectives for destination management

Destinations can be viewed as *complex planning systems*. There are *multiple stakeholders* with varying degrees of influence over decision-making – no individual stakeholder can fully control development and planning. Key stakeholders (e.g. airlines) are not always located at the destination and places may have to deal with impacts locally that stem from actions and pressures exerted elsewhere in a *local-global tourism system*. The globalization of capital, labour, people, information and culture industries adds further spatial and temporal *fragmentation* to planning under conditions where effects may be cumulative over time and extend from the local-regional to the transnational-global.

Collaborative planning organizations

Collaboration and continuous, integrated planning become even more important in these new globalisms: tourism must be integrated with other planning for social and economic development and modelled as an interactive system (Gunn, 2004). Murphy's (1985) ecological-community systems model and Inskeep's (1991) sustainability-oriented planning support such an interactive approach where sustainable tourism 'is envisaged as leading to management of all resources in such a way that economic, social, and aesthetic needs can be fulfilled while maintaining cultural integrity, essential ecological processes, biological diversity, and life support systems' (World Tourism Organization, 1997a, p.30).

Systems thinking becomes an imperative for destination management under the complex conditions outlined above – it requires understanding tourism as a networked system of interrelated and interactive components (Jamal et al., 2004). Yet, most destination tourist organizations focus on marketing and promotion; they are not properly involved in resource use, allocation and planning (Pearce, 1992). The resulting 'marketing-planning gap' has serious consequences for destination sustainability, as the Hawaii example below shows. Part of the problem lies in barriers to communicative planning, and community debate on sustainability choices (Healey, 2003). Traditional organizational structures and functions tend to isolate destination marketing, land-use planning, resource use and conservation from each other and from societal values and resident/visitor needs. Planning was seen as restrictive, while marketing was viewed as expansive.

Though momentum has built over the past two decades towards interdisciplinary integration, structural innovation, partnerships and collaboration to overcome such barriers, greater attention is required to their formation in tourism domains. Organization theory and research in inter-organization relations (e.g. Rahman et al., 2002) offer useful insights into new institutional arrangements. Complex social and sustainability domains range on a continuum from underorganized to organized. They exhibit two types of organizations which are complementary: one stays uncentred and retains a network character. The other displays some kind of centring through a self-regulating, collaborative body. The latter type (a *referent organization*) may have several functions: regulation, appreciation of trends and issues, providing leadership and direction and infrastructure support (Trist, 1983).

Similarly, Brown (1991, p.5) presents four kinds of *bridging organizations* that span the social gaps among organizations and constituencies to enable coordinated action. These vary from loosely structured networks to formally structured partners or coalitions. The case examples below illustrate two important modes of organizing, varying from a 'sustainable tourism committee' acting as a bridging organization in marketing-planning (Hawaii), to loosely structured community-policy networks (Palacios). These examples show the importance of approaching planning and marketing from an integrated perspective that facilitates sustainable use and development of a destination's tourism-related resources.

Sustainable tourism marketing

Traditionally, destination management/marketing organizations (DMOs) tend to represent the tourism industry's interests. Their mission is building and enhancing a favourable destination image to attract targeted tourists and increase visitor numbers. Even though product development is an essential component of marketing, the general public and some professionals equate marketing with promotion (and within promotion, primarily with advertising). Therefore, destination and state tourism agencies often focus their activities on tourism advertising campaigns, though their actual role should be more holistic and integrated. Historically, marketing focused on developing product, price, place and promotion 'to create exchanges that satisfy individual and organizational objectives' (American Marketing Association). Recently, marketing has been changed to 'an organizational function and a set of processes for creating, communicating, and delivering value to customers and for managing customer relationships in ways that benefit the organization and its stakeholders' (AMA, 2004). This reflects a shift away from mere economics towards creating value for a network of actors and environments. A marketing perspective on sustainable tourism has 'an overall management orientation reflecting corporate attitudes that … must balance the interests of shareholders/owners with the long-run environmental interests of a destination and at the same time meet the demands and expectations of customers' (Middleton and Hawkins, 1998, p.8).

The integrated destination management framework we propose brings in the destination's ecological-human communities as equitable and integrated members of planning-marketing and goal setting. The new approach integrates economic viability, social equity and environmental responsibilities towards achieving quality of life within *living systems*. Based on an ecosystem network model, a sustainable planning-marketing orientation does not just satisfy the needs and wants of individuals – it strives to sustain ecosystems. The marketing exchange does not just take place between consumers and businesses, it links self-generating networks of participants operating in diverse spatial and temporal spaces. The benefits are not just profits, but civic energy and social cohesion. Competition is replaced by dynamic interactions that aim at environmental, social and economic equity within the local-global network of living and physical (including built) structures. Therefore, sustainable tourism marketing's objectives are not to design a product, price, place and promotion of a tourism destination or attraction, but to ensure quality of life and environments through tourism development. Achieving this will be challenging; it involves developing an interactive product/place relationship that will provide value to visitors as well as to diverse community stakeholders. Communicating a sense of place and quality of life priorities to stakeholders becomes a key function of promotion.

An integrated destination management (IDM) framework

The tourism destination environment is a complex planning system due to various factors outlined above:

1. Interdependence among multiple stakeholders and industries
2. Fragmented control over planning/development
3. Culturally diverse values and different views
4. The traditional role of tourism destination marketing focused on growth and rapid development
5. Interrelated impacts in a local-global system.

The IDM framework proposed here takes these characteristics into account and sets as its objective an integrated approach to destination management and sustainability. Implementation of the framework requires the application of participatory principles based on a systems approach, cross-sectoral collaborative processes and principles that include equity and diversity:

■ A systems approach that effectively integrates planning, marketing and sustainable resource use and conservation. Adopting a systems view to destination management, multiple stakeholders can explore diverse views and develop a 'shared' appreciation and learning of the issues as well as joint solutions (Walker et al., 1999; Hall, 2000b). The Palacios and Hawaii examples below apply this systems-based principle in their participatory planning approach.
■ Sustainability-oriented processes, institutions and structures (formal/informal networks and partnerships) that address the interrelatedness of impacts and facilitate collaborative planning (Jamal and Getz, 1995). Collaborative initiatives are 'emergent interorganizational arrangements through which organizations collectively cope with the growing complexity of their environments' (Gray, 1989, p.236). The Sustainable Tourism Committee in the Hawaii process described below shows the application of this principle.
■ Resident involvement and community-based enterprise development based on local control, social equity and cultural diversity (Apo, 2004). Here, development draws upon principles that respect and celebrate the local community's sense(s) of place, diversity of cultural heritage, ethnicity and values and ecological-social relationships. Both of the examples below reflect this socially equitable approach, which is a *community-based* approach, focusing on sense of place, mutual respect, sharing, equity in employment and access to resources and benefits.

Case study 18.1 Palacios, Texas

Palacios, Texas, is a small coastal community of about 5000 people that is rich in history and cultural diversity. Its population is almost equally distributed among Hispanic, Anglo-American and Vietnamese. Globalization has severely impacted the town's shrimp-based economy. Its large shrimp industry struggles to survive as abundant, cheap shrimp imports and rising fuel costs diminish profits. However, Palacios is also a quaint and relaxing location for a small number of the region's recreational visitors as well as newcomer retirees. It also attracts some 'Winter Texans' (or 'snowbirds') who make the town their winter home. Its proximity to the Houston metropolitan area offers some growth potential. Community leaders are therefore looking to tourism to help diversify the town's struggling economy.

As a destination, the town is at the beginning of the tourism life cycle with little development, few tourist amenities and a small number of attractions such as sport and recreational fishing, birding and a museum representing its maritime heritage and history. A small urban design and tourism assessment project was undertaken in Spring 2003 to: (a) identify needs and wants of the community; (b) develop and discuss urban planning designs; and (c) discuss tourism impacts and potential tourism development initiatives.

Four resident committees explored and presented their views on downtown, waterfront, hike and bike trail, transportation and economic development issues.

Additionally, household, school and resident surveys were conducted to examine youth and adult opinions about community and tourism development. The project demonstrated collaboration between the community residents (the four committees taking a leadership role), the Economic Development Office (EDO) and other community leadership groups, business enterprises (particularly related to tourism and shrimping), and university planning and tourism faculty and students. The process emphasized the involvement of all diverse populations, the different activities valued and supported by these groups and the community's needs for protection, preservation and development. Rather than developing a standard tourism image ('City by the Sea') and advertising campaign, the project has focused on identifying a sense of place based on community needs and wants (quality of life issues) and initiating small enterprise for tourism development.

Palacios has therefore taken up the challenge of integrating its diverse historic, cultural and economic resources (e.g. shrimping and tourism) into the development processes in a way that hopes to ensure that tourism does not overrun the shrimping heritage and livelihood that much of its diverse populations rely upon.

Case study 18.2 Hawaii

Hawaii is a mature destination dealing with significant infrastructure, economic, environmental and sociocultural impacts. Tourism is the state's primary economic engine, accounting for 34 per cent of its diverse labour force and 28 per cent of total output ($10.9 billion) in 1997 (Konan and Kim, 2003/4). Its resources are stressed by almost seven million annual visitors, increasing population growth and urban development to accommodate a diverse group of residents. In Autumn 1999, the Hawaii Tourism Authority (HTA) awarded a three-year, $114 million contract to the Hawaii Visitors and Convention Bureau (VCB), aimed at adding nearly 30 000 visitors per day in 2005. In January 2000, the Sierra Club launched an unprecedented lawsuit against HTA, arguing that the state had to assess the environmental impact of projected visitor increases.

While the Supreme Court did not rule in favour of the Sierra Club, the long, drawn-out lawsuit 'further spurred interest in evaluating the impact of visitors on our environment, infrastructure, and our standard of living' (DBEDT, 2002). Act 259 of the 2001 Legislature requested the Department of Business, Economic Development and Tourism (DBEDT) to conduct a study on Hawaii's capacity to sustain future tourism growth. *Planning for Sustainable Tourism in Hawaii* was an innovative collaborative initiative, extensively documented and disseminated on http://www.hawaiitourismstudy.com/new.asp (accessed 20 June, 2004). The project included three major studies: (1) Infrastructure and Environmental Overview Study; (2) Economic and Environmental Modelling; (3) Public Input and SocioCultural Study. In addition to the scientific dimensions, therefore, the study aimed to identify key sociocultural impacts and provide guidelines and recommendations for addressing social issues, including Native Hawaiian issues (Knox, 2004).

From a process perspective, the ST Hawaii initiative involved a range of stakeholders, including public and private sector interests, academics, consultants, non-profit organizations, native and non-native groups, residents and communities across the various islands. Multi-stakeholder committees and advisory groups were set up to assist with the three studies. For example, the Hawaii Hotel Association, Hawaii Restaurant Association, HTA, VCB and various planning-related stakeholders participated in the Visitor Industry Advisory Committee. The Native Hawaiian Advisory Group contained an academic, a representative from Hilton Hotels, a Research and Development company representative and the Director of the Hawaii Hospitality Institute. The private consulting group retained for the sociocultural project convened a Sustainable Tourism Study Group comprised of diverse interests. Public input was facilitated by community meetings, e-mails and a statewide resident survey.

Discussions on implementation include re-envisioning the role of various marketing agencies better to integrate resource use and planning of this island paradise. New institutions, structures and roles are emerging to bridge the planning-marketing gap (what will be HTA's role in this?). A new state tourism liaison position was established in 2003 to facilitate tourism policy and cross-sectoral communication. Complementing these (inter-)organizational innovations with community-based tourism could enable Hawaii to set leadership for integrated destination management in the twenty-first century. Success will depend in part on how well its new institutional structures cope with the political landscape of planning-marketing in Hawaii, and its ethnic diversity.

Conclusions

This chapter presents an integrated destination management (IDM) framework based on:

1. A collaborative and systems-based approach that integrates previously disparate activities related to destination planning, marketing and management
2. Sustainable tourism and community-based principles (DBEDT, 2002) and
3. The destination's sense of place, as well as its economic and cultural diversity.

The new sustainability paradigm replaces the old 'sustainable development' paradigm that sought to 'balance' environment and economy, but lacked adequate attention to the growing diversity of social-cultural groups, their values and importance to sustainable resource use and conservation.

The task of integrated destination planning, marketing and management in this complex domain requires a variety of formal and informal processes and structures, including networks, partnerships, committees and other organizational forms. It also requires innovative planning tools, structures and systems-based processes for understanding impacts and making ethical choices for ecological and social sustainability. Diversity and equity have emerged as two increasingly important issues as globally mobile populations and technologies challenge traditional power structures and unsustainable business practices. This means re-orienting existing management practices around three key areas.

First, sustainable destination development requires closing the traditional marketing-planning gap using planning innovations (e.g. economic and environmental modelling, new collaborative forms), active debate and restructuring to integrate marketing and planning for sustainable tourism. The DMOs of the future will need to extend beyond the roles traditionally undertaken by tourist organizations and embrace a more holistic, integrated and communicative approach to destination management that is environmentally and socially equitable and embraces (celebrates) diversity.

Secondly, governance structures and processes are needed that enable informed participation in destination development. Rather than public 'input', communicative planning and joint decision-making is needed where residents are informed about the potential impacts of tourism development and can participate meaningfully in tourism decision-making. In the interdependent local-global tourism system of the twenty-first century, destination management must be re-envisioned from economic growth discourses towards building civil society and socially equitable forms of development that ensures the well-being of diverse human and ecological systems (see Figure 18.1).

Thirdly, enabling social equity in tourism development will be an increasingly important principle for socioeconomic sustainability as new values and ethnic voices arise through globalization. Conflicts related to the distribution of resources (including non-renewal resources) and the appropriation of cultural heritage for tourism can also be more effectively managed through sustainable planning and marketing, based on principles of social inclusion and equity.

Part Three: New Tools

19

Consumer Centric Tourism Marketing

Outi Niininen, Roger March and
Dimitrios Buhalis

Introduction

Consumer centric marketing (CCM) is a relatively
new trend in marketing that can be incorporated into
the customer relationship marketing (CRM) literature. While the ultimate aim of CCM is for companies
to gain insight into the general characteristics of their
individual clients, more specifically, CCM allows the
company to understand the motivations, habits, attitudes and values that shape consumers' opinions
about the brands the company is offering. Moreover,
the customers take an active role in the design of their
holidays by declaring their vacation preferences
and customizing their holiday packages accordingly.
Companies aim to establish regular communication
with their customers that will, hopefully, mature into
trust-based relationships (Maney et al., 2002; Lietz,
2003). As such, the concept of CCM alone is not new
in marketing; it is the combination of CCM philosophy and technological advancements that allows for a
more sophisticated data collection and manipulation
that whets the appetite of even seasoned marketing
managers.

Early stages of CCM

CCM builds on the techniques designed for customer relationship management (CRM). Furthermore, CCM derives from, and finds its natural home in, the packaged goods industry and much of the published work derives from this same sphere. Yet when the concept is extended into services, specifically tourism, it is apparent that CRM or the early stages of CCM have been practised in the travel sector for as long as people have used intermediaries to arrange their travel. In essence, CRM refers to the accumulation of knowledge about a consumer's needs and the utilization of that knowledge to deliver customer satisfaction. CCM takes this service even further by inviting the customers to become the 'architect' for their own vacations as well as being able to alter their vacation plans at short notice without great complication. Similar processes have been undertaken by counter staff in travel agents through time, yet changes to booked holidays were not always feasible. Arguably, therefore, CCM in the tourism context is the extension of the traditional travel agent role to the industry in general with greater flexibility and more opportunities for customization than in the past.

Loyalty programmes such as frequent-flyer programmes (FFPs) and hotel loyalty programmes are two examples of CRM in the tourism context. The frequent-flyer programmes, begun in the USA in the early 1980s, were loyalty-generation marketing initiatives conceived against a background of intensifying airline competition. FFPs gave airlines, for the first time, the means and the will to assess the value of the customers, classify them into segments and communicate through the medium of direct mail. The personalization of marketing communications to a relatively large customer segment had begun and the data collected detailed the guests' dietary and other personal needs, spending habits as well room type preferences and required business services. CCM is a more advanced marketing philosophy than CRM in the sense that CCM truly 'places the customer in the middle'. CCM also allows the organization to gather very detailed information on their customers and thus accumulate a very deep understanding of customers served. Yet the major advancement by CCM is that the customer is able to participate in the actual product design, thus achieving greater customization.

This chapter outlines the CCM process and its antecedents. The potential CCM for tourism businesses is then discussed with emphasis on future business opportunities made possible by the combined improvements in CCM and ICT.

Defining consumer centric marketing

In essence, CCM is a three-step process:

1. the collection and arrangement of information and data on individual customers
2. the utilization of that information to target more effectively those existing customers and
3. allowing the customer to customize and personalize the service to match their own needs and preferences.

Therefore, consumer centric marketing can be defined as 'the discipline of capturing and deploying consumer insights to enhance marketing effectiveness and better serve those consumers that are brand's best prospects' (Maney et al., 2002, p.3).

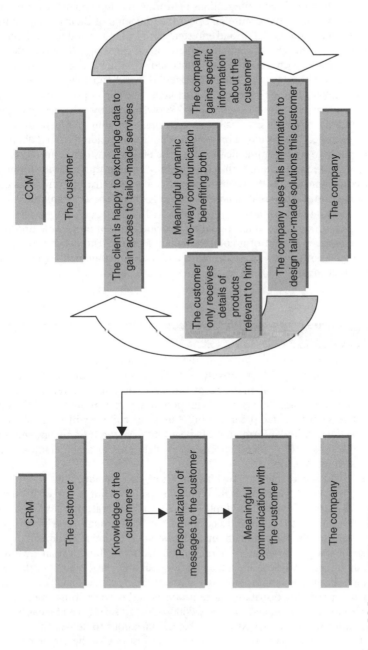

Figure 19.1 From CRM to CCM.

There are three prerequisites for successful CCM. First, the company needs to have a substantial amount of relevant information about the customers. Most companies do keep records/databases of some kind but fail to put this data into understandable information and actionable knowledge. Secondly, the company needs to offer their clients suitable communications platforms or selling points (e.g. Internet and call centres) where the client can select the elements of their travel product (transport, meals, accommodation and entertainment). Clients are able to customize their products. As with DELL computers where clients can design their own PC online by selecting alternative listed components and adjusting the price accordingly, many tourism organizations, e.g. Kuoni, Bridge the World and Tailor Made Travel, offer similar choices to their prospective customers and the opportunity to design their own vacations. Finally, the accumulated knowledge allows the design of personalized and meaningful messages to the customer regarding the features of the brand. To conclude, CCM is based on a cyclical notion of building from a database to meaningful (two-way) communication with the end-use customer. Furthermore, the dialogue created will reinforce the power of the database, thus allowing for more insightful communication with the customer and building his trust towards the company. Customer satisfaction is also increased through this process of communication and customization (Lietz, 2003).

However, tour operators cannot guarantee availability of perishable products in a similar manner to that of a computer manufacturer. The pricing for travel products is also influenced by seasonality and yield management operated by major travel businesses.

The emergence of CCM in tourism

Tourism is a unique product involving the sale of intangible dreams and fond memories. Customers spend a relatively large amount of their disposable income in this transaction where, at the time of purchase, they merely receive factual information of what their 'investment' can potentially mature into. Traditionally, these purchases have needed the use of brochures and contact with a travel agent, yet today all the required information can be found from the Internet and the consumer can compare the prices, suppliers, availabilities, product features and processes with relative ease.

In short, CCM is characterized by efficient knowledge management by efficiencies gained through 24/7 communication utilizing a single point of entry. This single interface will further reduce data duplication (e.g. for several Internet based services it is now a 'norm' to log on with a customer specific username) and increase the depth and value of the data held about each customer. Ultimately, tourism organizations can deal with a target segment of just one customer. Thus 'firms in the future will build their success on how much they know about their customers, how they will provide them [customers] with information about their products and services and how they will profitably distribute those products and services in an information based environment' (Olsen and Connolly, 2000, p.30). As service can be easily configured to individual needs, CCM will enable organizations to deliver this level of service. However, personalized travel products are just one of the segments available in the travel business and there will always be customers who wish to relieve themselves of the 'burden' of designing their own vacations and choose to purchase ready-made package trips, trusting the expertise of the professional who compiled this package.

Travel and tourism is one of the fastest growing sectors of the Internet (Buhalis, 2003). Already in 1996, 50 per cent of all Internet transactions were travel and tourism related. The expectation is that travel-related sales over the Internet in Europe alone will be €17.6 billion by 2006, while the on-line travel sales in the USA achieved $27 billion in 2002 (Marcussen, 2003). As Table 19.1 shows, a number of emerging tourism trends will further accelerate the use of ICT in tourism.

Relating CCM to traditional segmentation practice

Marketing has evolved from mass marketing to effective segmentation and targeting. This chapter advocates the 1-to-1 type of marketing by utilizing the latest ICT. Figure 19.2 demonstrates how CCM relates to mass/segmented marketing.

Mass marketing typically involves commodified products that hold little importance for the consumer (low involvement). The customer accepts marketing communications with no personalization and there is no need to cultivate relationships between the supplier and the end-user (e.g. sun-sand-sea packages). Targeted marketing is the classic segmentation approach where there is some understanding of the needs of the end-user and some degree of relationship may develop between customers and producers (e.g. pony trekking holidays targeted to riding club members). One-to-one type marketing is based on gaining real insight into the needs of the tourist with a high degree of personalization and allowing the client to customize his purchase by 'mixing and matching' different elements of the tourism product. A deep relationship between the tourist and the supplier of the holiday product may emerge (e.g. arranging a wedding in a foreign country). A 'cyber relationship' may also emerge between supplier and the traveller when the prospective client is allowed to customize very small details of their purchase over the Internet (e.g. Air India allows the clients to select from a menu of over twenty different types of meals).

However attractive may be the capability to identify a target segment of just one customer, it is not desirable to allow technology myopia to overshadow traditional marketing wisdom and challenge the requirement for long-term financial success for the company. It is therefore pertinent to revisit the segmentation concept. As a holiday purchase moves across the continuum towards the 1-to-1 type service model, the more important the traditional marketing wisdom and professional expertise related to the product on offer becomes. The whole target market can be divided into three key segments ranging from A to C:

- A-customers who are the perfect match to the product offering of the tourism company. These clients do not seem to have specialist demands on the service on offer as the product is already a match to their holiday requirements. The A-tourists make a definite positive contribution to the profits of the firm.
- The B-customers on the surface do not appear to be a good match to what the business is typically selling. There may be specialist requests and the impact

179

Table 19.1 Tourism trends influencing the adoption of CCM

Tourism trends	Industry response	Market implications
Brand and product proliferating	Low cost airlines Brand extensions in hotels and airlines Increasing competition among destinations, attractions and events	Consumers are bombarded by direct marketing communications Consumers become accustomed to SPAM Consumer awareness is harder to capture
Traditional media fragmenting	Digital radio and TV Interactive TV 3G mobile	Brand relationships are harder to establish and defend Database creation and knowledge management becoming easier
New media emerging	e-mail SPAM e-mail WAP WWW Increased transparency between substitute products	Permission-based communications increasing/ becoming a necessity Consumers appreciate personalized value adding services offering differentiated products Tourism products now follow their own fashion trends, the 'in place' to be
Consumers changing	Habitual buying of low importance products to 'free time' for more Leisure/holiday time increasingly important to consumers Instant gratification sought from holidays	Accelerating product life-cycles Customization and personalization encourage loyalty and customers feel more like 'being part of the brand'

	Greater experience in booking vacations independently Short break holidays Increasing demand for nature-based, cultural, spiritual and authentic experiences Greater fragmentation of segments by needs and benefits More savvy consumers	Consumers focus channel search to a …… Fairly predictable partners Consumers store details and preferences in 'My Product' type of on-line providers and expect them to filter out the 'information overload'
Increased channel power	Vertical integration across wholesaler and retailer/operator channels Tour operators can change the branding of a destination (e.g. identical BOGOFF (Buy One Get One For Free) to Spain and Greece campaigns)	Automated, on-line pricing is harder to achieve
Financial models	Yield management	Easier to compare the intangible and tangible elements of tourism product
ICT	ICT enables a more tangible presentation of the tourism product, e.g. 360° views of a destination Facilitates direct communication between customer and producers 'Me-too-ism' of consumers and tourism producers	Extended 'travel experience' when the tourist can belong to a virtual travel community before and after the trip as well as observe the destination on-line

Source: adapted from Maney et al., 2002, p.4

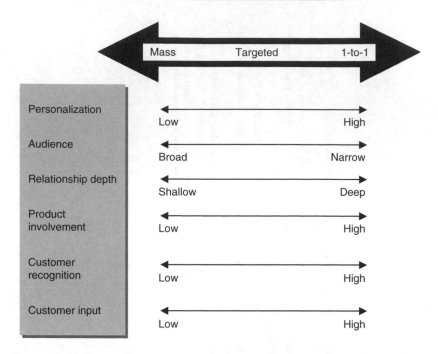

Figure 19.2 The marketing continuum. (Source: adapted from Maney et al., 2002, p.4)

on profits is questionable. However, these customers offer the firm a strategic advantage for the future.

■ Finally, the C-customers are beyond the target market of the organization and accepting bookings from these tourists will result in multiple specialist requests, complaints, dissatisfaction among other A/B-tourists at the tourism facility at the same time. The C-tourists will have a negative impact on the profits of the firm. Hence, implementation of these new applications needs to be exercised judiciously.

Information gathering strategies

Current use of the Internet is already educating the consumer how to exchange personal information in return for discounts, ease of service and customization. By signing-up for an account with e-retailers and logging-in to a personalized account consumers can store their details and preferences and organizations can track purchasing patterns to the degree of a 'segment of one'. Furthermore, incentives like discounts, air-miles and prizes can be used to entice the consumers to complete an on-line survey. For example, Eurostar allows registered customers to save regular services/purchases and retrieve them instantly on return log-in.

For consumers to gain from the CCM services, they must be signed up for such services, thus providing details of their preferred activities (or themes) during the trip, details of itinerary, contact details (mobile number and e-mail address), even details of accommodation and booked excursions to allow the company to match information offered to the required geographical location. The more sophisticated the data provided by the customers the more satisfaction the tourists can gain from their travel services. Hence it is in the consumer's best interest to provide accurate and detailed information about himself or herself and his or her product/experience/ travel preferences, thus creating the positive cycle of CCM. Increasingly, recommender services emerge that employ intelligent agents and artificial intelligence to 'cut through' unlimited information and reach personalized solutions (Ricci, 2004). Mobile phones are becoming an invaluable assistance and support for people on the move. The development of website services and a combination of 3G as well as location-based services will enable telecommunications networks and service providers to access customer profile, location as well as country and then send information of the relevant products and services.

Consumers will be happy to part with personal information only when this serves a clear objective of providing value adding services from specific organizations. If the organization misuses sensitive information or sells on to third parties it should be prepared to face the unhappy customers, negative word-of-mouth (WOM) and potential legal action. Most importantly, consumers will lose trust and will break the relationship with the organization. The Data Protection Act (in the UK) and other legislation also control the use of personal information.

Information utilization strategies

Tourism-related CCM applications feature services available to travellers before, during and after their trip. Much of today's CCM focuses on the before the trip services, e.g. Internet sites that track the availability of flights, accommodation and holiday packages according to the criteria set by users. CCM applications will follow the traveller while away from home and will include wireless technology applications and made-to-order products and services.

Wireless technology

Wireless technology is becoming more common, as third generation mobile services, WIFI and Bluetooth applications increasingly allow two-way-always-on connectivity regardless of location. The early adopters are already comfortable with wireless connectivity and soon the mass market will start to demand opportunities to connect to the Internet without being tied to a PC. There is a further trend of increasing use of hand-held devices that are becoming smaller and more affordable while mobile phones incorporating data-based applications are already regarded as a necessity rather than a luxury. Such data applications include logging expenditure; currency conversions; Location Based Services (LBS:GPS based tracking of location) and automated messages from local providers. Services controlled through Internet browsers are also becoming increasingly popular, thus emphasizing the importance of networking and sharing data about local attractions with global partners. Mobile applications will increasingly allow customers to check-in at airports and hotels, communicate boarding passes, vouchers and authentification information required for travel and immigration purposes. Furthermore, M-money can become the travel currency of the future. In this system consumers 'load up' currency to their mobile phones and then pay for services simply by dialling up the service provider's numbers.

Mobile application will enhance CCM as consumers will increasingly be able to communicate preferences electronically to service providers from where they are. For example, a customer carrying a Bluetooth enabled device will be automatically directed to a room of his preference when arriving in a CCM enabled hotel. Furthermore, this room will feature a customized welcome message including the customer's favourite picture, favourite music, room temperature is automatically adjusted to his preference and the customers preferred beverages will be available.

The made-to-order (MTO)

The made-to-order (MTO) concept appears to be at the centre of the customer centric philosophy and is already in some use in the tourism industry. Typically a holiday package comprises accommodation + transport + transfers, while meals + experience/entertainment are often included. Most of these sub-components of the vacation can be substituted by a competing supplier with no great complication. Internet providers such as expedia.co.uk and lastminute.com are already enabling this, while Kuoni allows for the customization of the holiday packages according to consumers' requests. These systems are gradually being adapted by learning from past experience and projecting the declared preferences.

By using intelligent agents (based on artificial intelligence and neural networks) travellers can 'educate' a software of their preferences. Initially the 'Shopbots' will seek services including specified attributes (e.g. adventurous holidays) and ignore other types of products. The programme monitors decisions made by the tourist and 'learns' from these transactions to be able to provide even more accurate matches to the search terms. This improves the suggestions offered to travellers while comparisons between users with similar profiles also educate the system about customer preferences, hence filtering away services that do not target individuals (Olsen and Connolly, 2000).

Electronic word-of-mouth

ICT is also allowing for positive and negative word-of-mouth (WOM) communication at an unprecedented scale across geographical borders. The Realholiday reports (http://www.realholidayreports.com/) displays feedback from ordinary tourists about the facilities in a destination. Internet search engines have also created unusual 'experts' of tourism products where a private web page or blog site may achieve the most hits for a destination. Moreover, the information-savvy tourists are well connected through virtual communities (e.g. www.virtualtourist.com) where members have the option to maintain their own travel web pages. These web pages can be visited and ranked by other users of this service, hence appealing to the competitive instinct of the tourist and providing an incentive to provide accurate and enjoyable reports on travel destinations and services. To conclude, such information-based services can also achieve the much coveted loyal clientele since 'the most successful competitors will collect and synthesize information about their customers' buying patterns and convert this knowledge to a highly personalized service' (Olsen and Connolly, 2000, p.31).

Case study 19.1 VirtualTourist.com

Virtual tourist.com, the award winning service, has over 400 000 members from 219 countries. Furthermore, the site claims to attract over 2 million visits each month. The members share insight into travel destinations, local customs and help each other to 'travel smarter' by stating the 'best places' for accommodation, car hire, airfares – in short – the most rewarding travel experiences. In total, visitors to the site can obtain unbiased travel reviews of over 19 000 destinations in over 220 countries or territories. The site has over 1 million travel photos, over 675 000 travel tips from the members, listings of over 2 million locations, travel resources etc. Furthermore, the Discussion Forum features over 1 million postings.

As a VirtualTourist you can:

1. Get inside info from fellow travellers about places you want to visit
2. Meet members from around the world and make friends
3. Build your own web pages and share your pictures and tips with friends and fellow travellers.

The services offered by VirtualTourist include over 875 000 travel tips in easily accessible format including:

- must see activities
- hotels and accommodation
- off the beaten track
- shopping
- restaurants
- nightlife
- travel photos searchable by keyword, destination or category
- deals on flights, car rental, hotels, etc.
- discounts from local businesses

For any company in the future, 'the ability to generate, store and analyse customer information is imperative. Competitive advantage will be based on intellect rather than assets and capital. While the latter two resources are necessary, they are no longer sufficient for competing successfully to attract the knowledge-based customer' (Olsen and Connolly, 2000, pp.39–40). Hence VirtualTourist.com has the opportunity to attract that difficult to attain customer loyalty since they have mastered the value-adding element of a travel purchase transaction (i.e. a match between the tourists' desires and experiences delivered in a situation where hype created by brochures is unlikely to bias tourists expectations of the travel service).

Caveats of CCM

Several caveats are worth mentioning. CCM is already happening. While we can label the concept an extension on an old theme, its increasing importance in a rapidly fragmenting marketplace makes it worthy of attention. Since ICT is putting CCM into the reach of everyone, competition is intensifying as technological means to access individual customers are becoming easier. This is a conundrum and a double-edged sword. Although the customers will be demanding the latest ICT solutions, the service industry may not be able to comply due to the initial investment required to achieve this, as well as the difficulty in calculating any rate of return for this investment (Olsen and Connolly, 2000, p.32). Business modelling becomes really complex as many partners need to be involved in order to deliver CCM. CCM is, at times, cost *in*efficient as customization has a higher per unit cost of production and this may affect the price of the product as well as its competitiveness. As with any new technology advance involving consumers' money, there will be initial resistance to sign-up for new services until the security of each transaction can be guaranteed. And finally, downloading speed, especially on mobiles, is still relatively slow, while data roaming is expensive, which limits the richness of data sent to the tourist while on vacation. The 'at destination' communication of today would involve mainly text, but once data roaming procedures and downloading times can be reduced more multimedia communications can be introduced and services such as 'virtual guides' and LBS will be introduced.

Conclusions: CCM as a marketing philosophy

Although ICT is not the panacea for all marketing ills, if properly used it can provide suitable solutions. Like marketing itself, CCM is a philosophy and approach that, if adopted and promoted throughout the firm, can enhance the value added offered by organizations. Understanding that the customer is actually in the driver's seat, surrounded by tools to identify suitable products and research transparent pricing, is an incredible challenge for the industry. Customizing products will require flexible production and marketing processes adaptable to consumer requirements. Hence, the need for and opportunities arising from individual consumer-focused marketing activities will prevail in tourism in the future.

20

Cross-Cultural Tourism Marketing

Po-Ju Chen and Abraham Pizam

Introduction

This chapter provides a review of culture and its effects on marketing in general and marketing of tourism, in particular. First, a definition of cross-cultural marketing is advanced and then the need for cross-cultural marketing strategies is explained. Second, the chapter examines the design and execution of culturally based marketing mix strategies. Third, the effect of culture on consumer behaviour in the hospitality and tourism industry is described and analysed. Lastly, the conclusion is reached that to be successful in international and cross-cultural markets, tourism and hospitality marketers have to devise marketing strategies that are geared to the needs and wants of the specific target markets, needs that are strongly affected by the consumers' national and/or ethnic culture.

Culture and cultural dimensions

Culture is an umbrella word that encompasses a whole set of implicit, widely shared beliefs, traditions, values and expectations that characterize a particular group of people. It identifies the uniqueness of the social unit, its values and beliefs (Leavitt and

Bahrami, 1988). Like nations, ethnic groups, organizations, industries and occupational groups have cultures too. Thus we can speak of the culture of African Americans, Hispanics, physicians, lawyers, engineers, etc. (Pizam, 1993).

The elements of culture such as language, tradition, family structure, society norms, gender role and time orientation impact on consumers' behaviour (Usunier, 2000; Hofstede, 2001). De Mooij (1998) argues that individuals' behaviour is influenced more by their culture than any other factors. Culture defines the character of a society and may change over periods of time (Peter and Olson, 1998; Hofstede, 2001). Thus culture change has significant implications on cross-cultural marketing and makes it imperative to adjust marketing strategies over time.

Alternative models are available to measure national cultural differences. Arguably, the most widely utilized dimensions of culture are the five presented by Hofstede (2001) and his colleagues from their instrument called the Values Survey Module (VSM). Briefly, they are:

- Individualism – the degree to which cultures encourage individual concerns as opposed to collectivist concerns
- Masculinity – the extent to which gender roles are clearly distinct, i.e. in masculine societies men are suppose to be assertive, tough and focused on material success, while in feminine societies social gender roles overlap
- Uncertainty avoidance – the extent to which the members of a culture feel threatened by uncertain or unknown situations
- Confucian dynamism – long- versus short-term orientation in life, and
- Power-distance – the extent to which the less powerful members of institutions and organizations within a society expect and accept that power is distributed unequally.

Cross-cultural marketing

Cross-cultural marketing can be applied to global as well as domestic-ethnic markets. Its application necessitates the use of knowledge and information for the purpose of customizing products/services and strategies according to national and ethnic cultural characteristics.

Cross-cultural marketing should not be thought synonymous with international marketing or globalization. International marketing may take one of two different approaches to market a product or service, standardization or adaptation. If the product or service is thought to be universally or globally applicable (i.e. culture free), the marketing manager will take the 'standardization' approach. Otherwise, the product or service must be modified for each market with considerations of the host country's cultural influences, thus, adaptation. McDonald's 100 per cent pure vegetarian dishes served in India are an example of such an adaptation approach. Cross-cultural marketing utilizes the product/service adaptation approach for cross-national borders markets, domestic-ethnic markets, or both.

Globalization has been linked to the view that the world is a single market of consumers with a single global culture. Thus, according to this school of thought the marketing mix can be standardized for the global market. Corporations such as Coca-Cola, McDonald's and IBM may have created a 'global culture of their own' (i.e. corporate culture of a global company), but this is not to imply that the world may soon become a single market with a homogeneous culture. Modernization does not automatically change, for example, collectivistic into individualistic values. The westernization in Japan is a good example of this. The Japanese have shown signs of westernizing – i.e. becoming individualistic – because young people in Japan are becoming more self-centred in their personal consumption behaviours, although their relationships to their families and employers are still traditional – i.e. collectivistic and hierarchical (De Mooij, 1998, p.287). World cultures may converge but they still retain their uniqueness.

International marketing implies marketing across the globe and cross-national borders. It does not intend to cover marketing efforts domestically within multicultural nations such as Britain and the USA. Multicultural marketing within the borders of a nation, the domestic-ethnic marketing, is aimed at various ethnic groups in the home country.

Ethnic minority groups have rapidly grown larger in size and gradually integrated into societies of their host countries. In the USA and other multi-ethnic countries many hospitality and tourism companies have tapped the exponentially increasing purchasing power of ethnic minorities. For example, Choice Hotels has 40 per cent of their hotels franchised to ethnic groups in the USA and Best Western has 28 per cent of their properties, worldwide, owned or franchised by Asian Americans. It is no secret that hotel properties that are owned, franchised, or managed by ethnic minorities are culturally acceptable to ethnic minority customers.

Cross-cultural differences between ethnic minority groups and the host nations' majorities affect marketing strategies (Lindridge and Dibb, 2003). Cross-cultural marketing research on ethnic minority groups has been growing during the last several decades. For example, Mulhern and Williams (1994) studied Hispanic and non-Hispanic consumer shopping behaviour.

Knowledge of cultural differences and similarities is important in the development of international and ethnic marketing strategies (De Mooij, 1998). In recent years, cross-cultural marketing has received attention from both business sectors and academia. Researchers have developed and applied cultural models (e.g. Hofstede, 2001) for cross-cultural consumer behaviour studies.

Cross-cultural consumer behaviour in hospitality and tourism

Until recently the role of national cultural characteristics in determining tourist behaviour had not been given much attention in hospitality and tourism research. However, the examination of cultural differences is especially relevant to tourism consumer behaviour. Several studies conducted by Pizam and colleagues from the UK (Pizam and Sussmann, 1995), Israel (Pizam and Reichel, 1996), Korea (Pizam and Jeong, 1996) and the Netherlands (Pizam et al., 1997), assessed the explanatory value of nationality in regard to tourist behaviour. These studies showed that nationality influences tourist behaviour and that there was a significant perceived difference between the tourist behaviours of the affected nationalities. Other researchers (e.g. Groetzbach, 1988) have also noted from their own structured observations, marked differences between the behaviour of Japanese, American, Western European and Arab tourists.

Culture not only influences destination choice, participation in tourist activities and other forms of tourist behaviour, but also determines expectations and perceptions of service quality that, in turn, determine satisfaction with services. For example, Mok and Armstrong (1998) found significant differences in expectations from hotel service quality among guests from the UK, USA, Australia, Japan and Taiwan. Tourists from these countries had different expectations for two of the service quality dimensions, namely 'tangibles' and 'empathy'. Tourists from different cultures might have different expectations of the physical facilities, equipment and appearance of the hospitality and tourism industry's personnel. Therefore, understanding the differences in cultural orientations would help to determine the type of services expected.

Crotts and Pizam (2002) found tentative evidence that national culture, as measured by Hofstede's framework, influences consumers' evaluation of services. More specifically the study discovered that respondents from medium power-distance/high-masculinity cultures (Japan and Italy) rated both airport and airline attributes more critically than those from small power-distance/low, medium and high masculinity cultures (UK, Germany, Australia, USA, Denmark, Netherlands, Norway, Sweden). Airlines and airports that serve visitors from countries with medium to large power-distance and high masculinity should expect more discerning passengers in terms of their service quality expectations when compared to visitors from smaller power-distance and low to high masculinity societies. Last, Choi and Chu (2000) investigated Asian and Western travellers' perceptions of service quality in Hong Kong hotels and found that Asian travellers' satisfaction was affected by the value factor, whereas Western travellers' satisfaction was influenced by the room quality factor.

Cross-cultural marketing and the hospitality and tourism industry

Marketing begins with the understanding of one's customers in terms of what, when, where, why, with what, and how they buy. But as will be further elucidated, these descriptors vary from culture to culture. To demonstrate that culture influences people's behaviour and, in turn, necessitates the design of culturally appropriate marketing strategies, Herbig (1998) uses the case of EuroDisney as an example of cultural misunderstandings in the process of designing a marketing strategy in the hospitality and tourism industry. Because the Disney Corporation negotiated the deal using a typical American rigid legal approach and insisted on duplicating its American management and marketing practices in the operation of the French park, the result was cultural friction and significant financial losses. Because of this and numerous other similar experiences, hospitality and tourism marketing professionals need to understand the importance of cross-cultural marketing for international and multi-cultural companies.

Cross-cultural marketing mix

In cross-cultural marketing the marketing mix consists of a set of tools or strategies designed to meet customers' expected values in a manner that is congruent with their culture. These strategies must match the customers' cultural preferences and expectations. For this to happen, the marketing mix designers have to understand not only the cultural characteristics of their intended customers but also the differences and similarities between the intended customers and the product/service provider. Because cultures are dynamic and change over time, the marketing mix should be periodically reviewed and modified to meet new challenges (e.g. the upward trend in Asians' focus on family values).

Product and service strategy

A product or a service is defined as 'a set of attributes which provide the purchaser/user with actual benefits' (Usunier, 2000, p.283). The products and services provided by the hospitality and tourism industry include lodging/resorts, food services, transport services, travel trade intermediaries, convention/events, etc. In a cross-cultural context, elements of product/service strategy include the decisions on product/service physical attributes such as the size, shape and colours of the guest room, the service attributes – i.e. a set of human resource qualities such as attention to the customer, courtesy, an atmosphere of hospitality, etc. – and the symbolic attributes such as branding and labelling.

There are three approaches used in the design of cross-cultural product/service strategies: global, national and combined. The global approach takes the stand that the world is a single market and, therefore, a standard products and marketing strategy on a global basis is more advantageous (e.g. Hilton International). The national approach focuses on designing products and the layout of marketing strategies according to specific nations (e.g. Sol Melia Hotels). The combined approach assumes that globalization is feasible for some of their products and other products are nation or culture-specific (e.g. McDonald's, Best Western International Hotels).

There are signs of a progressive convergence of globalization of some products. People's tastes worldwide on foods and electronic products, for example, are on the converging path. Music, DVDs, Chinese food, pizza, beefburgers, computers and travel bags are some examples of global products. However, corporations must comply with certain national regulations and local cultural considerations. Hence, product physical attributes adaptations remain subject to national regulations and cultural considerations in many situations. Usunier (2000) suggests that consumption patterns such as tastes, quantity and frequency of consumption affect the design of the product. McDonald's 100 per cent pure vegetarian dishes served in India demonstrate its adaptation to local consumers' tastes as well as the local cultural Hindu requirement of forbidding the consumption of beef. McDonald's 'curry' burger offered in the UK is another example of the need for adjusting to local cultural preferences. Products/services must adapt to local preferences and ways of using the product and must meet the national and local legal requirements. Further, the product/service design should also incorporate local traditional practice of usage. For example, hotels in Asian countries provide tea, rather than coffee, in guest rooms since tea is the local preferred beverage.

Service attributes specify what services and service quality levels are offered, but the tourists' expectations on the quality of these services vary by culture. For example, in relatively large power-distance countries such as China and India, hospitality customers come from higher status strata of the population and expect a high level of service from hospitality service employees who most likely come from people with a lower social status. This is in contrast to more egalitarian services provided by hospitality employees in the Western cultures where the difference between the employees and guest is often not noticeable (Mattila, 1999; Crotts and Pizam, 2002).

Symbolic attributes are powerful presentations of product/service brands. The use of native motifs is a good example for reinforcing the local flavour in global brand images. For example, Witkowski et al. (2003, p.77) report that 'a Starbuck's in Shanghai has a Ming Dynasty facade and the entrances of some Chinese KFC restaurants are guarded by full-size, fibreglass models of Colonel Sanders who, in his Asian reincarnation, looks a little portly like a Buddha'.

Branding strategy

A brand represents what the product/service is, what benefits it carries to the consumer and what differentiates the product/service from other products (Usunier, 2000). Branding has an important role in service companies. Brand enables consumers to visualize and understand the intangible aspects of the service including the quality of the people who provide the services.

Service branding is an effective technique in cross-cultural marketing. Hilton Hotels uses the service brand to guide their geographical and culturally different markets. For example, Hilton Hotel Corporation's service brand 'Equilibrium' (offered to guests to recharge their batteries and re-fulfil their lives) was aimed at catering to all types of customers. But its Japanese service brand 'Wa No Kutsurogi' was tailored specifically for serving Japanese tourists and business travellers. This special designed service brand emphasized distinctive service features appealing to Japanese travellers.

Pricing strategy

Consumers generally form their perceptions of products and services based on prices. Pricing products and services is a complex process. It is based on the uniqueness of product attributes and competing situations of similar products in the marketplace. Price is related to value also. The perceived value determines the price the consumer is willing to pay. Thus, pricing strategies are primarily aimed at conveying a message to consumers that they receive relevant values for the product and service.

There are several cross-cultural considerations when planning pricing strategies. Consumers' cultural norms and the host country political, social and legal environments affect pricing strategy (Maxwell, 2001). A cross-cultural product/service price strategy should not be just based on what the market can bear but also include other factors, such as GDP per capita, taxation levels, available discretionary income and the standard of living. Marketing professionals must be sensitive to the cultural norms and host country's environments. For example, state-controlled prices and consumers' attitudes toward quality and price relationships affect product and service pricing strategy.

Consumers from different cultures have different levels of 'trust' on imported products and services. In developing countries, where imported products are scarce, a low-priced product such as a budget hotel could be viewed as low quality. Consumers' attitudes toward price haggling vary from culture to culture. People in most Arab, Asian and Latin American countries are accustomed to price haggling while people in most European countries, the USA and Canada are not (Usunier, 2000). Thus, cross-cultural consumers' attitudes toward price negotiations are important factors in cross-cultural price strategies. Therefore, marketing professionals of hospitality and tourism companies need to understand the host country's attitudes and behaviour toward negotiations in order to conduct price-related negotiations.

Promotion strategy

Promotion strategy consists of a number of promotion mix components that marketing professionals can choose from. Cross-cultural considerations that need to be addressed in the design of the hospitality/tourism promotion mix include communications, advertising, personal selling and publicity and public relations.

Communications

The fundamental concept of marketing communications is to convey a message aimed at meeting consumers' interests, needs and values and to create consumers' trust in the products and services and the company. Unfortunately, marketing across cultures faces many communication barriers such as cultural barriers and source effects.

Cultural barriers exist because consumers' needs and values are formed from their cultures. Among all components of communications, language is the key component. It is also a major barrier. The spoken, written and symbolic languages are the vehicles for initiating interactions and cultural contacts. Using the language that the target consumers understand is vital in communications. Messages must use the language symbols (e.g. images) and styles that consumers in the host country can understand (De Mooij, 1998).

Another communication barrier is the 'source effect'. For example, the Coca-Cola Company's universal appeal, youth, sports and leisure theme in its branding message was designed to avoid consumers' 'source effect' (the idea of a strong association with American image) (Usunier, 2000). That is, the company downplayed its country of origin in their cross-cultural marketing strategy.

Advertising

Advertising is a form of non-personal communications that send messages about products, services and the company to potential consumers for their awareness of the product. The forms, styles and frequencies of advertising are important for effective cross-cultural advertising. For example, building trust and a relationship may be more important than product persuasion in certain cultural situations (De Mooij, 1998).

The trend in advertising has been toward an increased sensitivity to cultural diversity. Hospitality and tourism companies' cross-cultural marketing managers need to assess consumers' interests, needs, values and motivations according to cultural similarities and differences for developing an effective marketing adver-tising strategy. The advertising strategy should include the developing of a corporate platform with possibilities to incorporate meaningful host country extensions so that building a relationship and trust with consumers is possible (De Mooij, 1998, p.135). Some brands like Coca-Cola and Levi's jeans have very large market shares in Asia because consumers trust them implicitly.

Personal selling

Personal selling is an important marketing tool in the hospitality and tourism industry. The objective of personal selling is to locate the potential buyer, persuade the buyer to purchase the company's products or services and close the deal. Since people-to-people interactions are a major aspect of personal selling, it is of great importance to know and understand the buyers' cultural background and attitudes toward negotiation. (This is why local traders often ask travellers the question: 'Where are you from?') This means that personal selling processes will vary from culture to culture. The sales person needs to be aware, for example, that people in collectivistic and feminine cultures such as Latin Americans, are relationship builders and trust is the most important factor in negotiations. Therefore, the sales process in Latin America usually takes much longer than in most Western cultures (Darley and Luethge, 2003). Cultivating relationships and building trust are essential skills required for sales personnel to do personal selling in this type of cultural environment.

Publicity and public relations

Publicity involves non-paid communications to the public about the companies' products, services and matters associated with corporate reputation, identity and achievements. Public relations refers to all the activities that companies engage in to communicate with the public to maintain and improve their relationships and corporate images.

To gain positive publicity, hospitality and travel companies may engage in activ-ities such as press releases, event sponsorship, community involvement and good-will activities. Most hospitality and travel companies engage in sponsorships of goodwill activities in communities and host countries. McDonald's sponsors many sport teams as its public relations activity. The goodwill sporting sponsorships promote and enhance companies' favourable global images. Communicating effec-tively with international publics is important to corporate identity and reputation. The involvement with the host country community and government, especially with countries that have significant controls over foreign investments, is essential for building long-term relationships and enhancing corporate images.

Distribution strategy

Distribution systems, or channels serve as the intermediary between consumers and suppliers and are an essential part of the travel and hospitality marketing strategy. Many companies such as hotels or airlines use their central reservation systems to facilitate sales directly to customers. Customers may use toll-free telephone num-bers to make reservations or access the company's website through the Internet.

Cultural differences have many implications on Internet usage. Local culture considerations such as language should also be part of the distribution strategy. It is estimated that in the year 2004, out of a total of 730 million Internet users, only 35.8 per cent use English language websites. Therefore, many large Internet providers, such as Yahoo and Google, have localized their websites in various languages. Many hospitality companies also provide localized websites with several languages.

Conclusion and future perspectives

Culture has a significant effect on the tastes, preferences and behaviours of consumers of hospitality and tourism products and services. Therefore marketing managers have the responsibility of designing marketing strategies that are congruent with the values and norms of their target markets. Though in a minority of cases it would be possible to design a global marketing strategy that has the characteristic of 'one size fits all', for most hospitality/tourism products and services one would have to identify the cultural similarities and differences between their customers and then put in place as many strategies as the distinct cultural groups in their customer mix.

In conclusion, when marketing hospitality/tourism products cross-culturally it is necessary to adopt the 'riffle approach' which matches each individual marketing strategy with the values and norms of the target market. However, this approach can be successful only if the specific target market's needs and wants can be clearly identified. The unique cultural profile of each target market plays an essential role in the identification of the target market's needs and wants. Thus, if marketing managers can clearly identify the market segment's cultural profile, then they can tailor-make a marketing strategy that will meet the customers' specific needs and wants. One such technique is the Zaltman Metaphor Elicitation Technique (ZMET), which is designed to uncover the consumers' underlying feelings and thoughts that truly represent their unique needs and wants (Coulter et al., 2001). Therefore, understanding the targeted consumers' cultural profile and unique behaviour is essential in developing an effective cross-cultural marketing strategy. To this end marketing scholars are attempting to develop research techniques aimed at identifying and classifying consumer profiles.

21

Information Communication Technology – Revolutionizing Tourism

Dimitrios Buhalis and Peter O'Connor

Introduction

Information communication technologies (ICTs) have been transforming tourism globally. The ICT driven re-engineering has gradually generated a new paradigm-shift, altering the industry structure and developing a whole range of opportunities and threats. ICTs empower consumers to identify, customize and purchase tourism products and support the globalization of the industry by providing tools for developing, managing and distributing offerings worldwide. Increasingly ICTs play a critical role for the competitiveness of tourism organizations and destinations (Poon, 1993; Sheldon, 1997; Buhalis, 1998, 2003; O'Connor, 1999). ICTs are becoming a key determinant of organizational competitiveness and a wide range of technological developments propels this evolution. Successful ICT deployment requires innovative management constantly to review developments and adopt the suitable technological solutions in order to maximize organizational competitiveness.

Technological developments and ICT empowered change

Major hardware developments, including massive enhancements in processing capabilities, allow computers to handle complex algorithms with a constantly increasing speed of computation (Beekman, 2003). This allows organizations to centralize ICTs to units that control the entire organization and to outsource selected non-core functions to specialist businesses, which may simply host data or applications or handle the entire process. Scalable and 'on demand' technologies also allow organizations to switch computation power between applications, according to dynamic demand. The combination of enhancements in processing and flexibility of processing capability allows organizations to use their resources more wisely and profitably. Nanotechnologies facilitate the minimization of hardware and its mass production reduces production costs and improves the portability of devices. Nanoelectronics can provide the high-technology and low-cost manufacturing required and eventually will make systems become invisible and 'disappear' into the background. The development of mobile and portable devices, from laptops and tablet PCs to personal digital assistants (PDAs) and Smart Phones also offers significant computation power, storage and portability. Tablets are increasingly developing interfaces that simulate notebooks and palmtops and PDAs offer lightweight portable computing. As the distinction between PDAs and mobile phones becomes increasingly blurred, people will soon carry a device that incorporates both a mobile phone and a fairly powerful and permanently connected personal computer, enabling both voice and data communications.

Extensive networking is growing both within and between partner organizations (Amor, 2002). The proliferation of the Internet, intranets and extranets supports communications between employees, units, organizations, as well as with external partners and consumers. Intranets and enterprise resource planning (ERP) systems provide inter-organizational systems that support an integrated electronic infrastructure. Synergies and interoperability between processes, departments and functions enable enterprises to reduce labour costs, increase efficiency, enhance responsiveness and make better informed decisions. This empowers employees to improve their performance, increasing internal efficiency and effectiveness. Intra-organizational networking emerged through 'extranets' and enhances interactivity and interoperability between organizations and trusted partners. By linking and sharing data and processes electronically, organizations formulate alliances to build complementary services, expand reach and enhance collaboration. The Internet empowered the distribution of multimedia applications, such as textual data, graphics, pictures, video and sounds. Search engines such as Google and Yahoo provide unprecedented capability to find anything, including destination and product information. An electronic marketplace has gradually emerged and suppliers have developed Internet interfaces to communicate with clientele and partners to sell directly. New intermediaries also emerged to take advantage of the capabilities of the Internet and aggregate products through dynamic packaging.

The huge increase in digital information sent and received by households and businesses required an increase in bandwidth. Broadband provides fast 'always on' access to services, applications and content resulting in lifestyle and productivity benefits. Despite the initial massive investment required in new networks and infrastructure, as well as the development of new content, services and applications, broadband is expanding rapidly (EU, 2001). Broadband access is mostly charged based on flat access fees, resulting in both the expansion of time people spend online and e-commerce involvement. Wireless and mobile networks have also developed to allow access everywhere. The Global System for Mobile Communication (GSM) and the Wireless Application Protocol (WAP) allowed the communication of voice and data over mobile phones. General Packet Radio Service (GPRS) and Universal Mobile Telecommunications System (UMTS) as well as I-Mode in Japan introduce third generation (3G) mobile services, empowering multimedia communications on mobile devices. In addition, Wireless Local Area Networks (WLANs) allow connectivity of portable devices through wireless-radio connections (WiFi), while Bluetooth connects devices over short distances (Figure 21.1). Wireless LANs have limited area coverage while 3G networks enable continuous data transmission on the move. Increasingly devices are equipped with Bluetooth, WiFi and 3G capabilities and each technology will be used according to requirements, location and costs.

The development of digital television will effectively bring the Internet to the living room of most families. User friendly interfaces based on an advanced television set will be easily operated through a simplified keyboard and will enable the vast majority of the population to have direct access to organizations electronically. This will bring electronic commerce to the mass digital market.

Werthner and Klein (1999) have identified the most significant technological developments forcing a new wave of technological evolution (Figure 21.2). The underlying trend of all developments is the integration of hardware, software and intelligent applications through networking and advanced user interfaces. Technological convergence leads developments and only blurred boundaries between systems exist to illustrate dependencies and relationships. However, all technologies need improvements in order to enhance their speed, interoperability, reliability and adaptation to the industry and consumer needs. Fast and reliable networks need to emerge to support media-rich applications and on-line video presentations. Information management supported by object-oriented, relational

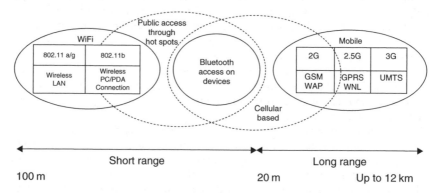

Figure 21.1 Wireless technologies convergence.

Network(ing)	Information management	Intelligent applications	User interface
ISO/OSI SGML	Databases relational, object-oriented	Artificial intelligence	What you see is what you get
Internet World Wide Web	Multimedia	Logics	Multimedia
Hypertext Markup Language	Data modelling	Optimization	Windowing
XML	Data mining and warehousing	Simulation	User modelling
Cryptography GSM, WAP	Unified modelling language	Statistics	Natural language processing
ATM ⟷ IPv6	Programming languages	Knowledge discovery and data mining	
System architectures	Java	Learning systems	Metaphors
Client–Server	CSCW (computer supported cooperative work)	Agents	Visualization
Distributed and mobile computing	Authoring tools Participatory design	Artificial life	Adaptive interfaces

Distributed architectures   *Object-orientation*   *Agents – Ontologies*   *Adaptive interfaces*

Integration
Metadata
Mediated architectures
Facilitators
Wrappers – legacy systems
Added services – e-payment and e-commerce

Figure 21.2 Lines of technological evolution.
(Source: adapted from Werthner and Klein, 1999).

databases are required to enable interlinking between all the information kept by organizations to generate synergies. Data modelling and knowledge management must enhance the use of operational data in the decision-making processes and enable better informed operational and strategic choices. Intelligent applications need to incorporate knowledge from all sections of an organization, use simulation techniques and the processing of statistics to improve the quality of information used for decision-making and enable organizations to adopt more proactive approaches to management and marketing problems. Knowledge discovery and data mining support management and marketing functions, while learning systems and agents increasingly accumulate and use knowledge productively to support employees and organizations.

User-friendly interfaces enable non-specialists to use computers without extensive training. Adaptive interfaces and the visualization of computing functions simplify processes and empower users to take advantage of systems and applications. Finally, integration of all applications and systems support interoperability on different platforms and through different media. Werthner and Klein (1999) define interoperability as 'the provision of a well defined and end-to-end service, in a consistent and predictable way. This covers not only technical features, but also for example in the case of electronic market environments, contractual features as well as a set of institutional rules'. Integration enables end-users to access a broad knowledge basis and empowers suppliers to appreciate the information as well as product and service needs of consumers and partners.

Perhaps the next major revolution will emerge in the form of ambient intelligence defined by ISTAG (2003) as 'a set of properties of an environment that we are

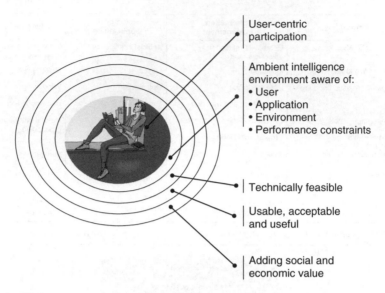

User-centric
participation

Ambient intelligence
environment aware of:
• User
• Application
• Environment
• Performance constraints

Technically feasible

Usable, acceptable
and useful

Adding social and
economic value

Figure 21.3 User-centred, participative, ambient intelligence.
Source: ISTAG, 2003.

in the process of creating'. This represents a new paradigm for how people can work and live together. According to the ISTAG vision statement, humans will, in an ambient intelligent environment, be surrounded by intelligent interfaces supported by computing and networking technology that is embedded in everyday objects, such as furniture, clothes, vehicles, roads and smart materials – even particles of decorative substances like paint. Humans will live in an ambient intelligence space in which there will be seamless interoperation between different environments – home, vehicle, public space, work, leisure space, tourism destination, etc. This implies a seamless environment of computing, advanced networking technology and specific interfaces which should be aware of the specific characteristics of human presence and personalities; adapt to the needs of users; be capable of responding intelligently to spoken or gestured indications of desire; and even result in systems that are capable of engaging in intelligent dialogue (Figure 21.3). Ambient intelligence facilitates participation by the individual – in society, in a multiplicity of social and business communities and in the administration and management of all aspects of their lives, from entertainment to governance. It should be unobtrusive and interaction should be relaxed and enjoyable rather than involve a steep learning curve. To be acceptable, ambient intelligence needs to be driven by humanistic concerns, not technologically determined ones and should be controllable by ordinary people.

Pursuit of the ambient intelligence vision will require contributions from many streams of research to realize both 'ambience' and 'intelligence'. The development of the ambient intelligence space will depend not simply on finding solutions to the research challenges for ambience and intelligence, but on the extent to which mechanisms can be found to ensure the successful, seamless, integration of components and their convergence into ambient intelligence systems. There are a number of research domains or components in which significant progress must be made in order to develop further and realize the ambient intelligence vision. Table 21.1

Table 21.1 Technology areas requiring further research for ambient intelligence

Components for ambiance	Components for intelligence
Smart materials that can emit light efficiently, e.g. electronic wallpaper or large synthetic foils that can emit light, materials that can be used for touch and tactile movement and synthetic materials that enable mass storage and processing of digital data and that can be integrated into fabrics	*Media management and handling* including presentation languages that support 'produce once' and 'present anywhere', methods and tools to analyse content and enrich it with metadata and tools to exploit the Semantic
MEMS and sensor technology, including ultra low-power (mechanical) effectuators, sensor devices bridging between the physical world and the cyber world, i.e. touch, vision, smell and technology for the integration of smart materials, micro systems and microelectronics into systems	*Natural interaction* that combines speech, vision, gesture and facial expression into a truly integrated multimodal interaction concept, allows human beings to interact with virtual through physical objects and that enables people to navigate the seemingly infinite information they will be able to acccss
Embedded systems development technology for re-configurable real-time embedded computing platforms, for remote diagnostics and repair of embedded systems and to build in security and trustworthiness to embedded systems	*Computational intelligence* including conversational search and dialogue systems, behavioural systems that can adapt to human behaviour and computational methods to support complex search and planning tasks
Ubiquitous communication including ubiquitous pico-radio networks for active and passive tagging, Internet accessibility for any physical object and ubiquitous broadband access to content and data	*Contextual awareness*, for instance systems support navigation in public environments, i.e. traffic, in airports and in hospitals, service discovery systems that enhance the shopping experience and context aware control and surveillance systems
Input/output device technology that supports ubiquitous hands-free speech control, ubiquitous touch pads and whiteboards and can turn any surface into a display	*Emotional computing* that models or embodies emotions in the computer and systems that respond to or recognize the moods of their users and systems that can express emotions
Adaptive software that is self-managing or has self-adjusting capabilities that can detect and adjust to the health or otherwise of its environment, re-allocating resources as required and automating much of the system configuration work that now has to be done manually	

Source: ISTAG, 2003.

indicates just some of the technologies for ambient intelligence that require significant research.

Eventually ambient intelligence will enable the formation of virtual enterprises, the fluid configuration of business processes and the seamless interoperation of underlying information systems. This will support organizations that are willing and able to accept organizational changes to participate in several networks simultaneously without the need radically to alter their company cultures and preferred methods of working. Whether people respond positively to the opportunities presented by ambient intelligence will depend heavily on the extent to which ambient intelligence complements rather than replaces existing methods of work and social discourse and the extent to which it requires fundamental changes to organizational structures. Therefore, ambient intelligence must be conceived holistically and, as it needs to be realized through highly complex systems, performing specific research, embodying results in particular technologies and products and then seeking to commercialize those products is an obsolete development process. The technical complexity of modern systems based on ICTs requires that all aspects of the innovation chain integrate their efforts and hence the engagement of both the research and business communities to integrate the rapid co-evolution of the technology, the market, and social and administrative requirements is critical for success (ISTAG, 2003).

Strategies for eTourism in the future

ICTs have profound implications for tourism and e-tourism reflects the digitization of all processes and value chains in the tourism, travel, hospitality and catering industries. Tactically, e-tourism enables organizations to manage their operations and undertake e-commerce. Strategically, e-tourism revolutionizes business processes, the entire value chain as well as strategic relationships with stakeholders. eTourism determines the competitiveness of organizations by taking advantage of intranets for reorganizing internal processes, extranets for developing transactions with trusted partners and the Internet for interacting with all stakeholders (Buhalis, 2003). ICT developments generate both opportunities and challenges for tourism organizations and the most significant emerging trends can be examined within the framework of change (Figure 21.4). Increasingly tourism organizations need to use ICTs to develop strategies that are customer centric, profitability driven and partnership enabled. This will assist them to focus on their customers, organizational needs and distribution strategies, respectively.

Consumer centric

ICTs should place users in the middle of their functionality and product delivery. Every tourist is different, carrying a unique blend of experiences, motivations and desires. The population in general is travelling more frequently, becoming more linguistically and technologically skilled and can function in multicultural and demanding environments overseas. The Internet empowers such 'new' tourists with more knowledge and encourages them to seek exceptional value for money and time. Experienced, sophisticated, demanding travellers require interaction with suppliers to satisfy their specific needs and wishes. Living a hectic life,

CONSUMER Customer centric
- Personalization – CRM
- Location/context/mood aware
- Proactive/anticipatory
- Reactive/adaptive to consumer needs
- System integrated
- Satisfaction driven

eTourism
TRENDS

COMPANY Profitability driven

Revenue
- Expansion of markets and operations
- Marketing and promotion
- Direct distribution
- Yield management/revenue management
- Extensive distribution strategy

Cost
- Internal integration
- Reduction of intermediation
- Intelligent procurement
- ASPs

DISTRIBUTION Partnership enabled
- Virtual organizations
- Interoperability
- Developing a value system

Figure 21.4 ICT enabled eTourism trends.

consumers have shorter periods of time to recharge batteries and to engage in their favourite activities. Leisure time is used more for 'edutainment' (the exploration of personal interests for both personal and professional development) and independently organized tourism facilitated by dynamic packaging, while rigidly packaged mass tours are in decline. The contemporary/connected consumer is far less willing to wait or put up with delays, to the point where patience is a disappearing virtue. Hence the key to success lies in the quick and accurate identification of consumer needs and in reaching potential clients with comprehensive, personalized and up-to-date products and services that satisfy those needs.

Tourism organizations need to develop technology-supported personalized services to address individual needs. They should collect customer information at each stage of service – before, during and after a visit – in order to understand better consumer behaviour choices, concerns and determinants. Personalized services driven by advanced customer relationship management systems should record customer preferences and requirements for present and future usage. Systems need to be location, context and mood aware in order to provide sensible advice. Proactive services may be offered based on the anticipated needs resulting from known/declared or previously experienced customer profiles. Reactive services should be designed to meet the needs of customers following incidents or external environment factors. To achieve customer centricity, organizations need to integrate their systems and develop mechanisms for both recording customer reaction to stimulus and also to develop tools to allow consumers to customize their desired products to personal preferences.

- User-friendly and customized interfaces (e.g. MyHilton)

- Consumers have more information and enjoy greater choice

- Accurate and richer marketing research by collecting data from all transactions and enquiries

- Better understanding of consumer needs based on research interaction and data mining

- Differentiated and customized services according to personal preferences and attitudes

- Pricing becomes more flexible and transparent

- Reduction of bureaucracy and paper-work frees employee time for better customer service

- Customizing the product and establishing 'one-to-one' marketing through loyalty schemes

- New personalized value-added services (e.g. personalized in-flight or in-room entertainment and information channels)

- Automation of repetitive operational tasks through ITs (e.g. in-room TV checkout)

- Personalized services (e.g. telephone operator acknowledges guest by name or waiter knows dietary preferences or requirements)

- Language barriers reduced through interfaces that market through automatic translations.

Figure 21.5 IT empowered developments enhancing customer satisfaction.

Customer satisfaction depends highly on the accuracy and comprehensiveness of tourism information and the ability of organizations to provide tools for customization. Consumers not only require value for money, but also value for time for the entire range of their dealings with organizations. ICTs enable travellers to access reliable and accurate information as well as to undertake reservations in a fraction of time, cost and inconvenience required by conventional methods. Transparency between product characteristics and pricing also empowers customers. ICTs can assist the customization of service quality and contribute to higher guest/traveller satisfaction. Consumers can personalize not only their choice of products but also the essence of the product itself by customizing the layout of hotel rooms, the channels available on the TV or the drawings on the wall. A wide range of developments empowers consumers, as indicated in Figure 21.5.

Powerful databases, supported by innovative decision support systems, should therefore drive organizations to personalize services and to match consumer needs with organizational capabilities and offerings. ICT-supported, consumer-centric, flexible service delivery is critical and the industry needs to become more flexible, efficient and quicker in responding to consumer requests as well as to offer ICTs tools and mechanisms for product customization.

Profitability driven

Tourism is a profit-driven industry and ICTs should contribute to profitability. This can be achieved through driving increases in revenue, reductions of production and operational cost and an increase in awareness and promotion. Emerging tools can support production increase, improvement of load factor/occupancy levels and enhance scheduling. Airlines, for example, use technology to forecast demand, schedule and monitor load factors before deciding on route capacity, frequency, hub and spoke operations. Other types of organizations can similarly manage capacity more efficiently as well as expand to new markets using similar ICT based tools. ICTs also facilitate direct distribution – a critical function for increasing revenue. By distributing directly organizations can save commission and fees and reinforce their brand throughout the process, engage in relationships with consumers, satisfy personalized needs and better understand consumer preference and price elasticity. Selling products directly also increases customer loyalty and reduces leakages to competing organizations.

Technology empowered yield/revenue management supports accurate demand estimates and decisions either to fluctuate capacity (in the case of transportation) and/or price to optimize revenue. Yield management is about coordinating 5Cs: calendar, clock, capacity, cost and customer. Strategically, levels of yield management are geared to matching service timing and pricing to customers' willingness to pay in relation to its timing and demand from other customers (Enz and Withiam, 2001). Historical demand patterns, competitor pricing, as well as events and occurrences affecting demand, can be scanned electronically to provide revenue-management critical information. Constant interactivity with consumers and partners supports flexible and competitive pricing. Monitoring sales allows marketers to adjust the product and price and/or to initiate promotional campaigns. ICTs can also alert organizations about excess capacity or demand. Multi-location organizations (e.g. tour operators or airlines) can then divert capacity to profitable segments or regions. On-line auctions and last-minute offers can provide additional revenue streams and new avenues for disposing of distressed capacity. Specialist organizations such as lastminute.com and QXL.com have developed their entire business model around this proposition and dispose of distressed inventory without spoiling suppliers' brands.

Tourism organizations can also use ICTs for building awareness and promotion through newsletters, pop-ups and search engine optimization strategies. Regardless of size they can build and maintain websites, either internally or through partners. ICTs enable tourism organizations to have a global presence and partnerships around the world in an efficient and cost effective manner enabling small firms to build their virtual size. Until recently global distribution systems (GDS) were the only widely spread electronic distribution channel, despite being limited to the distribution of scheduled airlines, city hotel chains and large car rental companies. The Internet enables all types of organizations to distribute products directly to consumers and to link with emerging intermediaries (such as lastminute.com, Expedia, eBookers and Hotels.com), expanding their value chain and promoting their products through a combination of systems and partners (Kärcher, 1997; Buhalis and Licata, 2001; O'Connor, 2003).

Despite expensive initial investments, ICTs can reduce administration and production costs by integrating internal data and processes. Operational and communication costs can be reduced by integrating operational systems, maximizing internal efficiencies, decreasing back-office labour costs, reducing number and length of personal communications and enabling consumers to have direct access to information. Disintermediation and reduction of commission and fees for intermediaries also reduce costs. Despite the cost of developing e-commerce platforms, many firms achieved savings by direct distribution. Many have passed a proportion of savings to consumers to maintain competitiveness. As more consumers are able to serve themselves, on-line distribution costs are declining. On the procurement side, organizations will increasingly purchase products from global electronic marketplaces. Systematizing the procurement function through electronic connections with regular suppliers can also reduce processing and administration costs. Finally, Application Service Providers (ASPs) allow organizations to 'rent' ICT applications developed and hosted by specialized professionals (Paraskevas and Buhalis, 2002). This enables them to share the development and maintenance cost of such software. Hence, ICTs should contribute to profitability through increase of revenue and reduction of costs.

Partnership enabled

Few other industries depend on partnerships as much as tourism. ICTs empower networking throughout the industry and also improve the interactivity between tourism production and distribution partners, supporting a closer cooperation towards the provision of seamless products (Figure 21.6).

The creation and delivery of tourism products is based on partnerships between a range of organizations, including transportation, accommodation, catering, entertainment and cultural heritage. Taking advantage of the characteristics of virtual organizations will force firms to adapt their product constantly to satisfy tourism demand; use information extensively; develop partnerships; and outsource a significant amount of functions in order to achieve economies of scope (Hale and Whitlam, 1997). Virtual organizations will allow tourism firms to develop extended products and services, produced independently and instantaneously, in response to customer demand. Informational networks can link up and bring together the core competence of independent firms breaking traditional organizational boundaries. Trusted partners can offer flexible and speedy value-added products and services, through accessing world-class competencies, exploiting fast-changing opportunities by sharing costs, skills and by accessing global markets. These corporations do not necessarily need to be located near the consumer, as ICT networks and tools empower corporations to develop a virtual proximity to consumers and their needs.

Networking allows the outsourcing of non-core functions to specialists, while value-added services products can be sourced from competent trusted partners. Distribution is the obvious function that benefits from virtual organizations. The globalization of the industry intensifies the information required for all tourism transactions and requires instant confirmation and purchasing abilities. As distribution has changed from facilitation of information exchange and reservations to a sophisticated mechanism for dynamic personalization of added-value services, virtual corporations enable tourism firms to expand their value chain and include endless products and services. Intermediaries have access to endless inventory while suppliers become intermediaries by augmenting their product by selling complementary products and services from partners. Organizations need therefore to appreciate the benefits of coopetition and codestiny, when organizations need to collaborate with players that they would normally regard as competitors.

Virtual corporations and globalization bring more market participants and complicate distribution channels further (Figure 21.6), increasing heterogeneity

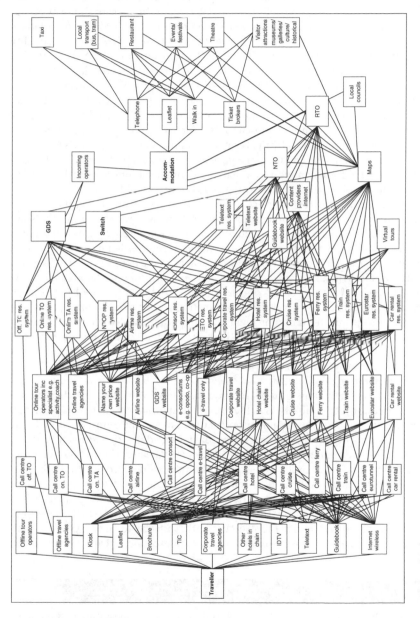

Figure 21.6 Consumer path to tourism provider and interconnectivity required in the tourism industry.

and requiring standardization and interconnectivity. The virtualization of the tourism value chain will depend on the degree of interconnectivity and interoperability between organizations to allow the flow of information and data in this complex value process. To ensure interoperability, data from a variety of independent sources have to be collated and delivered to final users and distribution systems in a consistent format. Hitherto a number of standardization initiatives (such as IFITT Reference Model Special Interest Group (RMSIG), Hospitality Industry Technology Integration Standards (HITIS), Open Travel Alliance (OTA) and the Travel Technology Initiative (TTI), the Hotel Electronic Distribution Network Association (HEDNA) and Hotel Technology – Next Generation) have developed standards to promote communication between different data structures and organizations. However, these programmes have faced adoption challenges in different countries and cultures. Moreover, standardization initiatives are in general being driven by the big players in the market and SMEs have little choice but to adopt the changes, irrespective of their suitability, or be left behind. There is a need for a common tool that allows organizations to recognize and to communicate with each other allowing wide interoperability.

The advent of new technical frameworks (XML, Semantic integration) raises new expectations on the integration process. Semantic reconciliation tools are being developed, such as a data mediator computer program that translates data between systems with different data exchange formats/schemas. This approach depends on a shared, conceptual reference schema – the ontology of the domain – and allows individual organizations to keep their proprietary data format while exchanging information based on the ontology. A mediation tool is based on three major technologies: XML, for information coding and exchange; ontology, for knowledge and content management; integration of *heterogeneous information sources*, for the reconciliation method. The mediator automatically generates data translations from descriptions of the data in the source and the receiver schemas, allowing users to keep their proprietary data formats while allowing interaction among their data.

ICTs increasingly transform distribution to a global value system, where access to information and ubiquity is achieved, while interactivity between principals and consumers provides major opportunities. Hence, the Internet propels the re-engineering of the entire process of producing and delivering tourism products, as well as boosting interactivity between partners that can design specialized products and promotion in order to maximize the value-added provided to individual consumers. Ultimately, ICT tools reinvent the packaging of tourism to a much more individual-focused activity, offering great opportunities for principals and intermediaries and enhancing the total quality of the final product (fitness to purpose). Equally, it is changing the structure of the industry to an ecosystem of individual but interrelated organisms and nodes, all interconnected and interoperable.

Conclusions – IT trends and implications for tourism

ICTs evolve constantly, providing new tools for tourism marketing and management. They support the interactivity between tourism enterprises and consumers and, as a result, they re-engineer the entire process of developing, managing and marketing tourism products and destinations. This chapter has identified a number of key changes in hardware, software and networking that will impact on the tourism industry in the future. Although the exact impacts are far from clear, the future of e-tourism will be focused on *consumer centric* technologies that will enable organizations to focus on their profitability through a network of partnerships. Consumers will be more sophisticated and experienced and therefore more difficult to please. The availability of powerful ICTs empowers both suppliers and destinations to enhance their efficiency and re-engineer their communication strategies. Increasingly ICTs will provide the 'info-structure' for the entire industry and will take over all mechanistic aspects of tourism transactions. Innovative tourism enterprises will have the ability to divert resources and expertise to servicing consumers and provide higher value-added transactions. Agile strategies are required at both strategic and tactical management levels to ensure that the ICT-raised opportunities and challenges are turned to the advantage of tourism organizations to enhance their innovation and competitiveness.

22

Tourism Marketing Information System: Decision Support for the Tourism Manager

Karl W Wöber

Introduction: information needs of tourism managers

Tourism marketing is becoming increasingly sophisticated as a result of greater importance attached to the reliability of information and competent analysis for the effective planning, monitoring and management of tourism enterprises (Bar-On, 1989; Buhalis, 2003). Decisions concerning investments in tourism developments, such as infrastructure for major new regions or individual resorts, transportation facilities, accommodation facilities including new hotels, self-catering apartments and camp sites, museums or theme parks as well as advertising investments made by destination marketing organizations (DMOs) are crucial because they are very cost intensive. In the planning phase, a careful consideration of potential customer benefits, technological expertise and the identification of a unique competitive positioning are necessary. To avoid investment failures the target market has to be clearly defined and its potential estimated and forecasted.

Many DMOs have special information needs, particularly if they are non-profit organizations with the responsibility of providing marketing guidance for the industry. These needs arise from the nature of the tourism product (intangibility, perishability, heterogeneity and multitude of components) and the complexity of the industry structure. However, to serve the business information needs of the industry, in addition to those of the consumers, managers working in DMOs require information and decision support in the fields of market intelligence, training and education and investment decisions.

The working style of tourism managers appears not very different from that of any other managers. Tourism managers work at an unrelenting pace and at a high level of intensity. Their activities are characterized by variety, fragmentation and brevity. Managers working at top management levels of destination marketing simply have not enough time to get deeply involved in the wide range of issues they are facing on a daily basis.

Tourism managers like to work on issues that are current and directly related to a specific, strategic goal of their company. They prefer uncertain information based on speculation, hearsay and gossip in brief over historical, certain and standardized information. The main reason why routine information receives less attention from tourism managers is probably because their expertise becomes less important for tasks where enough routine information is available. In order to fulfil their tasks they operate a network of contacts throughout their organization and environment and they exchange information with colleagues, competitors, partners, visitors, secretaries, government officials and so forth. Therefore, communication is the primary work of a tourism manager and he or she uses whatever tools are available to be an effective communicator.

However, communication and processing information become more and more difficult. Not only are the decisions tourism marketing managers facing more complex than a few years ago, but also the volume of data available to them makes it increasingly difficult to focus on the most relevant and useful data to analyse to an organization's best advantage. Finding and processing the correct data, therefore, is one of the principal problems of tourism managers during their daily work (Wöber, 2003). This problem has a number of dimensions:

1. The manager may not know what data sources are available; therefore he/she does not know where to search or even whether the data might exist
2. The manager may be faced with a variety of different data sources with deviating results
3. The manager may not know enough about the subject material to choose the correct source
4. The manager may require access to subsidiary information to interpret correctly the primary data he/she is processing.

While the information to help the managers may be available in publications of various sorts, at present little of this secondary information is available on-line with the data.

As the decisions become more difficult, marketing managers in general and tourism managers in particular, need assistance in making the most effective and efficient use of the available data to support marketing decisions (Little, 1979). Information technology has been helping marketers by developing databases, more advanced marketing information systems (MIS) that draw on the various internal and external data resources available to a company and by automating approved analytical methods and marketing theories by means of decision support systems (DSS).

From marketing information systems to marketing decision support systems

There are three broad types of information systems that support marketing managers at their work (Figure 22.1). In order of complexity and presentation, these types are (Wierenga and van Bruggen, 2000):

1. Marketing information systems (MkIS, MIS)
2. Marketing decision support systems (MDSS) and
3. Marketing group decision support systems (MGDSS).

Marketing information systems

According to the American Marketing Association (AMA), 'A Marketing Information System (MkIS, MIS) is a set of procedures and methods for the regular, planned collection, analysis and presentation of information for use in marketing decisions' (see www.marketingpower.com/live/mg-dictionary.php). Conceptually, it is a framework for the day-to-day management and structuring of information gathered regularly from sources both inside and outside an organization (Laudon and Laudon, 2003). An MIS provides a continuous flow of information about prices, advertising expenditures, sales, competition, and distribution expenses. Since the main focus of an MIS is on data processing and retrieval, it consists of a powerful database and an inquiry system that delivers regular reports of sales by product or market categories, data on inventory levels and records of sales people's activities.

Marketing information systems (MIS) came into vogue in the 1970s with the ability to place marketing data in a file or database and then to allow different users to gain access to the data in the same time frame. They opened a new door for marketing managers because they allowed them to access the information when they needed it in the form that they needed. However, the early systems did not live up to this promise because they had restricted capabilities due to the lack of computing skills by marketing managers and analysts. These systems tended to allow the managers to produce and print a limited number of standard reports. Managers would use a terminal to select the desired report type, enter several parameters that specified the brand, styles, flavours, time periods and regions. Sometime later, a screen full of numbers would appear on the manager's terminal. Such systems were the dominant ones in use by marketing managers in the mid-1980s.

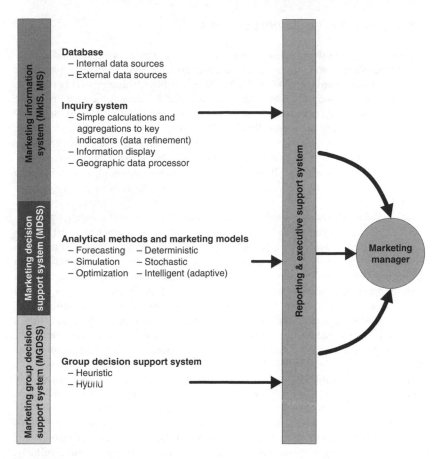

Figure 22.1 Types of marketing information systems.

The latter part of the 1980s saw an evolution in the power and ease of use of marketing information systems. Ease of use was dramatically improved from earlier systems via flexible pop-up menus and the iconic interface employed by operating systems and applications. These inventions allow marketing managers to start using the system after a short training period and provide a large degree of freedom in the types of reports that can be generated. By the early 1990s, many tourism organizations had acquired and made use of database solutions that allowed easy access to internal business data and research information acquired from market research companies and publicly available tourism statistics (Ritchie and Ritchie, 2002).

Data refinement procedures like simple calculations of key indicators are often the first type of computer support systems and the information they provide supports decision-making. Moreover, tremendous progress has recently been made in graphical displays of data, including geographic data mapping and three-dimensional, multicolour displays. These features are greatly enhancing the decision-making value that reporting and inquiry systems hold for tourism marketing managers.

Marketing decision support systems

When a marketing information system is enhanced by more sophisticated analytical features than simple data refinement procedures, then it becomes a marketing decision support system (MDSS). An MDSS is a set of 'problem-solving technology consisting of people, knowledge, software and hardware successfully wired into the management process' (Little, 1979) to facilitate improved decision-making by marketing managers. While MDSSs help marketers making decisions, they do not replace managerial judgement. Much of this utility comes from the ability to allow decision-makers to interact with models or other forms of analysis. This interaction provides the flexibility in data analysis that is necessary because of the ad hoc nature of marketing questions and the changeable nature of marketing environments.

Analytical methods and marketing models are the principal components of an MDSS. The latter is the logical representation of the marketing organization and its real-world marketing environment. Mathematical and/or statistical methods provide analytical tools which allow us to solve forecasting, optimization and simulation tasks usually found in marketing decision problems. Both analytical methods and marketing models allow marketers to experiment more quickly, and at less cost and risk, than is possible by experimenting in the real world. Sophisticated systems for optimizing the regular media budget allocation task of a national tourist office, for instance, have been developed to help diagnose potential growth markets and maximize the impact of advertising campaigns (Mazanec, 1986).

Mathematical, statistical, econometric and financial models which can be frequently found in MDSSs are time series models, brand switching models, linear programming models, elasticity models (price, incomes, demand, supply, etc.), regression and correlation models, analysis of variance models, sensitivity analysis and spreadsheet similar 'what if' models. Some of the models used are stochastic, i.e. those containing a probabilistic element, whereas others are deterministic models where chance plays no part. Brand or destination switching models, for instance, are usually stochastic since these express brand choices in probabilities. Models that support the selection of benchmarking partners based on linear programming tools are deterministic in that the relationships between variables are expressed in exact mathematical terms (Wöber, 2000). Moreover, some MDSSs that incorporate artificial intelligence and other advanced computer technologies can automatically adapt to changes in the marketing environment (Moutinho et al., 1996).

Marketing group decision support systems

Many marketing decisions are made not in isolation but, rather, in collaboration with several other members of an organization. To support collaboration, group decision support systems have recently begun to be used as a supplement to individual-oriented systems (DeSanctis and Gallupe, 1987), also in tourism (Calantone and di Benedetto, 1991; Wöber, 2001). A marketing group decision support system (MGDSS) is a computer-based system that assists with problem-solving activities involving multiple marketing managers. Most frequently, an MGDSS consists of software that supports electronic meetings and facilitates group interaction and data exchange, determines group preferences and generates and processes information from the individuals in the group. The dramatic success of the Internet and the World Wide Web has brought new opportunities for disseminating and exchanging information between groups of managers over long distances at considerably lower costs.

Management information systems in tourism

Given the importance of information and information management for tourism organizations, their need for successful marketing decision support system solutions seems to be obvious. In practice, however, the majority of tourism organizations do not yet use such systems and many have not even thought about installing one. Also literature on marketing decision support projects in tourism can rarely be found and usually refers to demand-oriented systems like destination management or consumer oriented travel counselling systems. Nevertheless, a few particularly innovative marketing information and decision support system applications have emerged in the following areas:

1. Statistical database systems for exchanging and disseminating market research information in tourism (Navarro and Rubio, 2000; Wöber, 2003)
2. Systems supporting marketing decisions in national tourism organizations (Mazanec, 1986; Rita, 1993; Wöber, 1998)
3. Travel counselling systems for travel agents (Hruschka and Mazanec, 1990)
4. Systems supporting regional planning regarding the optimal selection of locations for investment projects (Calantone and di Benedetto, 1991; Walker et al., 1999)
5. Simulation tools for forecasting travel behaviour in certain regions (Middelkoop, 2001).

Case study 22.1 TourMIS – A Freely Accessible Tourism Marketing Information System

In 1996, the Austrian National Tourist Office (ANTO) initiated the development of a web-based Tourism Marketing Information System – TourMIS (www.tourmis.info, see Figure 22.2).

In 1998, the two most significant international tourism organization networks, European Cities Tourism (www.europeancitiestourism.com) and the European Travel Commission (www.etc-corporate.org), joined the project and since then have been using TourMIS as a platform for exchanging tourism statistics (Wöber, 2003). Today, TourMIS provides market research information for more than 5000 tourism managers, researchers and students from all over the world and plays an important role in exchanging experiences among the participating users. Since its official Internet launch in 1999, the number of international enquiries and users has grown steadily up to 70 000 enquiries in 2003. The growing proportion of tourism professionals registered in TourMIS is

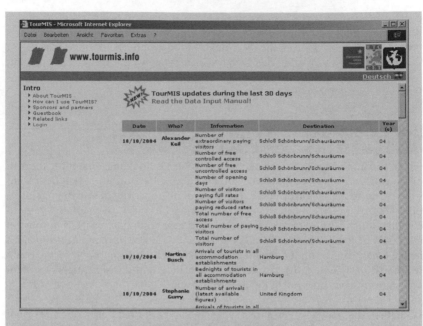

Figure 22.2 The TourMIS homepage (www.tourmis.info).

indicating that the system is increasingly being used by tourism managers in Austria and elsewhere.

Tourism managers use TourMIS to generate 'reports' that contain rows and columns of numbers. It includes dozens of information displays which can be produced by selecting the display type from a menu and then using other menus to specify the destination, type of accommodation, scope of information, market, periods and measures. Representative reports are general performance newsletters, guest mix, market share and fair share summaries, benchmarking tables, trend indicators based on time series analysis, capacity utilization reports, seasonal variation reports, etc. The manager thus has an opportunity to examine many aspects of a DMO in varying levels of detail.

Table 22.1 shows a typical report that the marketing manager of the Berlin Tourist Board might produce using TourMIS. Having produced this report, the manager can: do an analysis; learn from unexpected developments; attach meaning to the information; gain insights from this information. The following would be such an analysis: 'I see that although we experienced an increase on bednights generated by visitors from Portugal (+6.4 per cent), we actually have lost market share since our competitors (56 other European cities) have performed even better (+8.1 per cent)'. The manager has generated new insights from the information in the report.

What does the manager then do with these insights? They either remain with the manager, they are communicated to others, or they are used for operational decisions within their company. The tourism manager of Berlin, for instance, may use TourMIS to investigate further the competitive cities which have been

Table 22.1 Example for a TourMIS report generated on www.tourmis.info

City tourism statistics compiled by European Cities Tourism Destination: Berlin
Information: Bednights of tourists in all accommodation establishments Period:
2002

Cities	Berlin			Other cities	
	absolute	+/−	% p.y.	% p.y. (1)	Number (2)
Austria	97095	−9745	−9.1	−1.3	61
Belgium	70089	3992	6.0	4.4	61
Czech Republic	21393	1416	7.1	4.6	53
Denmark	173330	8857	5.4	−1.4	60
Finland	35015	1475	4.4	0.9	58
France	151244	8962	6.3	6.2	64
Germany	7795373	−520049	−6.3	−1.3	64
Greece	35412	6912	24.3	11.6	56
Hungary	17164	1052	6.5	0.6	54
Ireland Republic of	12685	−3611	−22.2	14.8	55
Italy	245527	5106	2.1	2.2	64
Luxembourg	11901	−1074	−8.3	−3.9	55
Netherlands	237740	15962	7.2	5.8	63
Norway	61355	15251	33.1	4.3	58
Poland	54757	3243	6.3	−1.9	57
Portugal	24393	1477	6.4	8.1	56
Russia (GUS)	64178	7752	13.7	5.4	54
Spain	156972	18236	13.1	11.5	61
Sweden	136578	−7375	−5.1	−4.1	60
Switzerland	178189	1982	1.1	4.8	63
United Kingdom	335504	19952	6.3	2.5	61
Europe	9915894	−420227	−4.1	1.3	64
Canada	54670	8155	17.5	− 3.7	61
United States	393743	7104	1.8	−7.1	64
America	448413	15259	3.5	− 3.3	64
Japan	109275	−5107	−4.5	−1.6	63
Asia	109275	−5107	−4.5	23.0	64
Australia	53955	8636	19.1	1.1	47
Oceania	53955	8636	19.1	7.5	55
Total foreign	3220191	190318	6.3	0.4	63
Total domestic	7795373	−520049	−6.3	−0.4	63
Total foreign and domestic	11015564	−329731	−2.9	−0.7	68

(1) = Mean change rate (median) compared to previous year.
(2) = Number of cities TourMIS could calculate a change rate.
Table: ECT-J7

particularly successful in the Portuguese market and may observe or interview
the respective marketing managers in order to gain knowledge about their marketing strategy in this market segment. Then he or she may decide to use a new
promotional strategy in order better to process this market and, finally, prepare
a presentation in order to propose this new concept to the management board

of the organization. Thus we can view the manager's job as both generating insights from information, sharing these insights via communications, using it for business decision-making and for persuading other people to follow these decisions.

Emerging trends and future developments

The major reason for the poor application of management science models and methodologies in tourism management is the insufficient education of practitioners and the inadequacy of problem-solving features of standard software solutions. Marketing information systems and marketing decision support systems provide a set of techniques which supports managers in accomplishing their marketing planning tasks and stimulates its users to learn more about the data, methodologies and models available in the system.

TourMIS is an example of a successful implementation of a marketing information system in tourism which is freely accessible on the Internet. The advantage of the TourMIS approach is that it represents an adaptive process which creates a learning environment for all participating tourism managers in Europe. Aside from the direct advantages of having a comprehensive and complete data set of tourism development for urban marketing analysis and planning, the high involvement of tourism marketers in the harmonization and rectification procedure and the regular reporting of market volume and market share analysis stimulates critical discussions and behavioural learning among all participants. Thus, TourMIS does not substitute current initiatives to establish a common system of tourism statistics, but rather supports them through direct involvement of all people working in the tourism field.

Technological progress will offer further benefits for the electronic transmission of market data. Interdisciplinary research projects will be challenged with tourism, statistics and commercial information technology. For example, there are still a number of problems to be solved in order to use jointly ecoscopic and demoscopic tourism data within a marketing information system. These combination options require a constant standardization of information sources as well as new approaches towards the methodological processing of data gained from various studies.

The development of information systems through research on knowledge presentation methodologies and service quality in information services will support the utilization and acceptance of decision support systems. Advanced user tracking techniques will support systematic analysis and understanding of managerial information needs. Technological improvements and a better understanding of managerial information needs will support the development of more powerful decision support systems and make these systems essential for tourism destination marketers.

23

Forecasting Tourism Demand Using Econometric Models

Gang Li, Haiyan Song and
Stephen F Witt

Introduction: forecasting is important for decision-making

Demand is the foundation on which all business decisions ultimately rest. Practitioners are interested in forecasting for numerous reasons. First, tourism suppliers are interested in the demand for their products. Their success depends largely on demand and management failure is often due to an overestimation or underestimation of demand. Estimates of expected future demand are critical in all planning activities and accurate forecasts are essential for efficient planning. Secondly, at the macro level, forecasting is important for investments in destination infrastructure, such as airports, highways and rail-links, which require long-term financial commitments from public finances. The prediction of long-term demand for tourism-related infrastructures often forms an important part of project appraisals. Thirdly, governmental macroeconomic policies depend largely on the relative importance of individual sectors within the economy. Hence, accurate forecasts of the demand situation in the tourism sector of the economy will help governments in formulating and implementing appropriate medium- and long-term tourism and regional development strategies.

Tourism forecasting methods fall into two major categories: quantitative and qualitative approaches. Empirical studies on qualitative tourism forecasting have centred on Delphi surveys and scenarios (see, for example, Müller, 1998). Within the quantitative framework, in addition to econometric models, time series and artificial neural network models have also been applied to tourism forecasting studies (see, for example, Turner and Witt, 2001 and Law, 2000, respectively). Since the majority of tourism demand forecasting papers involve econometric studies, this chapter focuses on modern econometric models and their applications to tourism demand analysis and forecasting. A number of econometric models are used to explain the relationship between tourism demand and the influencing factors, including income, price and substitute prices, and to generate future forecasts.

Econometric models

Econometric models accommodate scores of different specifications. This chapter, however, only presents those modern econometric models that have previously been used in tourism demand analysis and evaluates their abilities to generate accurate forecasts. The specifications of these models are described below and a full account of these approaches can be found in Song and Witt (2000). The models used are complementary in nature and often econometricians choose the best performing model for a particular situation based on accuracy of past performance.

Autoregressive distributed lag (ADL) model

In the single-equation modelling approach, the ADL model is the most general form that encompasses many of the existing model specifications. Therefore, a general ADL model is used as a starting point for determining a specific form. According to the general-to-specific modelling approach (Hendry, 1995), a general ADL model should include as many variables as possible suggested by economic theory. It takes the form:

$$Q_t = \alpha + \sum_{j=1}^{k}\sum_{i=0}^{p} \beta_{ji} x_{jt-i} + \sum_{i=1}^{p} \Phi_i Q_{t-i} + \varepsilon_t \tag{1}$$

where Q is the quantity of tourism demanded, the xs are explanatory variables, p is the lag length, k is the number of explanatory variables, α, β and Φ are parameters that need to be estimated and ε is an error term that is assumed to be normally distributed with zero mean and constant variance. With respect to the explanatory variables, income levels of the potential tourists, tourism prices in the destination (own price) and in the competing countries (substitute prices), travel costs and marketing expenditure are considered most frequently in tourism studies.

With different restrictions on the parameters in Equation (1), the general ADL model can be transformed into various specific forms (Hendry, 1995; Song and Witt, 2000), reflecting different dynamic features involved in the demand. The final model for forecasting from among these specific models is determined by both theoretical and statistical criteria.

Cointegration (CI) and error correction models (ECMs)

Policy makers and planners are often interested in the long-run equilibrium relationship between economic variables, while marketers are mainly concerned with the short-run disequilibrium behaviour of markets and consumers. The cointegration technique is used to examine the long-run equilibrium relationship. By transforming the cointegration regression into an ECM, both the long-run equilibrium relationship and short-run dynamics are traced.

Given the general ADL model in Equation (1), an ECM can be written in the following form:

$$\Delta Q_t = (current\ and\ lagged\ \Delta x_{jt}s,\ lagged\ \Delta Q_t s)$$

$$- (1 - \Phi_1)(Q_{t-1} - \sum_{j=1}^{k} \gamma_j x_{j,t-1}) + \varepsilon_t \tag{2}$$

where $\Delta Q_t = Q_t - Q_{t-1}$ and $\Delta x_{jt} = x_{jt} - x_{jt-1}$.

Three types of cointegration-ECM analysis are examined in this chapter and they are the Wickens-Breusch one-stage approach (WB-ECM) (Wickens and Breusch, 1988), the ADL two-step approach (ADL-ECM) (Pesaran and Shin, 1995) and the Johansen (1988) maximum likelihood approach (JO-ECM). Unlike the WB and ADL approaches, the Johansen method can detect more than one cointegration relationship if more than two explanatory variables exist in the cointegration regression. The ADL approach involves estimating both the long-run cointegration relationship and the short-run ECM based on an ADL model with the optimal lag structure. However, this approach tends to suffer from small-sample bias. The WB method estimates both long-run and short-run parameters in a single step. When the sample size is relatively small, the WB approach is more appropriate.

Time varying parameter (TVP) model

Forecasting failure and the apparent coefficient changes exhibited in a tourism demand model may well be a reflection of underlying structural change in the data-generating process. Even if the justification for the structural change is not strong, a safer way forward would be to use the TVP approach to deal with the possible structural instability. Unlike fixed-parameter regression models, the TVP model allows the coefficients of the explanatory variables to change over time.

The TVP model can be specified in state space form:

$$Q_t = \alpha + \sum_{j=1}^{k} \beta_{jt} x_{jt} + \varepsilon_t \tag{3}$$

$$\beta_{jt} = \delta_{j0} + \sum_{l=1}^{m} \delta_{jl}\beta_{jt-l} + \omega_{jt} \qquad (j = 1,2,\ldots,k) \qquad (4)$$

Equation (3) is called the observation equation and Equation (4) the state equation. The most commonly used specification for the state equation is the random walk process:

$$\beta_{jt} = \beta_{jt-1} + \omega_{jt} \qquad (5)$$

Applications of the TVP model to tourism demand analysis are still rare. The exceptions include Riddington (1999), Song and Witt (2000), Song et al. (2003a) and Song and Wong (2003). All of these studies find that the TVP model performs well especially in short-term forecasting.

Vector autoregressive (VAR) model

Instead of assuming that the explanatory variables in the single equation model are exogenous, the VAR model treats all of the variables as endogenous variables. This avoids the possibility of obtaining biased and inconsistent estimates when some of the explanatory variables on the right-hand side of the single equation model are endogenous. The VAR specification starts with a vector of unrestricted autoregressive models involving as many variables as possible suggested by economic theory and with the longest possible lag length permitted by the degrees of freedom. Then following some statistical criteria, the optimal lag structure will be decided.

A general VAR model can be written as:

$$Y_t = \Pi_0 + \sum_{i=0}^{p} \Pi_i Y_{t-i} \qquad (6)$$

where Y_t is the vector of endogenous variables and Π_0 and Π_i are parameters to be estimated. Although this approach has attracted much attention in macroeconomic modelling, little research has been done in the tourism context. Exceptions include Song and Witt (2000) and Song et al. (2003a).

Table 23.1 summarizes the applicability of the above models under different conditions.

Elasticity analysis

One of the advantages of using econometric forecasting models is the ability to analyse demand elasticities, which are of great importance for policy makers and planners. The income elasticity (ε_{ix}) shows to what extent a percentage change in income results in a change in tourism demand, with prices held constant. The own-price elasticity (ε_{ij}) measures how a percentage change in the price of tourism (p_i) affects the quantity demanded of tourism (Q_i) with other factors held constant. The own-price elasticity is generally expected to be negative. The cross-price

Table 23.1 Summary of model selection criteria

Model	When to use
ADL model	1. When the dynamics of tourism demand are of interest 2. When the specific model structure is to be determined
Engle-Granger ECM	1. When the sample size is large 2. When there are a maximum of two explanatory variables in the cointegration regression or if more than two only one cointegration relationship is identified 3. When it is necessary to examine both the long-run equilibrium relationship and short-run dynamics of the tourism demand model 4. When both policy evaluation and forecasting are of interest
Wickens-Breusch ECM	1. When the sample size is small (less than 40 annual or 80 quarterly observations for each of the variables in the model) 2–4. Same as above
Johansen ECM	1. Ideally, the sample size should be a minimum of 40 annual or 80 quarterly observations for each of the variables in the model 2. When there are more than two explanatory variables in the model 3–4. Same as above
VAR model	1. When the distinction between endogenous and exogenous variables is not clear 2. When the effects of policy 'shocks' on forecasting are of interest
TVP model	1. When the structure of the model is unstable 2. When the effects of policy changes on demand elasticities are of interest 3. When short-term forecasts are of interest

Source: adapted from Song and Witt (2000, p.158).

elasticity measures the impact on tourism demand of a percentage change in price of a different holiday and a positive sign suggests that the holidays are substitutes, whereas a negative sign indicates that the holidays are complements. The magnitudes of demand elasticities can provide useful information for pricing and promotion strategies in destinations. In a log-linear model where both dependent and independent variables are transformed into logarithms, demand elasticities can be obtained directly from the estimated coefficients of the independent variables.

Evaluation of forecasting performance

Where alternative econometric models are considered, evaluation of their *ex post* forecasting performance contributes to the selection of the best models for *ex ante* forecasting. The actual tourism demand is compared with the forecast values from the estimated models over the same period (i.e. *ex post* forecasting). A recursive forecasting procedure is followed to obtain one-period-ahead, two-periods-ahead, three-periods-ahead forecasts and so on. The forecasting performance is then evaluated according to the length of the forecasting horizon. The error measures used for forecast comparison are usually the mean absolute percentage error (MAPE) and the root mean squared percentage error (RMSPE) (for a detailed explanation, see Witt and Witt, 1992).

Once the best econometric model is selected, it can be employed to forecast the future trends of tourism demand (i.e. *ex ante* forecasting) and the corresponding growth rates of demand can be further calculated. Before the forecasts of the dependent variable are generated, the explanatory variables need to be forecast using appropriate time-series techniques, or based on particular scenarios analysis. Sometimes forecasts of important economic variables are available from official sources.

Case study 23.1 Forecasting Thai Inbound Tourism Demand

Introduction

Thailand was one of the first countries that promoted tourism wholeheartedly and became the third largest tourism receiving country in the East Asia and Pacific region in 1999. Tourism has become a key source of Thailand's foreign exchange earnings. This empirical research is conducted by the authors, aiming to examine the performance of econometric models in forecasting inbound tourism demand in Thailand from seven major source markets: Australia, Japan, Korea, Malaysia, Singapore, the UK and the USA.

Econometric models

International tourism demand in Thailand can be described by the following log-linear function:

$$LTOU_{jt} = f(LGDP_{jt}, LRRCP_{jt}, LRSUB_{jt}, DUM74, DUM79) \quad (j = 1, 2, ..., 7) \quad (7)$$

where the letter L in front of the variable names in Equation (7) stands for logarithm, TOU_{jt} is tourist arrivals from origin country j, GDP_{jt} is the income in origin country, measured by gross domestic product (GDP); $RRCP_{jt}$ is the tourism price level in Thailand relative to that of the origin country j and is calculated by dividing the consumer price index (CPI) in Thailand by the CPI in the origin country j and then adjusting by the relevant exchange rate; $RSUB_{jt}$ represents the relative substitute price level of tourism in competing destinations and is measured by a weighted price index of the main alternative destinations for Thailand (Malaysia, Indonesia, Philippines and Singapore) divided by the price in the origin country; and $DUM74$ and $DUM79$ are dummy variables capturing the effects of the two oil crises in 1974 and 1979.

Table 23.2 Estimates of reduced ADL models

	Australia	Japan	Korea	Malaysia	Singapore	UK	USA
Constant	−0.194	4.993	1.581	−0.366	0.165	−15.007	1.855
	(1.563)	(1.352)	(1.872)	(1.307)	(0.340)	(2.870)	(0.745)
LTOU(−1)	0.589	0.594	0.710	0.499	0.795	0.332	0.593
	(0.120)	(0.062)	(0.094)	(0.111)	(0.078)	(0.122)	(0.092)
LGDP	1.446				0.438		0.223
	(0.502)				(0.179)		(0.117)
LGDP(−1)			0.592	0.607		3.489	
			(0.206)	(0.190)		(0.631)	
LRRCP		−0.709		−1.242		−0.312	
		(0.314)		(0.543)		(0.155)	
LRRCP(−1)	−1.472	−0.925					
	(0.543)	(0.205)					
LRSUB		0.772	−0.926	2.446	0.460		
		(0.320)	(0.243)	(0.656)	(0.211)		
LRSUB(−1)	1.686			−1.370		0.452	−1.234
	(0.553)			(0.565)		(0.170)	(0.298)
DUM74		−0.258					0.188
		(0.088)					(0.101)
DUM79		−0.202	−0.314				−0.157
		(0.086)	(0.133)				(0.087)

Note: values in parentheses are standard errors.

Estimates of econometric models

Following the general-to-specific methodology, the general ADL model for each origin country is reduced to a specific one, in which all the coefficients of the remaining variables are statistically significant (Table 23.2). The results show that the lagged dependent variable, LTOU(−1), measuring the demand in the previous year, is the most important determinant of tourism demand in Thailand. It suggests that habit persistence and word-of-mouth recommendation play an important role in the determination of international tourism demand in Thailand. The substitute price variable also features in all models, the income variable is found to be significant in all models except the Japanese model and the own price variable appears in four out of seven final models. In terms of the one-off events, the second oil crisis had an adverse impact on the demand for Thai tourism by residents of Japan, Korea and the USA. The first oil crisis dummy also features in the Japan and USA models.

Elasticity analysis

The derived long-run income elasticities show that the demand for Thai tourism by residents from Australia, Korea, Malaysia, Singapore and the UK is highly income elastic (elasticity > 1). With regard to the own-price elasticities, the estimates of the average values suggest that the demand for Thai tourism by Australian, Japanese and Malaysian travellers is highly sensitive to price changes in Thailand

Table 23.3 Forecasting accuracy over different forecasting horizons

	Measure	VAR	No change	ARIMA	Static	Reduced ADL	WB-ECM	JO-ECM	ADL-ECM	TVP
1 year ahead	MAPE	0.919 (3)	0.973 (6)	0.971 (5)	1.947 (9)	1.023 (7)	0.928 (4)	0.857 (1)	1.113 (8)	0.903 (2)
	RMSPE	1.551 (4)	1.494 (3)	1.798 (7)	2.303 (9)	1.558 (5)	1.465 (2)	1.560 (6)	1.865 (8)	1.136 (1)
2 years ahead	MAPE	1.711 (6)	1.707 (5)	1.813 (7)	2.003 (9)	1.680 (4)	1.634 (3)	1.594 (2)	1.925 (8)	1.193 (1)
	RMSPE	2.550 (6)	2.310 (2)	3.304 (9)	2.384 (5)	2.353 (4)	2.335 (3)	2.556 (7)	2.872 (8)	1.519 (1)
3 years ahead	MAPE	2.356 (8)	2.287 (6)	2.024 (2)	2.024 (3)	2.185 (4)	2.185 (5)	2.314 (7)	2.409 (9)	1.250 (1)
	RMSPE	3.378 (7)	2.675 (3)	2.924 (5)	2.287 (2)	2.904 (4)	2.946 (6)	3.440 (9)	3.421 (8)	1.523 (1)
4 years ahead	MAPE	2.889 (9)	2.358 (6)	1.999 (2)	2.249 (5)	2.127 (3)	2.183 (4)	2.426 (7)	2.485 (8)	1.290 (1)
	RMSPE	3.525 (9)	2.327 (2)	2.582 (5)	2.576 (4)	2.447 (3)	2.597 (6)	3.237 (8)	2.972 (7)	1.730 (1)
5 years ahead	MAPE	3.040 (9)	2.591 (7)	2.451 (5)	2.462 (6)	2.134 (2)	2.207 (3)	2.803 (8)	2.446 (4)	1.246 (1)
	RMSPE	3.585 (9)	3.051 (7)	2.938 (6)	2.871 (4)	2.396 (2)	2.596 (3)	3.382 (8)	2.918 (5)	1.546 (1)
Overall	MAPE	2.183 (9)	1.983 (5)	1.852 (4)	2.137 (8)	1.830 (3)	1.827 (2)	1.999 (6)	2.075 (7)	1.176 (1)
	RMSPE	3.030 (9)	2.487 (5)	2.750 (6)	2.483 (4)	2.373 (2)	2.440 (3)	2.923 (8)	2.867 (7)	1.487 (1)

Note: values in parentheses are rankings. MAPE denotes mean absolute percentage error and RMSPE denotes root mean squared percentage error.

(elasticity > 1). The cross-price elasticities indicate that the alternative destinations are complementary to Thailand in the Korea and USA models, while the substitute effect is in force in the other models. It seems that tourists from Korea and the USA prefer to travel to a number of destinations on the same trip to Thailand, while tourists from other origins tend to substitute Thailand with alternative destinations.

Comparison of forecasting performance

One- to five-years-ahead forecasting performance of the seven econometric models (VAR, TVP, reduced ADL, static and three error correction models) during 1996–2000 is examined. Two univariate time series models (ARIMA and no-change models) are also included in the evaluation as benchmarks (Table 23.3). The results show that for one-year-ahead forecasts the Johansen ECM (JO-ECM) and TVP models are the most accurate forecasting models according to both MAPE and RMSPE. For longer-term forecasting horizons, the TVP model always outperforms the other models. The performance of the JO-ECM and VAR declines while that of the reduced ADL model increases with increases in the length of the forecasting horizon. As for the other models, there is no clear-cut trend and the performance fluctuates over time. When the overall forecasting performance is considered, the TVP model generates the most accurate forecasts. The poor forecasting performance of the VAR model in the cases of Japan and Korea reduces its overall ranking among the competing models. These results suggest that the TVP model is a preferred specification in forecasting the demand for Thai tourism.

Case study 23.2 Forecasting Hong Kong Tourist Inflows

Hong Kong has a unique culture that combines western life style with Chinese traditions. International tourist arrivals in Hong Kong increased from 0.93 million in 1975 to 13.06 million in 2000, representing an average annual growth rate of around 9.2 per cent. Tourism has become the second largest foreign currency earner since 1995 and the income generated from tourism has contributed around 6 per cent to Hong Kong's GDP over the last decade.

In a study conducted by Song et al. (2003b), the determinants of international tourism demand in Hong Kong were identified and the future trends of tourism demand over the period 2001–2008 by 16 major origin countries/regions are forecast. Following the general-to-specific modelling approach, the reduced ADL models were established and estimated. The empirical results show that the most important factors that determine the demand for Hong Kong tourism are the costs of tourism in Hong Kong, the income level in the origin countries/regions, the costs of tourism in the competing destinations and the 'word of mouth' effect (or the behavioural persistence of tourists). The policy implication of this is that Hong Kong should maintain its price competitiveness against its competitors and the suppliers of tourism products/services should improve their service quality and upgrade their brand images.

The forecasts show that the number of tourists from India will grow the fastest while China is predicted to be the largest source market for Hong Kong tourism over the forecasting period. The top 5 source markets for Hong Kong tourism in 2008 are predicted to be China (7.99 million), Taiwan (3.86 million), Japan (2.37 million), the USA (1.77 million) and the UK (0.97 million), respectively. The total tourist arrivals in Hong Kong are likely to reach 23 million in 2008, which will be 10 million more tourists visiting Hong Kong compared with the number in 2000.

Future trends

The continuing growth of global tourism demand stimulates studies of tourism forecasting. The increasing uncertainty calls for more accurate forecasts of tourism demand, especially in the short term. Broader applications and further developments of these advanced forecasting techniques are likely to benefit tourism forecasting research and practice. For example, the TVP model has shown its superiority over other econometric models in most cases. Its combination with other advanced time-series forecasting techniques, such as the structural time series model (STSM), is likely to generate more accurate forecasts for seasonal demand. The almost ideal demand system (AIDS) model has strong theoretical underpinnings and is useful for analysing the competitiveness between neighbouring destinations. By forecasting the variation in market share among the competing destinations in attracting tourist expenditure from a particular source market, the AIDS model can provide important information for policy making in these destinations. Li (2004) shows that the incorporation of the TVP technique into the AIDS model results in substantial improvements in forecasting accuracy. This study will inspire more research in examining the forecasting performance of the TVP AIDS in the tourism context. Moreover, since qualitative surveys could gather inputs from key industries in the forecasting process, an integrative forecasting method that combines both quantitative and qualitative approaches should be given more attention in future tourism forecasting practice.

Conclusions

This chapter presents some commonly used econometric models in tourism demand modelling and forecasting. The chapter demonstrates that econometric forecasting techniques can be useful for managers to predict demand levels and to adopt suitable managerial actions. Their applications are illustrated in two cases studies of international tourism demand. In particular, the TVP model shows its outstanding forecasting performance. Further improvements of econometric techniques are expected in order to facilitate more accurate forecasts and provide reliable recommendations for tourism policy making.

24

Managing Economic Impacts, Tourism Satellite Accounts and Observatories

Antonio Massieu

Introduction

The tourism industry is increasingly demanding governments for more recognition of the economic contribution of tourism. By and large, the justification for this demand is the large volume of activity of those companies that satisfy visitor demand (whether resident or non-resident, tourists or same-day visitors). A large portion of the production of the accommodation, restaurant, passenger transport, vehicle rental and other industries is geared towards meeting the demand of such segments (WTO, 2001).

This demand on the part of the corresponding business lobbies initially takes the form of requesting a proper estimation of the contribution of this production to the Gross Domestic Product as a basic indicator for identifying the importance of the tourism industry in the overall economic activity. Subsequently, such requests to National Tourism Administrations (NTAs) for more information can be geared towards other uses, for example, estimates of incomes government attribute to tourism, the measurement of specific types of tourism industries (as the organization, promotion or management of events such as conventions, conferences and meetings, business and trade shows), the development of financial-economic indicators for loans requests from tourism companies, etc. (Smale and Candance, 2001).

NTAs also aim to highlight, within the government context, the fact that tourism is an economic factor of primary importance for the development of the overall economic activity of the country. This alignment of interests explains the fact that the type of data on tourism required both by the public and the private sector has changed in nature. Besides quantitative information on the flow of visitors, such as arrivals and overnights and descriptive information on the conditions in which visitors are received and served, countries now need robust information and indicators to enhance the credibility of the measurements concerning the economic importance of tourism (Statistics Canada, 1998; Hunn and Mangan, 2002; Manente, 2003; Wilton, 2004; Deery et al., 2005).

The interest over the past few years in the Tourism Satellite Account (TSA) is explained by this alignment of interests and by the approval by the UN Statistical Commission in 2000 of a conceptual framework supported by the UN, OECD, Eurostat and the World Tourism Organization (WTO/OMT) itself. Although there are antecedents of the TSA in France (late 1970s) and in Canada (late 1980s), it was not until the beginning of the twenty-first century that this new statistical instrument made its debut.

In these few years, the WTO/OMT has been able to mobilize NTAs (the main users of the TSA) to assume a leadership role in this project. They had to create a stable inter-institutional mechanism of cooperation with other governmental organizations (such as National Statistical Offices (NSO) and Central Banks (CB)), jointly with tourism industry representatives.

Generally, in most countries, the NSO is in charge of preparing the National Accounts (of which TSAs are satellite accounts) and it normally shares responsibility for tourism statistics with the NTA. In some countries, however, the CB, besides being responsible for preparing the balance of payments (a key source of information on tourism expenditure associated with inbound and outbound tourism), also takes responsibility for drawing up the national accounts.

It is not always obvious to whom, i.e. which national institution, the task of launching the TSA should fall. This will largely depend on the institutional and administrative set-up of the country in question and on the technical-administrative development of its National Tourism Administration and other institutions.

Some of the previously mentioned stakeholder interests are set out as follows:

■ National Tourism Administration: should be able to meet many of the long-standing demands of the sector for information on the performance of inbound visitor expenditure in terms of main source markets, destinations and tourism products consumed.
■ National Statistical Office: satellite accounts (tourism, education, health, etc.) represent a valuable tool when it comes to coordinating statistics linked with a vast amount of dispersed data relative to horizontal and cross-cutting activities. The NSO itself can turn this type of exercise to good account, with a view both

to enhancing its estimates of some of the national account headings and to strengthening coordination in the field of the general system of statistics.

■ Central Bank: should develop an alternative source of information other than bank records, which are used in practically all countries, for estimating the 'travel' item of the balance of payments.

■ Tourism industry businesses: demands for specific information that attest to the importance of tourism and that can serve to improve the design of business strategies for operating in national and international markets.

Cooperation between all stakeholders can take different forms, normally a commission or a committee. In countries where tourism is especially important and those where there is a strong geographical concentration of tourism in certain regions, national tourism observatories (with strong regional representation) play an important role. The pioneering example is that of France. Other countries such as Portugal and Morocco have also followed this model.

Tourism analysis

Economic impact analysis is usually referred to as those techniques which attempt to measure the effects on a regional or local economy of a given change in economic activity. These techniques (traditionally associated with multiplier and input-output analysis) try to describe the final sum of effects of the economic transactions generated by that change (Fletcher, 1989; Hughes, 1994; Andersson, 1998). The multiplier in its simplest form describes the final economic effects, without considering what particular industry benefits from the direct effects or from the final effects. On the other hand, input-output analysis is based on a detailed analysis of the propensity to consume by each particular sector of the economy (Archer and Fletcher, 1990; Wanhill, 1994).

Although these methodologies have also been applied to tourism, only a small number of such exercises have been carried out and only in a few countries. Furthermore, they have been of limited application for the purpose of designing specific tourism policies on the part of NTAs. They have also experienced difficulties in terms of the acceptance of their results due to the low level of development of systems of tourism statistics in many of the countries.

The truth is that between this type of exercise and the traditional way in which NTAs evaluate tourism activity (mainly based on physical indicators – arrivals and overnights data, plus the *travel* item of the balance of payments as an approximation of expenditure associated with inbound and outbound tourism) there is a vacuum in terms of conceptualization and from the analytical perspective. One of the main contributions of the TSA is that it makes it possible to bridge this gap in a scientific way.

TSA has a very important statistical function by serving as a coordinating framework for tourism and general economic statistics (UN, 2001; CRT, 2003; Jones, 2003). First, the conceptual framework ensures the consistency of the definitions and classification used in both types of statistics. Secondly, the accounting framework ensures the numerical consistency of data drawn from different sources, such as general or tourist ad hoc surveys and other administrative sources. Moreover,

TSAs support the measurement of so-called 'aggregates' or macroeconomic indicators that are politically important, because they are measures of the quantitative importance of tourism in a country. These indicators include tourism value-added, tourism GDP, tourism employment, etc.

The descriptive power of the results obtained should not be dismissed, since they could offer new policy-relevant insights into the nature and role of tourism in the region of reference and into its contribution to the region's overall economic activity. The enormous amount of elementary data (or micro-data) used to prepare them allows other types of analysis.

TSA adoption and limitations

Another important contribution of the TSA is the possibility of achieving the international comparability of tourism activity measurements from a macroeconomic perspective. This cannot be done by comparing the results obtained from different modelling exercises. For example, the use of input-output tables (which exist in a number of countries) for estimating tourism aggregates cannot hide the fact that there are substantial differences in this type of instrument relative to the definitions used, the level of disaggregation of economic activities, tourism variables estimation methods, their degree of integration in the country's system of national accounts, etc. Table 24.1 shows the approximate state of development of the TSA in the different countries of the world.

The TSA can also be viewed as a synthesis of national systems of tourism statistics. Therefore, interest in developing the TSA is driving the expansion and improvement of the available statistical sources. An initial step is obtaining credible figures for non-resident visitor arrivals and a set of basic surveys. On the demand side, surveys are what makes it possible to estimate the expenditure associated with the different forms of tourism (inbound, domestic and outbound). On the supply side, surveys of establishments in tourism characteristic industries are needed.

Table 24.1 Advanced countries in adopting the TSA

Argentina	Ecuador	Malta	Senegal
Australia	Egypt	Martinique	Singapore
Austria	Finland	Mexico	Spain
Barbados	France	Morocco	Sweden
Belize	Ghana	Namibia	Switzerland
Brazil	India	New Zealand	Thailand
Canada	Indonesia	Norway	Trinidad/Tobago
Chile	Hong Kong, China	Panama	United States
Colombia	Israel	Peru	Zambia
Costa Rica	Jamaica	Philippines	
Cuba	Korea, Republic of	Saint Lucia	
Dominican Republic	Malaysia	Saudi Arabia	

Note: The list of countries corresponds to those that can be included in one of the following categories: countries with an established Tourism Satellite Account; countries expecting that the implementation of their TSA will be highly developed during the period 2004/2005; countries that have recently developed relevant macroeconomic studies on the economic importance of tourism.

Limitations are evident even in many of the approximately forty countries mentioned, such as the lack of adequate sources, the partial covering of the different
groups of visitors associated with each form of tourism, difficulties in adapting data
at disaggregated levels to tourism industries and products classification lists, etc.
This situation mirrors the global context in which efforts still need to be made to
establish a more solid foundation on which to build a sufficient and credible set of
indicators for the purpose of international comparability. Table 24.2 summarizes

Table 24.2 Availability of basic indicators of tourism activity 1999–2001 (numbers by countries)

Basic indicator (20)	Total number of countries[a]	EU		OECD
	207	15 MS[d]	10 CC[e]	30 MS[d]
Inbound tourism				
Arrivals				
Visitors	111	6	10	17
Tourists (overnight visitors)	184	14	10	26
Same-day visitors	91[b]	7	6	14
Arrivals by country of origin	193[c]	14	10	29
Arrivals by mode of transport	150	9	10	21
Arrivals by purpose of visit				
Leisure, recreation and holidays	134	7	6	15
Business and professional	128	7	6	15
Other purpose	123	7	5	15
Overnight stays and length of stay				
Overnight stays in H&S	116	14	10	24
Overnight stays in CE	73	14	10	25
ALS of non-resident tourists	103	8	9	17
Tourism expenditure in country of reference	176	15	10	30
Domestic tourism				
Overnight stay in H&S	85	14	9	26
Overnight stay in CE	51	14	9	25
Outbound tourism				
Departures	100	12	10	26
Tourism expenditure in other countries	148	15	10	30
Tourism activities				
Hotels and similar establishments				
Number of rooms	167	13	9	28
Number of bed places	139	12	10	22
Occupancy rate	149	14	10	29
Average length of stay (residents and non-residents)	101	7	10	18

Notes:

[a] Only eight having the whole set of basic indicators.

[b] For 25 countries, referring to cruise passengers.

[c] For 88 countries, arrivals by country of nationality; for 96, by country of residence; and for 9, both by country of nationality and by country of residence.

[d] Member States.

[e] Candidate countries.

the availability to a number of countries of the basic set of indicators that support at present the international comparability of tourism activity.

In the same way that an inter-institutional cooperation project is needed at the national level to advance the development of the tourism statistics system as a necessary condition for undertaking the TSA project, at the international level it is also necessary for the proper international organizations to cooperate in order to promote the comparability of these types of indicators. In fact, several International Organizations (IIOO) are promoting initiatives for having more credible and comparable tourism statistics (the perspective of GATS negotiations is a central argument).

In this process of expanding the number of information sources as a necessary condition for developing the TSA, the confrontation between estimates from the demand and the supply side is unavoidable. It is not only an accounting exercise that may question the credibility of some data sources, but also the incorporation of a statistical culture that is almost missing in tourism statistics.

TSA future developments

In the future, the TSA will also be regarded as a powerful database, which will support and range other types of analysis. One of them could be the measurement of non-desirable economic effects of tourism. For instance, cost-benefit analysis will pay special attention to the pressure on land and natural resources brought about by tourism development. The consideration of the existence of so-called 'negative externalities' is in opposition to the approach of those who equate tourism expenditures with the benefits provided by tourism. Cost-benefit analysis will try to measure these negative externalities in order to 'deduct' them from the purely monetary benefits of tourism activity.

The extension of the present conceptual framework, focused on a national perspective, an annual timeframe and an economic approach. In the future, this should include other realities: first priorities could be the adaptation to a regional level, the development of short-term indicators to update the basic TSA aggregates and the design of a tourism balance of payments. In a regional framework, different perspectives are also possible. For instance, the perspective of sustainable tourism development should work towards the formulation of a new paradigm for tourism with an integral vision on sustainability, aiming to reach the greatest socioeconomic efficiency in a given territory. Special attention should be given to expanding the current statistical base as a necessary condition for the successive TSA exercises. This will enable TSA to have greater coverage of the groups studied, greater precision in the disaggregation of tourism industries, new analytical possibilities, etc., and should strengthen the economic analysis of tourism.

The increasing use of data from administrative records will be a support for extremely useful statistical information, because it is impossible for the development of the system of tourism statistics (STS) and the TSA to be based exclusively on surveys. The WTO has included the use of administrative records produced by some traffic regulating authorities in designing its general guidelines for the measurement of visitor expenditures associated with inbound tourism as well as the improvements of arrival figures at national borders. These guidelines focused basically on international arrivals by air and by road and analysed the best way of integrating statistical surveys with such administrative records.

One important outcome developed from the model border survey has been the design of guidelines for the creation of a statistical universe that can be used for obtaining random samples for different surveys associated with inbound tourism and for upgrading the sample data. This would lead not only to credibility for basic tourism statistics (international arrivals and tourism expenditure associated with inbound tourism flows) but also assist in measuring non-residents tourism activity.

From the supply side, the use of tax records is also an important area for developing more accurate and detailed tourism statistics. The exhaustive nature of tax sources makes them useful for the structural analysis of tourism industries and, in the case of value added tax, also timeliness is a basic comparative advantage. Obviously, there are also limitations using administrative records: inconsistency over time, lack of standardization between reporting units, quality of the associated activity code, etc., are some relevant examples that users must have in mind.

Conclusions: TSAs as a tool for better tourism management

In many countries, tourism has suffered from a lack of political and popular support because its true economic significance has often been underestimated. It has hitherto been approached mainly as a consumer activity, hence the focus of analyses on the traveller, trip characteristics and other demand-side aspects. Now there is increasing awareness of tourism's role as a productive activity and its potential to generate value added, employment, government income and other benefits whether directly or through induced effects in the economy.

There is therefore a radical change of focus. The approval of the conceptual framework of the Tourism Satellite Account (TSA) by the United Nations Statistical Commission in 2000 was a response to this situation. The TSA is a statistical instrument, a 'satellite' revolving around the concepts, definitions and aggregates of the system of national accounts, that makes it possible to make valid comparisons with other industries, as well as between countries or groups of countries.

25

Tourism Planning, Development and the Territory

Carlos Costa

Introduction

The beginning of the twentieth-first century has been characterized by massive changes that are determining the future of the tourism sector. Competition is becoming increasingly global rather than regional; governments are losing their capacity to intervene in markets and political practice creates policies based on administration principles rather than ideologies. Within this environment, the re-invention of tourism planning has come to the top of the planners' agenda. Physical and normative approaches that dominated tourism planning theory and practice for decades are now being challenged. Physical planning is still a dominant objective of most tourism planning schools, because of the need to ensure ecologically and socially sustainable environments. However, planning is now moving towards creating new models capable of bringing together the regulation of the destination alongside the coordination and stimulation of private sector and public participation. Sustainable economic growth, through sufficient return on investment for enterprises and improvement of social capital are top priorities. Self-sustained and sustainable destinations are now seen as a product of responsible markets and responsive citizens.

The evolution of tourism planning

Tourism is the world's largest industry and will become the world's leading business, as a result of the overwhelming rates of growth foreseen by the WTO. According to forecasts, international arrivals will sharply increase from 700 million in early 2000 to 1.6 billion by the year 2020.

The origin of this rapid expansion of the tourism industry can be traced back to the 1950s and 1960s, with the explosion of mass tourism. Between the 1950s and 1970s, the world's international arrivals climbed from 25 million to 165 million and receipts rose from US$ 2 billion to US$ 18 billion. During the following decade, tourism continued to progress very rapidly and in 1980 reached 284 million international arrivals and US$ 103 billion receipt (WTO, 2004). Several books published in the area show how social, economic, technological and political situations prompted the rapid expansion of tourism during this phase (Murphy, 1985; Torkildsen, 1999; Cooper et al., 2005).

Early days of tourism planning: 1950s–1970s

During the early days, the tourism sector expanded almost on its own, without the support of proper planning and development policies. WTO (1980) concluded from 1619 plans that 'few destinations forecast integrated tourism within the socio-economic objectives for country development, and also that tourism plans where social aspects have priority over direct profitability are even more exceptional'. Other conclusions also point out that even if 'it is possible to observe an increasing awareness worldwide, environmental strategies are rarely associated with tourist policies'. The absence of specific tourism planning controls, the inadequacy of legislation, poor and ineffective tourism organizations in many Mediterranean resorts that were desperate for economic growth and prosperity, were responsible for the failure of tourism planning. Such forms of development created negative impacts at destinations located around the Mediterranean basin and in the Caribbean and have jeopardized the long-term prosperity of those regions and damaged resources severely.

The absence of proper planning policies, vision and knowledge of what tourism was all about, helps to explain why, during this period, some forms of development were responsible for causing so many negative environmental, sociocultural and economic impacts. Nevertheless, tourism as an academic discipline and body of knowledge was still in its infancy and therefore many mistakes were inevitable and lessons had to be learned.

Up to the 1970s tourism planning evolved alongside urban and regional planning.

When compared to the approach that was launched after the Industrial Revolution, and despite (the) rapid expansion of tourism, it can be observed that the planning and management of the tourism sector did not progress that much. 'Tourism planning' continued to be viewed, and thus undertaken, under the umbrella of town planning. It was still believed that the expansion of tourism was equivalent to the growth of urban developments set aside for tourism purposes. In the absence of particular planning instruments capable of coordinating and regulating the development of resorts, the expansion of the tourism sector was left in the hands of entrepreneurs interested in short-term profit, and, thus, not concerned with the long-term impact on the physical and social environment and on the long-term survival of the economic structure of the destination areas (Costa, 2001).

Market economies therefore capitalized on local capital and exploited resources belonging to local populations. As a result of this, tourism planning failed to control tourism developments.

Tourism planning towards maturity: 1980s–1990s

Research on tourism economics started to emerge only after the 1970s and, as a result, it was only after the 1980s that tourism planning theory and practice started to emerge supported by evidence and research through a specific body of knowledge. The PASOLP diagrammatic approach (Baud-Bovy, 1982), the integrative systems model of tourism theory and practice (Getz, 1986), the tourism policy model (Mill and Morrison, 1985) and Inskeep's (1991) schematic representation focusing on the components of a tourism plan, illustrate the emergence of a specialized body of knowledge, approaching destinations as systems, that bring together town planning, economics, geography, sociology, psychology, etc. Such models also provide evidence that tourism planning started to emerge as a distinct and differentiated discipline, even if very close liaisons to its town planning counterpart can be registered.

These models also provide evidence that, since the 1980s, tourism planning began to be viewed much more from a strategic rather than a physical point of view. Until then, tourism planners were mainly concerned with physical issues, a situation that may be explained as a result of their main background in town planning and the non-existence of well-structured tourism schools. Governments became progressively aware of the economic advantages that tourism could bring to national and regional balance-of-payments, income, employment, investment and regional development. They also regarded tourism as potential to stimulating economic development in areas where agriculture, fishing and industry were declining.

Modern tourism planning: after the 1990s

Tourism planners have realized that their agenda is changing considerably. While in the recent past their actions were geared towards the design of physical plans and the zoning of infrastructure and equipment, the trend is now for planners to follow a different approach. Government budgets are shrinking, which means that planners have limited resources to implement policies. In addition, private sector organizations and citizens are increasingly playing a more influential role in designing the future course of actions. When analysing the way tourism is developed and organized around the world, there is evidence to suggest that private sector organizations are indeed intervening decisively in the way in which tourism is planned and developed, as they play a prominent and influential role in the decision-making process (Pearce, 1992; Costa, 1996). This means that the rational and technical approaches traditionally followed by planners in previous decades will have to take into consideration the interests of private sector organizations and local communities.

Such awareness is well mirrored in the contemporary tourism research. An intensive interest placed by academics on new areas of tourism economics is prompting the development of new knowledge for tourism planning. Greater emphasis on matters concerning partnerships, networks, clusters, strategic planning, innovation, self-sustained growth, SMEs, quality control and policy evaluation is noticed.

The economics of development

How forms of sustained development can be designed to boost development is a matter that is gaining increasing importance in the planners' agenda. Globalization, fierce competition among destinations, the failure of the welfare state, the states' fiscal crisis and the emergence of 'region-states' are leading planners to divert their attention from forms of extensive planning to more flexible, adaptable, creative and participative planning policy, capable of prompting self-sustained growth. Leverage or entrepreneurial planning and public-investment planning directing the development process, are among the strategies most cited by planners in comparison to 'classical' regulative and interventionist planning (Brindley et al., 1989; Stoker and Young, 1993).

Dealing with smaller budgets and aware of the states' incapacity to channel large amounts of investment to the 'periphery', planners have realized that forms of self-sustained economic growth should be achieved. However, a number of conditions are required. First, regions that would like to develop their destinations should create capacity to lure external investment into the area. Tourism plays a prominent role since it has the capacity to attract investment and labour from outside. As this takes place, regions also improve their accessibility and links to the world market.

Furthermore, regions with endogenous and rich tourism resources may specialize in the 'production' and 'exportation' of products that give them competitive advantage. Planners are conscious that tourism offers enormous potential since, when compared to manufacturing, products are less subject to competition, because they are interconnected to the destination. In other words, the business of tourism is very much oriented towards the commercialization of non-comparable and differentiated territories, such as Côte d'Azur, Bath, Miami, Algarve, Crete, Costa del Sol, etc. This means that planners must place the emphasis on the development and promotion of territories rather than products, since products may be sold 'independently' of the place.

The success of tourism depends very much on its authenticity and uniqueness. To succeed, regions must make the best use of their own internal resources and should avoid, as far as they can, imports. Raw materials ought to be produced and provided locally, while locals should be given priority for employment. This will help to strengthen the local economic basis and to support economic multipliers, boosting cumulative growth, stimulating exportation and gradually leading to the attraction of human resources, capital, investment and knowledge into the area.

Moreover, planners are also aware that such forms of cumulative growth will, sooner or later, spill over to other parts of the territory. Development is then induced from the centre to the periphery and not the other way round, as it is observed in forms of subsidized or centrally directed forms of planning.

The development theories that support most of these approaches are linked to the 'classical' development theory of the export-based theory, the Heckscher-Ohlin theorem and the growth poles theory (Armstrong and Taylor, 2000). Nevertheless, issues related to productivity, technology, innovation and capacity to bring together private and public sector organizations have to be seen alongside classical theories if sustained and sustainable planning is to be achieved.

Development theories concerning partnerships, networks, clusters and governance are flourishing worldwide. Planners have realized that development must be stimulated at the regional level, which comprehends the management of its endogenous resources (physical planning) and from the angle of the organization and coordination of the territory, which includes the superstructure responsible for its planning and management (strategic planning). Planning must be seen therefore in an interconnected way: from the side of the performance of the 'hardware' (infrastructure and superstructure) that supports the system, and from the angle of the 'software' (coordination and management) that induces and stimulates its operation.

Emergent trends in tourism planning

The future of tourism planning lies in the way in which tourism resources and systems may be regulated and coordinated. Baldwin and Cave (1999) argue that 'regulation's purpose is to achieve certain publicly desired results in circumstances where, for instance, the market would fail to yield those'. They go even beyond this statement and affirm that 'regulatory competition is the competitive adjustment of rules, processes, or enforcement regimes, in order to secure an advantage, and thus regulation leads to rigour, accountability, creation and diffusion of innovation'.

Hostility towards governmental action was partially based on ideology and on observed government failures in the centrally planned Soviet bloc. Such a point of view was perhaps supported on the often negative language of regulation, frequently seen as 'intervention', 'interference', 'restricting', and 'constraining'. It is worth emphasizing that 'entrepreneurship may be, in large measure, a function of an institutionalized socio-political structure' (Schumpeter, 1983). However, regulation should offer destinations a strategic direction by providing a comprehensive framework for strategic management of territories and resources and by bringing together public, private, non-profit organizations, residents, policies and rules that safeguard the long-term benefit of all stakeholders involved in the tourism industry and lead to the sustainability of resources.

National, regional and local level tourism organizations are often set up seeking such objectives. However, it is also noticed that their operating philosophies are, in a number of situations, becoming obsolete. First, their functioning is often too bureaucratic and political. Hence, they cannot respond with the speed, efficiency and effectiveness required by markets. There is also strong controversy on whether their associates represent legitimate interests, since their accountability is often questioned. Most national tourism organizations stress their operation on marketing and promotional matters, while neglecting the provision of strategic vision for the destination. They also fail to take measures to optimize the multiplier effects that may emerge if proper and interconnected networks integrating the entire economy are set up.

The operation of most regional and local tourism organizations in countries such as Spain, Portugal, France, etc., is based on 'administrative territories' rather than 'product-based territories'. Tourism organizations are created in accordance with existing administrative borders set up for other purposes (e.g. town planning, environment, education, health, etc.). However, it is becoming clear that tourism clusters often do not coincide with borders established for other administrative purposes, which means that collaboration between counties, regions, or even between countries is required. Rethinking the way in which 'tourist territories' are established is critical.

It is unquestionable that tourism planning has much to benefit it if it is designed and managed alongside other forms of planning. Tourism involves core business activities addressing tourist needs. However, infrastructure should also be used for improving the living standards of the local population and for stimulating regional development. The benefits of designing policies able to meet the demands of both tourists and residents are enormous, from an economic point of view (more users and thus more income is generated and therefore the multiplier effect is maximized), from a social perspective (forms of dual development and antagonism towards tourism may be avoided) and also from a development point of view (investment is concentrated at spots and scale economies can be achieved).

While it is important to plan, especially regional, tourism planning alongside other forms of regional planning (town, health, environment, etc.), it must be said that at local level greater flexibility should be introduced, in order to allow businesses and organizations to organize themselves within economic, social and physical viable and sustainable clusters. While forms of strategic planning ought to be considered at regional level alongside regional planning, greater levels of freedom should be allowed at local level, because actors must organize themselves in viable clusters that depend very much on their own wishes and on their investment capacities.

There is evidence that this tendency is already emerging and gaining popularity worldwide. The Tourism Satellite Accounts developed by the WTO provide a great step forward in this area because, contrary to the fragmented demand-side definitions that have dominated tourism planning theory and practice over the last decades, they bring focus and clarification to what tourism businesses and activities are all about. The new supply-side definitions highlight that the core of the tourism activity comprehends seven main economic activities:

1. accommodation
2. food and beverage
3. transportation
4. intermediaries, tour operators, travel agencies and tourist guides
5. rent-a-car
6. cultural services and
7. leisure and recreation activities.

By placing the emphasis on the tourism core businesses, the new definitions clearly suggest that tourism policies and investment should be directed to its core.

With regard to this, research and data are central to rational planning. Tourism Observatories have been launched in countries such as France, Italy, Portugal, and Spain, acting as leading agencies for the governance of tourism destinations. They provide entrepreneurs, public and non-profit organizations with management and planning information and can create intelligence that supports the strengthening of competitiveness against competing destinations.

The trend towards the creation of more flexible forms of strategic planning is also observed in the way in which Regional Tourism Boards are also evolving in several countries. The tendency registered, for instance, in Britain and Portugal, is a good example of that. In the British Northwest, regional level organizations have strengthened their relationships with the aim of creating more coherent and competitive tourism clusters. The same is observed in Portugal, where the tendency is for regions to merge with the aim of creating stronger and more viable economic clusters. In both countries the idea is to boost the creation of 'product-space' against 'space-product' organizations. 'Product-based territories' are then emerging in substitution of 'administrative territories'. Product-based territories are made of viable, well-identified, distinct and, as far as possible, unique, tourism products and they are responsible for polarizing tourism businesses around them.

Following these trends tourism planning will gradually assume contemporary philosophies. At a regional level, tourism planning will be integrated alongside other forms of urban and regional planning. Physical planning, including decisions on where superstructure and infrastructure should be located, will be mainly left to local authorities, responsible for tourism zoning. Within this context sub-regional level organizations will gradually be shaped following market dynamics and viable tourism clusters. The concept of sustainable competitive destinations will tend to mean sub-regional level and product-based territories, responsible for governing economically viable tourism territories and for sustaining valuable resources for the future.

Case study 25.1 The Tourism Policy for the Peneda-Geres National Park (Portugal)

The Peneda-Geres National Park is the largest Portuguese natural park. The park includes a fully protected area, with a wide variety of world-protected fauna and flora species and places where (small numbers of) visitors are allowed to enter. The park offers some recreational opportunities and there are five traditional villages located in the outskirts of the protected area. The park is embedded in an exuberant landscape dominated by forms of rural tourism. The area was ranked among the 12 best world ecotourism projects in the 1999 British Airways Tourism Awards, as a result of its capacity to articulate rural development, tourism and environmental protection.

At the end of 1999 a sustainable tourism plan was completed for the park. The policy was designed by a team headed by the University of Aveiro and the Park Authority and brought together public sector agencies and investors. The project includes a tourism policy endorsed by all agencies intervening in the Park and a €62.5 million investment plan, made up of 60 per cent private sector investment and 40 per cent public sector investment.

Further sources of information: Costa (2004); Home page: www.adere-pg.pt

Case study 25.2 The Tourism Policy for the Caramulo Region (Portugal)

The Caramulo Tourism Development Plan incorporates a tourism policy designed for the four Caramulo municipalities. The policy was designed by the University of Aveiro and was approved by the regional and national tourism authorities in charge of the area. In order to put the policy into practice an investment plan amounting to €60 million (60 per cent private sector investment and 40 per cent public sector investment) was launched in the area.

The policy aims to stimulate economic development in an area with few investment opportunities. The region is located outside the most developed Portuguese areas. As a result of the lack of industrial and social development and being an unspoiled place, the region offers a number of tourist attractions. Forest recreational land, heritage, gastronomy and a wide network of rivers are among the most sought tourist resources.
Further reading:

Breda et al., 2005

Conclusion

Tourism planning is maturing as a discipline and new paradigms will undoubtedly emerge in the area. While tourism planning theory and practice are still very much influenced by town planning, the present evolution points towards the creation of new paradigms that will be determined by market-led approaches. Tourism destinations will become planned and managed by emerging models that place the emphasis on the coordination and stimulation of private sector organizations and also that bring public participation right into the core of the decision-making process. The emerging approaches will give priority to methodologies that improve the coordination between private and public sector organizations and also that place the citizens, both residents and visitors, right in the core of the decision-making process. The governance of tourism destinations, their capacity to become more sustainable, competitive and profitable and the design of self-sustained developments will become the priority of tourism planning models. Organizations polarized by tourism clusters ('product-space organizations') will replace the old bureaucratic organizations ('space-product organizations'). In the future, therefore, tourism administrations will adjust to this trend and will be set up according to coherent clusters of products rather than following mere administrative procedures set up years ago for other bureaucratic purposes.

Part Four: Conclusion

26

Conclusion: Tourism Management Dynamics

Carlos Costa and Dimitrios Buhalis

The *Tourism Management Dynamics: Trends, management and tools* book provides a vision for the way in which the external environment of the tourism industry will be progressing in the future through the examination of key trends. It then provides a range of implements to equip businessmen, politicians, managers and academics with innovative management techniques and business tools that will enable them to take better advantage of these trends and strengthen their competitiveness.

The book demonstrates that the future management dynamics of the tourism industry will result from a group of external and a group of internal *new trends*. The external new trends influence dramatically the tourism industry through changing demand patterns, resources available as well as legislation and regulation. One of the most influential trends is demographics (Chapter 2). The changing profile of the world population and the ageing of several main markets as a result of low birth rates will drive the tourism industry in search for new leisure markets. Senior tourism will emerge thanks to the growing availability of free time and disposable income in this market segment, although this market will require different products and services. However, a life course approach seeks not to impose a normal or ideal life path as articulated in traditional life-cycle models, but to explore the transition periods in people's lives which influence their needs, preferences and consumer behaviour. Yet, growing numbers of new travellers appear as a result of the changing profile of the world working population. Consumption of leisure and tourism will increasingly become more inelastic in the future as, on the one hand, consumers satisfy all their needs for basic products and, on the other, work-related stress generates relaxation needs. In addition, globalization will continue making businesses migrate to a number of new locations, collaborate internationally as well as sell products and services on a global basis. A growing number of workers will therefore be travelling around the world following career and business opportunities.

Mother nature will continue to provide not only resources for tourism but also determinants for travel. Therefore a second main external new trend that will strongly affect the tourism industry is climate change (Chapter 5). There is clear evidence that climate is changing rapidly around the globe with both temperatures and sea levels rising. Destinations such as the Maldives, Venice and other seaside places may experience land loss, the temperature in the Mediterranean may become uncomfortable in the summer months, while alpine resorts may experience changes in the snowfall patterns. This will affect landscapes at the sea-shores, snowfall, temperatures and other factors that determine tourism activity. Climate change may also have negative impacts on small islands and other low-lying areas, including loss of land, increased storm surge damage and saltwater intrusion into fresh groundwater aquifers. The implications of this situation to the tourism sector are enormous since some well-established seaside resorts and mountain regions may radically change their profile and thus will have to adjust, whenever they can, in search for new products and markets.

Safety and security concerns (Chapter 3) will also assume mounting importance in the future. Following 11 September 2001 and other terrorism attacks, where the tourism and travel industries have been targeted due to their international profile, a number of global initiatives have been emerging. Perceived safety and security in the eyes of the consumer naturally determines the attractiveness and success of tourism destinations. Although different nationalities and cultures perceive and deal with insecurity differently, it is evident that at times of uncertainty travellers prefer to holiday in familiar environments, boosting domestic and interregional tourism. The importance played by the globalized media (Chapter 7) is also related to this issue as increasingly events are covered almost live. Graphic pictures and commentary often exaggerate situations to ensure higher visibility ratings for television stations, causing incredible and long-lasting effects on destinations. Few people can forget the images of 11 September 2001, the tsunami disaster, the avalanches in St Anton and foot-and-mouth disease in the UK, even years after they have occurred. Destinations will therefore become increasingly scrutinized by the media, which will result in mounting pressure for competition, exposure to the public and protection of consumers' rights. Hence an escalating fierce competition, associated with concerns about massive investments involved at most destinations, will lead to an increasing pressure for the tourism industry to get ready to manage unpredictable situations that may arise from natural disasters, civil conflicts, epidemics and technology failures. Risk and crisis management will therefore become one of the most important priorities of the tourism sector in future (Chapter 4). Consequently, the tendency for destinations to pay more attention to safety, security and to the media and communication will grow in the future.

A second large group of *new internal trends* that will emerge are changes that will be operated within the tourism industry. Liberalization and deregulation (Chapter 8) emerging through international collaboration propelled by World Trade Organization agreements, the strengthening of the European Union and Mercul as well as bilateral agreements, will fuel both competition and collaboration. This will push the introduction of greater levels of efficiency, further globalization of products and services as well as a new wave of alliances, mergers and acquisitions throughout the industry. The tendency for diagonal (horizontal and vertical) integration of the tourism industry will continue while global players will gradually offer integrated solutions to their clientele. Within this environment small family-size businesses will struggle to survive. They will need either to develop alliances with the larger players in the marketplace to offer complementary niche products and services or to pull their resources together in search of economies of scope, productivity gains and enhancing professionalism and innovation.

These trends have great impacts on the emerging tourism research agenda (Chapter 9). While at present most tourism research has been geared towards matters related to geography, economics and anthropology, in the near future investigation will bring about new research areas centred on emerging issues such as productivity, the systems within which the tourism industry operates, conflict between stakeholders, technology and strategies. Instead of researching what has happened, innovative research should be building scenarios to guide the tourism industry towards proactive and reactive strategies in order to optimize its operations and strategies. Research results will need to be implemented by tourism organizations and destinations if they are to strengthen their competitiveness.

The rising pressure on the tourism industry brought about by the new consumer requirements and external environment trends, will result in radical changes in the *management* of the tourism sector. Notably organizations will be pushed to achieve greater levels of efficiency, effectiveness, productivity and profitability. In a global world and in face of a delocalized industry, involving widespread chains with operating branches in generating countries, transit regions and destinations, the tendency is for organizations to abandon forms of formal planning and engage in new managerial approaches based on decentralization, flexibility and rapid decisions (Chapter 10). More turbulent, competitive environments will demand greater strategic adaptability, operational flexibility and service customization and these, in turn, are more effectively delivered by decentralized, performance-driven organizations. Empowering and providing tools for front-line employees will be critical for the success of the future tourism organizations.

Understanding the evolution of the tourism industry through the needs of consumers as well as the external environment at each era of development would enable organizations to appreciate better future directions. Constant product and process innovation will therefore be essential for encouraging creativity and enhancing competitiveness (Chapter 11). A number of emerging trends, approaches, models and paradigms arise to take tourism organizations beyond the millennium and enable them to to expand and adjust to the evolution of the market ('learning organizations'). Chaos theory (Chapter 12), for example, proposes that everything exists in a state of flux, that any appearance of a steady state, in the usual sense, is illusory and that catalysts pop up to dislodge the system from its quasi-rest. Depending on whether the catalyst is negative or positive the response may be immediately disadvantageous or profitable.

Within this environment, the vast majority of tourism enterprises are small, family run and often lifestyle driven (Chapter 13). As the tourism sector is still a young industry with low barriers to entry, there will always be the tendency for the rapid emergence of new businesses. Unfortunately, only a few of the SMEs currently in tourism are truly innovative and competitive. The vast majority of players are not motivated by growth or economic benefits, lack knowledge and skills and are unable to follow the global developments. These organizations will find it increasingly difficult to compete in the future and will either disappear or under-perform producing inadequate return on investment. The ability of SMEs to explore the global trends and develop innovative products and services to address them will be critical for their own competitiveness as well as the competitiveness of the destination and the value systems they operate in. Hence, the tendency is for an evolution that will push tourism businesses to grow, while forms of horizontal integration bringing together small businesses will be evident in the future.

A major tendency will be towards the creation of forms of horizontal and vertical integration. Gradually, most tourism organizations will, to a greater or lesser extent, become integrated in alliances bringing together private, public and non-profit organizations. Organizational forms based on partnerships and networks will then emerge (Chapters 14 and 18) to take advantage of clusters at the destination level and to create co-destiny for all their participants. While partnerships, mergers, alliances and other formal organizational forms will become more popular among businesses, the tendency is for the establishment of networks or clusters at destinations, involving private, public, and non-profit organizations. They will aim at bringing strategy, guidance and community involvement for the economic and social clusters set up at local level while creating a dynamic platform for creating, adopting and disseminating innovation. This will represent a great breakthrough towards the implementation of forms of sustained and sustainable growth and for the achievement of integrated total quality management at the destination level. Perhaps, more importantly, organizations need to get used to the idea of coopetition, where they compete and cooperate at the same time. By interconnecting their resources and by collaborating for serving particular needs, target markets and events, they can increase the size of the market and increase their collective profitability rather than compete constantly for merely an increase in their market share. Smaller players would benefit particularly from those arrangements as they will be able to increase their virtual size through participating in an organized 'business ecosystem' that is supporting its parts. Technology will be critical for supporting such networking organizations as it will provide the tools for interconnectivity and interoperability to sustain an agile network.

Successful organizations of the future will require better educated human resources with knowledge and interest in getting involved in the decision-making and in the decision-taking process (Chapter 14). Educated workers, with international experience, operating in interconnected organizational networks will introduce great advantages for the tourism sector. Not only will they support business to operate within a globalized environment but they will also ensure that professional management is applied (Chapter 15). Yet, they will make organizations better adjusted to manage situations of instability at any place in the network

(Chapter 12). Further, they will create the opportunity for organizations to manage the environment in which they are operating and also to respect and support the destination resources (Chapter 16). Providing equitable returns for the resources utilized should be one of the main priorities of the future tourism industry, to ensure sustainability and long-term prosperity.

The growing dynamics and fierce competition that will be registered in the world tourism market will push entrepreneurs, managers and planners towards new management tools that will enable them to manage their internal operations, devise suitable strategies and establish relationships with consumers. The success of the tourism industry will be determined by the ability to attract better customers for the destination, who will enjoy the experience, respect the resources and thus increase their levels of spending. Future businesses, therefore, will mainly be concerned with knowing the needs of consumers, developing innovative and suitable products (while taking into consideration the resource constraints) and delivering personalized products. Delighting the customer of the future will be increasingly difficult as immense competition from professionally run organizations and destinations globally will make differentiating and excelling difficult. Nevertheless consumer-centric tourism marketing will not only target individual consumer preferences but will also encourage consumers proactively to personalize the products and services they would like to consume (Chapter 19).

A global tourism industry responsible for moving people (both consumers and employees) from their usual place of residence and for placing them in different cultural environments will also push cross-cultural marketing strategies (Chapter 20). Highlighting and recognizing the different places and cultures available around the world and addressing particular needs and requirements will be critical for success. Hence, cross-cultural hospitality will dominate the way in which tourism marketing will evolve in the future. This will involve both the adaptation of the product as well as of the communication, pricing and distribution strategies. Therefore to the degree that global organizations target a great proportion of the world, they will have to 'glocalize' their strategies.

Few other tools have such an impact on tourism as information communication technologies and the Internet in particular (Chapter 21). Increasingly technologies transform distribution to a global value system, where access to information and ubiquity is achieved, while interactivity between principals and consumers provides major opportunities. Hence, the Internet propels the re-engineering of the entire process of producing, marketing and delivering tourism products, as well as boosting interactivity between partners towards the design of specialized products and the maximization of the value-added provided to individual consumers. This effectively changes the structure of the industry to an ecosystem of individual but interrelated organisms and nodes all interconnected and interoperable that can enhance their collective competitiveness and profitability. In addition, marketing information systems will set a much-needed intelligent network for data collection and information dissemination. They are set to perform decision support functions for managers and planners (Chapter 22) and they will provide the infostructure for the collection and analysis of critical information from a number of sources as well as for the dissemination of processed information back to the industry. Better and up-to-date information will ensure that decision-makers can take proactive and reactive managerial actions fast enough to meet market requirements and at the same time to maximize the benefit from their organizations and destinations.

There is currently a profound rethinking about tourism applied research and information required for strategic and tactical decisions around the world. Global competition propels the need for marketing and economic applied research that provides a comprehensive information base for decision-making by both planners and managers. The rapid expansion of tourism marketing, the need to make places attractive for tourists to choose them and greater concern in managing tourist flows appropriately to maximize benefits and optimize impacts is also prompting the creation of tourism observatories at many destinations. Tourism observatories tend to follow the supply-side tourism definitions and the principles set up by the WTO's Tourism Satellite Account Methodology (Chapter 24). The aim is to understand how much tourism contributes to the nations' and regions' development and, above all, to unveil the interconnected economic relationships created by networks of businesses. Moreover, powerful tourism forecasting methods also emerge capable of monitoring and informing how many visitors destinations may attract (Chapter 23). They will be developed alongside the collection and analysis of how tourists interact with local economies and society at destinations.

Better information will encourage better planning and management of tourism at the macro level. In the future the management and the planning of destinations will emphasize the tourists' interaction with the space, and future tourism territories' administration will be set up according to tourism products rather than following classical administrative boundaries (Chapter 25). Managing and planning the territory will require understanding of what products tourists choose and why, the territories they comprehend and the economic, social and political forces that influence their evolution. Planning will have as its top mission to interpret and make social and economic forces to 'land' on the territory and not to fight against it.

The future will be bright for those tourist organizations and destinations that explore trends and take advantage of the emerging management techniques and tools for developing suitable proactive and reactive strategies in order to enhance their competitiveness. It is increasingly becoming evident that only organizations and destinations that have the knowledge and the capacity to deal with tourism professionally will be able to develop their competitive advantage and achieve their objectives in the future. In spite of the growth rates expected for the tourism industry, destinations and businesses that fail to predict the future and to develop proactive and reactive strategies will be unable to benefit. It is within this framework that competitiveness, efficiency, effectiveness, long-term profitability, ethics and sustainability are the main themes that will ensure the long-term prosperity of tourism organizations and destinations.

Although predicting the future is always a hazardous occupation the *Tourism Management Dynamics: Trends, Management and Tools* book together with its affiliate publication *Tourism Business Frontiers: Consumers, Products and Industry*, provide a comprehensive analysis of both supply and demand trends as well as of the emerging issues in the tourism external environment. They also demonstrate a wide range of management mechanisms and tools that will enable tourism organizations and destinations to strengthen their competitiveness for the future.

References

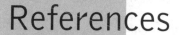

Abernathy, V.D. (2004) Not tonight, sweetie; no energy. *World Watch*, September/October.

Agnew, M. and Viner, D. (2001) Potential impacts of climate change on international tourism. *Tourism and Hospitality Research*, **3**(1), 37–61.

Allaby, M. (ed.) (1998) *A Dictionary of Ecology* (electronic source). New York: Oxford University Press. http://0-www.netlibrary.com.catalogue.library.brocku.ca/EbookDetails.aspx, (accessed 30 July, 2004).

AMA (American Marketing Association) (2004) What is the meaning of 'marketing'? *Marketing News*, 14 September, p. 18.

American Marketing Association (AMA) www.ama.org, www.marketingpower.com (accessed 28 April, 2005).

Amor, D. (2002) *Internet future strategies*. New Jersey: Prentice Hall.

Anderson, B. (2004) Observations on International Tourism Communications. *First World Conference on Tourism Communications* (Klancnik R, ed.), Madrid, 29–30 January, pp. 59–61.

Andersson, T. (1998) *An alternative model of economic impact analysis – using 'dividends' instead of 'multipliers'*. Sweden: The European Tourism Research Institute (ETOUR).

Apo, P. (2004) *Community Tourism: Empowering communities to tell their own stories*. Honolulu: Hawaiian Hospitality Institute.

Appadurai, A. (1996) *Modernity at Large Cultural Dimensions of Globalisation*. Miineapolis:University of Minnesota Press.

Archer, B.H. and Fletcher, J. (1990) *Multiplier Analysis in Tourism (Les Cahiers du Tourisme)*. Aix-en-Provence: Centre des Hautes Etudes Touristiques.

Armstrong, H. and Taylor, J. (2000) *Regional Economics and Policy*, 3rd edn. Oxford: Blackwell.

Ashkenas, R., Ulrich, D., Jick, T. and Kerr, S. (1995) *The Boundaryless Organization: Breaking the Chains of Organizational Structure*. San Francisco: Jossey-Bass.

Ateljevic, I. and Doorne, S. (2000) Staying with the fence: lifestyle entrepreneurship in tourism. *Journal of Sustainable Tourism*, **8**(5), 378–392.

Augustyn, M.M. (2004) Coping with resource scarcity: the experience of UK tourism SMEs. In *Small Firms in Tourism: International Perspectives* (Thomas R, ed.). Amsterdam: Elsevier, pp. 257–275.

Austin, J.E. (1990) *Managing in Developing Countries Strategic Analysis and Operating Techniques*. New York: The Free Press.

Bakewell, C. and Mitchell, V. (2003) Generation Y female consumer decision-making styles. *International Journal of Retail & Distribution Management*, **31**(2), 95–106.

Baldwin, R. and Cave, M. (1999) *Understanding Regulation-Theory, Strategy and Practice*. Oxford: Oxford University Press, pp. 7–63.

Bar-On, R. (1989) *Travel and Tourism Data*. Phoenix: Oryx Press.

Barton, L. (1994) *Crisis Management: Preparing for and Managing Disasters. The Cornell Hotel and Restaurant Administration Quarterly*, April, 59–65.

Baud-Bovy, M. (1982) New concepts in planning for tourism and recreation. *Tourism Management*, **3**(4), 308–313.

Baum, T. (1987) Introducing educational innovation in hospitality studies: a case study in practical curriculum change. *International Journal of Hospitality Management*, **6**(2), 97–102.

Baum, T. (1995) Managing cultural diversity in tourism. *Insights*, November, A-77–A-84.

Baum, T. and Odgers, P. (2001) Benchmarking best practice in hotel front office: The Western European Experience. *Journal of Quality Assurance in Hospitality and Tourism*, **2**(3/4), 93–109.

Baumol, W.J. (1982) Contestable markets: an uprising in the theory of industry structure. *American Economic Review*, **72**, 1–15.

Becherel, L. and Cooper, C. (2002) The Impact of globalisation on HR management in the tourism sector. *Tourism Recreation Research*, **27**(1), 3–16.

Becken, S. (2004) How tourists and tourism experts perceive climate change and carbon-offsetting schemes. *Journal of Sustainable Tourism*, **12**(4), 332–345.

Beekman, G. (2003) *Computer Confluence: Exploring tomorrow's Technology*, 5th edn. New Jersey: Prentice Hall.

Beirman, D. (2003a) *Restoring Tourism Destination in Crisis*. Oxford: CABI Publishing.

Beirman, D. (2003b) *Restoring Tourism Destinations in Crisis: A Strategic Marketing Approach*. Sydney: Allen & Unwin.

Beni, M. (1996) Travel Trade and Globalization: Communication and Competition on the International Market. *AIEST Congress Report 46*, Vol. 38. New Zealand, St Gall.

Benjamin, W. (1935) *The Work of Art in the Age of Mechanical Reproduction* http://www.student.cs.uwaterloo.ca/~cs492/01public_html/Benjamin.html (accessed 10 June, 2004).

Bentley, T.A. and Page, S.J. (2001) Scoping the extent of adventure tourism accidents. *Annals of Tourism Research*, **28**, 705–726.

Berenschot Consultancy (2004) I am sterdam. Municipality of Amsterdam (October).

Bhushan, N. and Subbarao, V. Mobile Commerce: Killer Applications. *Infosys*, http://www.infy.com/knowledge_capital/thought-papers/mcommerce.pdf; (accessed 10th August, 2004).

Blake, A. and Sinclair, M.T. (2003) Tourism crisis management: US response to September 11. *Annals of Tourism Research*, **30**, 813–832.

Bordas, E. (1990) Marketing Research – Marketing Strategy: Design of a Communication Strategy for a Tourist Destination. *AIEST Congress Report 32*, (Tourist Research as a Commitment). St Gall.

Brackenbury, M. (2004) Observations on International Tourism Communications. *First World Conference on Tourism Communications* (Klancnik R, ed.), Madrid, 29–30 January, pp. 32–33.

Bramwell, B. (ed.) (2004) The policy context for tourism and sustainability in southern Europe's coastal regions. In *Coastal Mass Tourism. Diversification and Sustainable Development in Southern Europe*. Clevedon: Channel View, pp. 32–47.

Bramwell, B. and Lane, B. (eds) (2000) Collaboration and partnerships in tourism planning, In *Tourism Collaboration and Partnerships: Politics Practices and Sustainability*. Clevedon: Channel View Publications, pp. 1–19.

Braun, P. (2002) Networking tourism SMEs: E-commerce and E-marketing issues in regional Australia. *Information Technology & Tourism*, **59**(1), 13–24.

Breda, Z., Costa, R. and Costa, C. (2005) Do clusters and networks make small places beautiful? The case of Caramulo (Portugal). In *Tourism Local Systems and Networking* (Lazzeretti, I and Petrillo, C.S. eds). London: Elsevier.

Briassoulis, H. (2002) Sustainable tourism and the question of the commons. *Annals of Toursim Research*, **29**(4), 1065–1085.

Briggs, J. and Peat, F.D. (1999) *Seven life lessons of Chaos: Timeless wisdom from the science of change*. St Leonards: Allen & Unwin.

Brindley, T., Rydin, Y. and Stoker, G. (1989) *Remaking Planning*. London: Unwin Hyman.

Britton, S. (1990) Tourism, capital and place: towards a critical geography of tourism. *Environment and Planning: Society and Space*, **9**(4), 451–478.

Brown, J.S. and Duguid, P. (2002) *The Social Life of Information*. Boston: Harvard Business School Press.

Brown, L.D. (1991) Bridging organisations and sustainable development. *Human Relations*, **44**(8), 807–831.

Brusco, M.J., Johns, T. and Reed, J.H. (1998) Cross-utilization of a two-skilled workforce. *International Journal of Operations and Production Management*, **18**(6), 555–564.

Bryman, A., Bytheway, B., Allatt, P. and Keil, T. (eds) (1987) Introduction. In: *Rethinking the Life Cycle*. Basingstoke: Macmillan, pp. 1–16.

Budowski, G. (1976) Tourism and environmental conservation: Conflict, co-existence or symbiosis? *Environmental Conservation*, **3**(1), 27–31.

Buhalis, D. (1998) Strategic use of information technologies in the tourism industry. *Tourism Management*, **19**(3), 409–423.

Buhalis, D. (1999) Information technology for small and medium sized tourism enterprises: adaptation and benefits. *Information Technology & Tourism*, **2**(2), 79–95.

Buhalis, D. (2003) *eTourism: Information Technology for Strategic Tourism Management*. London: Financial Times/Prentice Hall.

Buhalis, D. and Licata, C. (2002) The future of eTourism intermediaries. *Tourism Management*, **23**(3), 207–220.

Burns, P. (1999) Paradoxes in planning, tourism elitism or brutalism. *Annals of Tourism Research*, **26**(2), 329–348.

Burns, P. (2001) *Entrepreneurship and Small Business*. Tavistock and Rochdale: Palgrave, Macmillan.

Byers, T. and Slack, T. (2001) Strategic decision-making in small businesses within the leisure industry. *Journal of Leisure Research*, **22**(2), 121–136.

Calantone, R.J. and di Benedetto, C.A. (1991) Knowledge acquisition modeling in tourism. *Annals of Tourism Research*, **18**(2), 202–212.

Callon, M., Law, J. and Rip, A. (eds) (1986) *Mapping the Dynamics of Science and Technology*. London: Macmillan.

Capra, F. (1982) *The Turning Point*. London: Flamingo.

Castells, M. (2001) Information technology and global capitalism. In: *On the Edge Living with global capitalism* (Hutton, W. and Giddens, A. eds). London: Vintage.

Caulkin, S. (2004) To Lose a Customer Please Press… *The Observer*, 29th August.

Chen, R.J.C. and Noriega, P. (2003) The impacts of terrorism: perceptions of faculty and students on safety and security in tourism. *Journal of Travel and Tourism Marketing*, **15**(2/3), 81–97.

Chien, C.L. and Law, R. (2003) The impact of the Severe Acute Respiratory Syndrome on hotels: a case study of Hong Kong. *International Journal of Hospitality Management*, **22**(3), 327–332.

Choi, T.Y. and Chu, R. (2000) Levels of satisfaction among Asian and Western travellers. *International Journal of Quality and Reliability Management*, **7**(2), 116–131.

Churchill, N.C. and Lewis, V.L. (1983) The five stages of small business growth. *Harvard Business Review,* **61**(3), 33–51.

Cohen, E. (1972) Towards a sociology of international tourism. *Social Research*, **39**(1), 64–82.

Coles, T. (2003) A local reading of a global disaster: some lessons on tourism management from an *annus horribilis* in south west England. *Journal of Travel and Tourism Marketing*, **15**(2/3), 173–197.

Competition Commission (1997) *Foreign Package Holidays: A Report on the Supply in the UK of Tour Operators' Services and Travel Agents' Services in Relation to Foreign Package Holidays*. London: Competition Commission.

Cooper, C., Fletcher, J., Gilbert, D., Shepherd, R. and Whanhill, S. (2005) *Tourism: Principles and Philosophies*, 3rd edn. Harlow: Pearson.

Costa, C.M.M. (1996) Towards the improvement of the efficiency and effectiveness of tourism planning and development at the regional level: planning, organisations and networks. The case of Portugal. *PhD Thesis*. Guildford: University of Surrey.

Costa, C.M.M. (2001), An emerging tourism planning paradigm? A comparative analysis between town and tourism planning. *International Journal of Tourism Research*, **3**(6), 425–441.

Costa, C. (2004) The management of eco-tourism destinations through policies of investment. In *Ecotourism: Management and Assessment* (Diamantis, D. and Geldenhuys, S. eds). London: Continuum, Ch. 13.

Coulter, R.A., Zaltman, G. and Coulter, K. (2001) Interpreting consumer perceptions of advertising: An application of the Zaltman Metaphor Elicitation Technique. *Journal of Advertising,* **30**(4), 1–21.

Craik, J. (1995) Are there cultural limits to tourism. *Journal of Sustainable Tourism.* **3**(2), 87–98.

Crotts, J. and Pizam, A. (2002) The effect of national culture on consumers' evaluation of travel services. *Tourism Culture and Communication,* **4**(1), 17–28.

CRT (2003) *Du Système de statistiques du tourisme (SST) au compte régional du tourisme.* Riviera Côte d'Azur: Comité régional du tourisme.

Darley, W. and Luethge, D. (2003) Cross-cultural communications and promotion. In *Cross-cultural Marketing* (Rugimbana R, Nwankwo S, eds.) London: Thomson, pp. 141–179.

Davies, B. (1999) Industrial Organization: The UK Hotel Sector. *Annals of Tourism Research,* **26**(2), 294–311.

Dawson, C. (2001) Ecotourism and nature-based tourism: One end of the tourism opportunity spectrum. In *Tourism, Recreation and Sustainability, Linking Culture and the Environment* (McCool, S. and Moisey, R.N. eds). Wallingford: CABI Publishing, pp. 41–53.

DBEDT (Department of Business, Economic Development and Tourism) (2002) Progress on the Study: Planning for Sustainable Tourism in Hawaii. Report to the Legislature, January 2002. http://www.hawaii.gov/dbedt/sustainable/index.html (accessed 15 June, 2004).

de Albuquerque, K. and McElroy, J. (1999) Tourism and crime in the Caribbean. *Annals of Tourism Research,* **26**(4), 968–984.

Deery, M., Jago, L., Fredline, L. and Dwyer, L. (2005). *The National Business Events Study: An Evaluation of the Australian Business Events Industry.* Sustainable Business Cooperative, Gold Coast, Australia.

De Mooij, M. (1998) *Global Marketing and Advertising. Understanding Cultural Paradoxes.* London: Sage.

Department for Environment, Food & Rural Affairs (2004) http://www.defra. gov.uk/footandmouth/contingency/contplan.pdf

DeSanctis, G. and Gallupe, R.B. (1987) A foundation for the study of group decision support systems. *Management Science,* **33**(5), 589–609.

Diamond, J. (1998) *Guns, Germs and Steel. A short history of everybody for the last 13,000 years.* London: Vintage.

Draper, D. (2004) Niagara Falls skyline in danger. *Pulse Niagara,* February 5–11, **18**(8), 7.

Elder, G.H. Jr (1994) Time, human agency and social change: Perspectives on the life course. *Social Psychology Quarterly,* **57**(1), 4–15.

Elsasser, H. and Messerli, P. (2001) The vulnerability of the snow industry in the Swiss Alps. *Mountain Research and Development,* **21**(4), 335–339.

Engle, R.F. and Granger, C.W.J. (1987) Cointegration and error correction: representation, estimation and testing. *Econometrica,* **55**, 251–276.

English Heritage (2002) *The Heritage Dividend.* London: English Heritage.

Enz, C. and Witham, G. (2001) *Yield Management.* Cornell University: CHR Reports.

EU (2001) *The Development of Broadband Access Platforms in Europe: Technologies, Services, Markets, Final Report.* Brussels: Information Society, IST, European Commission.

European Commission (2004) http://europa.eu.int/comm/enterprise/enterprise_ policy/sme_definition/presentation.pdf.

Eurostat (2003) *Europäische Unternehmen: Zahlen und Fakten. Teil 5: Handel und Tourismus*. Luxembourg: European Commission.

Evans, P. (1999) *Recent Developments in Trade and Competition Issues in the Services Sector: A Review of Practices in Travel and Tourism*. UNCTAD Series on Issues in Competition Law and Policy. New York and Geneva: United Nations.

Farrell, B.H. and Twining-Ward, L. (2004) Reconceptualizing tourism. *Annals of Tourism Research*, **31**(2), 274–295.

Faulkner, B. (2001) Towards a framework for tourism disaster management. *Tourism Management*, **22**, 135–147.

Fayos-Sola, E. (2004) The role of knowledge in destination policy formulation. BEST Sustainable Tourism Think Tank IV June 30–July 4, 2004, University of Southern Denmark, Esbjerg.

Finley, L. (1990) *Entrepreneurial Strategies: Text and Cases*. Boston: P.W.S. Kent.

Flamholtz, E.G. (1990) *Growing Pains*. Oxford: Jossey-Bassimc.

Fletcher, J. (1989) Input-output analysis and tourism impact studies. *Annals of Tourism Research*, **16**(4), 514–529. http://www.world-tourism.org/statistics/tsa_ project/basic_references/index-en.htm.

Floyd, M.F., Gibson, H., Pennington-Gray, L. and Thapa, B. (2003) The effect of risk perceptions on intensions to travel in the aftermath of September 11, 2001. *Journal of Travel and Tourism Marketing*, **15**(2/3), 19–38.

Foot, D.K. and Stoffman, D. (1996) *Boom, Bust and Echo*. Toronto: Macfarlane Walter & Ross.

Frangialli, F. (ed.) (2001) A vision, three worksites and a strategy. In: *Observations on International Tourism*. Madrid: WTO, pp. 573–599.

Furr, H., Bonn, M. and Hausman, A. (2002) A generational and geographical analysis of internet travel service usage. *Tourism Analysis*, **6**(2), 139–174.

Gabriel, Y. (1988) *Working Lives in Catering*. London: Routledge and Kegan Paul.

Gallouj, F. (2002) Innovation in services and the attendant old and new myths. *Journal of Socio-economics*, **31**, 137–154.

Gartner, W.C. (1993) Image formation process. *Journal of Travel and Tourism Marketing*, **2**(2/3), 191–215.

Getz, D. (1986) Models in tourism planning: towards integration of theory and practice. *Tourism Management*, **7**(1), 21–32.

Giles, A.R. and Perry, A.H. (1998) The use of a temporal analogue to investigate the possible impact of projected global warming on the UK tourist industry. *Tourism Management*, **19**(1), 75–80.

Gilloch, G. (1996) *Myth and Metropolis: Walter Benjamin and the City*. Cambridge: Polity Press.

Gleick, J. (1987) *Chaos: Making a New Science*. London: Heinemann.

Glick, P. (1947) The family life cycle. *American Sociological Review*, **12**, 164–174.

Go, F.M. and Fenema, P.C. (2003) *Moving bodies and connecting minds in space: a matter of mind over matter*. Paper presented at the 19th EGOS Conference, Copenhagen, 3–5 July.

Go, F.M., Lee, R.M. and Russo, A.P. (2003) E-heritage in the globalizing society: enabling cross-cultural engagement through ICT. *Information Technology & Tourism*, **6**(1), 55–68.

Goffee, R. and Scase, R. (1995) *Corporate Realities*. London: Routledge.

Goodrich, J.N. (2002) September 11, 2001 attack on America: a record of the immediate impacts and reactions in the USA travel and tourism industry. *Tourism Management*, **23**, 573–580.

Gössling, S. (2002) Global environmental consequences of tourism. *Global Environmental Change*, **12**(4), 283–302.

Govers, R. and Go, F.M. (2004) Cultural identities constructed, imagined and experienced: A three-gap tourism destination image model. *Tourism*, **52**(2), 165–182.

Graham, A. (2003) *Managing Airports – An International Perspective*, 2nd edn. Oxford: Butterworth-Heinemann.

Graham, B. (1998) Liberalization, regional economic development and the geography of demand for air transport in the European Union. *Journal of Transport Geography*, **6**(2), 87–104.

Gray, B. (1989) *Collaborating: Finding common ground for multiparty problems*. San Francisco: Jossey-Bass.

Green, C.G., Bartholomew, P. and Murrmann, S. (2003) New York restaurant industry: strategic responses to September 11, 2001. *Journal of Travel and Tourism Marketing*, **15**(2/3), 63–79.

Groetzbach, E. (1988) Erholungsverhalten und Tourismusstile am Beispiel Orientalischer Lander. In: *Berichte und Materialien* (Ritter, W. and Milelitz, G. eds). Berlin: Institut fur Tourismus, Freie Universitat.

Gronroos, C. and Ojasalo, K. (2004) Service productivity. Towards a conceptualization of the transformation of inputs into economic results in services. *Journal of Business Research*, **57**, 414–423.

Grumbine, R.E. (1994) What is ecosystem management? *Conservation Biology*, **8**(1), 27–38.

Guerrier, Y. and Adib, A. (2001) Working in the hospitality industry. In: *In Search of Hospitality* (Lashley, C. and Morrison, A. eds). Oxford: Butterworth-Heinemann, pp. 255–275.

Gunn, C. (2004) *Tourism Planning*, 4th edn. New York: Routledge.

Hale, R. and Whitlam, P. (1997) *Towards the Virtual Organisation*. London: McGraw-Hill International.

Hales, C. (2000) Management and empowerment programmes. *Work, Employment and Society*, **14**(3), 501–519.

Hales, C. (2001a) *Managing Through Organization*, 2nd edn. London: Thomson Learning Business Press.

Hales, C. (2001b) Organizational futures: E-cultures, N-forms, M-forms or bureaucracies? *Business Strategy Review*, **12**(3), 53–59.

Hales, C. (2002) Bureaucracy–lite and continuities in managerial work. *British Journal of Management*, **13**(1), 51–66.

Hall, C.M. (2000a) The future of tourism: a personal speculation. *Tourism Recreation Research*, **25**, 85–95.

Hall, C.M. (2000b) *Tourism Planning: Policies, Processes and Relationships*. Harlow: Prentice-Hall.

Hall, C.M. (2005) *Tourism: Rethinking the Social Science of Mobility*. Harlow: Prentice Hall.

Hall, C.M. and Higham, J. (2005) *Tourism, Recreation and Climate Change*. Clevedon: Channel View Publications.

Hall, C.M. and Jenkins, J. (2004) Tourism and public policy. In: *A Companion to Tourism* (Lew, A.A., Hall, C.M. and Williams, A.M. eds). Oxford: Blackwell, pp. 525–540.

Hall, C.M. and Müller, D. (eds) (2004) *Tourism, Mobility and Second Homes: Between Elite Landscape and Common Ground*. Clevedon: Channelview Publications.

Hall, C.M., Timothy, D.J. and Duval, D.T. (eds) (2003) *Safety and Security in Tourism: Relationships, Management, and Marketing*. New York: Haworth.

Hamel, G. and Prahalad, C.K. (1994) *Competing for the Future: Breakthrough strategies for seizing control of your industry and creating the markets of tomorrow*. Boston: Harvard Business School Press.

Hanlon, P. (1999) *Global Airlines – Competition in a transnational industry*, 2nd edn. Oxford: Butterworth-Heinemann.

Harrison, S.J., Winterbottom, S.J. and Sheppard, C. (1999) The potential effects of climate change on the Scottish tourist industry. *Tourism Management*, **20**, 203–211.

Hart, M. (1999) *Guide To Sustainable Community Indicators*, 2nd edn. North Andover: Hart Environmental Data http://www.sustainablemeasures.com (accessed 16 March, 2002).

Hashimoto, A. (2002) Tourism and socio-cultural development issues. In: *Tourism and Development: Concepts and Issues* (Sharpley R, Telfer D, eds). Clevedon: Channel View Publications, pp. 202–230.

Hatten, T. (1997) *Small Business: entrepreneurship and beyond*. London: Prentice Hall.

Healey, P. (2003) Collaborative planning in perspective. *Planning Theory*, **2**(2), 101–123.

Hecksher, C. and Donnellon, A. (eds) (1994) *The Post-Bureaucratic Organization: New Perspectives on Organizational Change*. London: Sage Publications.

Hein, W. (ed) (1997) Tourism and sustainable development: empirical analysis and concepts of sustainability – a systems approach. In: *Tourism and Sustainable Development*. Hamburg: Schriften Des Deutschen Übersee-Instituts, no. 41, pp. 359–400.

Held, D., McGrew, A., Goldblatt, D. and Perraton, J. (2000). *Global Transformations Politics, Economics and Cultures*. Cambridge: Polity.

Henderson, J.C. (2003) Communicating in a crisis: flight SQ006. *Tourism Management*, **24**, 279–287.

Hendry, D.F. (1995) *Dynamics Economics: Advanced Text in Econometrics*. Oxford: Oxford University Press.

Herbig, P. (1998) *Handbook of Cross-Cultural Marketing*. New York: The International Business Press.

Hetherington, K. and Law, J. (2000) After networks. *Environment and Planning D: Society and Space*, **18**, 127–132.

Hilmer, F.G. and Donaldson, L. (1996) *Management Redeemed: Debunking the Fads that Undermine Corporate Performance*. New York: Free Press.

Hochschild, A.R. (1983) *The Managed Heart: Commercialisation of Human Feeling*. Berkley: University of California Press.

Hofstede, G. (2001) *Culture's consequences: Comparing values, behaviors, institutions, and organizations across nations*. Thousand Oaks: Sage.

Holden, A. (2002) *Environment and Tourism*. London: Routledge.

Hong Kong Tourism Board (2003) http://www.Partnernet.hktb.com

Hruschka, H. and Mazanec, J. (1990) Computer-assisted travel counselling. *Annals of Tourism Research*, **17**(2), 208–27.

Hsieh, S. and O'Leary, T. (1993) Communication channels to segment pleasure travellers. *Journal of Travel and Tourism Marketing*, The Haworth Press. pp. 57–74.

Hughes, H.L. (1994) Tourism multiplier studies: a more judicious approach. *Tourism Management*, **15**(16), 403–406.

Hume, C. (2004) An unsightly view of Niagara Falls, Parks Commission wants a gondola ride. *Toronto Star*. www.thestar.com (accessed 10 August, 2004).

Hunn, C. and Mangan, J. (2002) Estimating the economic impact of tourism at the local, regional and State or Territory level, including consideration of the multiplier effect. Australia: Bureau of Tourism Research.

Hutton, W. (1995) The 30/30/40 Labour Market. http://www.jobsletter.org.nz/ jbl03010.htm. First published in *The Jobs Letter* no.30, 15 December 1995 (accessed 30 July, 2004).

Inskeep, E. (1991) Tourism planning: An integrated and sustainable development approach. New York: Van Nostrand Reinhold.

Ioannides, D. and Debbage, K.G. (1998) *The Economic Geography of the Tourism Industry – A Supply Side Analysis*. London: Routledge.

IPCC (2000) *IPCC Special Report on Emissions Scenarios: Summary for Policymakers*. Geneva: IPCC.

IPCC (2001) *Climate Change 2001: The Scientific Basis, Contribution of Working Group I to the Third Assessment Report of the Intergovernmental Panel on Climate Change* (Houghton JT, Ding Y, Griggs DJ et al. (eds.)). Cambridge and New York: Cambridge University Press.

ISTAG (2003) *Ambient Intelligence: from vision to reality For participation in society & business*. Draft report. Brussels: IST Advisory Group, European Commission.

Jamal, T. and Getz, D. (1995) Collaboration theory and community tourism planning. *Annals of Tourism Research*, **22**(1), 186–204.

Jamal, T., Borges, M. and Figueiredo, R. (2004) Systems-based modeling for participatory tourism planning and destination management. *Tourism Analysis*, **9**(1–2), 77–90.

Jamieson, W. and Mandke, P. (2000) Urban tourism and environmental sustainability – taking an integrated approach. In *Developments in Urban and Regional Tourism* (Robinson, M., Sharpley, R., Evans, N., Long, P. and Swarbrooke, J. eds). Sunderland: The Centre for Travel and Tourism and Distance Education Publishers Ltd.

Johansen, S. (1988) A statistical analysis of cointegration vectors. *Journal of Economic Dynamics and Control*, **12**, 231–254.

Johnson, P., Conway, C. and Kattuman, P. (1999) Small business growth in the short run. *Small Business Economics*, **12**(1), 103–112.

Jones, C. (2003) Regional Tourism Satellite Accounts in the UK: issues and challenges. Cardiff: Cardiff University.

Jones, P.D. and Moberg, A. (2003) Hemispheric and large-scale surface air temperature variations: An extensive revision and an update to 2001. *Journal of Climate*, **16**, 206–223.

Jones, P.D., New, M., Parker, D.E., Martin, S. and Rigor, I.G. (1999) Surface air temperature and its changes over the past 150 years. *Reviews of Geophysics*, **37**, 173–199.

Jong, P. (2004) Keynote speech delivered by Mr Peter de Jong, CEO of PATA at the CAUTHE Conference in Brisbane, Australia on 11 February, 2004.

Kanter, R.M. (2001) *Evolve! Succeeding in the Digital Culture of Tomorrow*. Boston: Harvard Business School Press.

Kärcher, K. (1997) *Reinventing Package Holiday Business*. Berlin: Deutscher Universitäts Verlag.

Kickert, W., Klijn, E-H. and Koppenjan, J. (1997) *Managing Complex Networks. Strategies for the Public Sector*. London: Sage.

King, R., Warnes, A.M. and Williams, A.M. (2000) *Sunset Lives: British Retirement to the Mediterranean*. London: Berg.

Kirby, D. (2003) *Entrepreneurship*. London: McGrawHill.

Klancnik, R. (ed) (2004), Executive Summary. In: *Observations on International Tourism Communications, First World Conference on Tourism Communications*, Madrid, 29–30 January, pp. 15–25.

Knox, J. (2004) *Sustainable Tourism in Hawaii: Socio-Cultural and Public Input Component: Volume 1: Summary Report*. Honolulu: John M. Knox & Associates, Inc. Draft April 2004.

Konan, D. and Kim, K. (2003/4) Transportation and Tourism I Hawaii: Computable General Equilibrium Model. Transportation Research Record 1839, Paper No. 03-3987. University of Hawaii, Honolulu.

Korczynski, M. (2002) *Human Resource Management in Service Work*. Basingstoke: Palgrave.

Kwan, M-P. (2000) Gender differences in space-time contraint. *Area*, **32**(2), 145–56.

Lai, P. and Baum, T. (2005) Just-In-Time Labour in the Hospitality Sector? *Employee Relations*, **27**(1), 86–102.

Laudon, K.C. and Laudon, J.P. (2003) *Management Information Systems*, 8th edn. London: Prentice Hall.

Law, J. and Hassard, J. (1999) *Actor Network Theory and After*. Oxford: Blackwell.

Law, R. (2000) Back-propagation learning in improving the accuracy of neural network-based tourism demand forecasting. *Tourism Management*, **21**, 331–340.

Leavitt, H.J. and Bahrami, H. (1988) *Managerial Psychology: Managing Behaviour in Organizations*, 5th edn. Chicago: University of Chicago Press.

Legohérel, P., Callot, P., Gallopel, K. and Peters, M. (2004) Personality characteristics, attitude toward risk, and decisional orientation of small business entrepreneur: a study of hospitality managers. *Journal of Hospitality & Tourism Research*, **28**(1), 109–120.

Leslie, D. (1999) Terrorism and tourism: the Northern Ireland situation – a look behind the veil of certainty. *Journal of Travel Research*, **38**, August, 37–40.

Lettenblicher, M. (2004) Speech delivered by Mr Mark Lettenblicher, Chairman of the Hong Kong Hotels Association at the Association's annual gala dinner in Hong Kong on 18 March, 2004.

Lew, A.A., Hall, C.M. and Williams, A. (2004) *A Companion to Tourism*. Oxford: Blackwell.

Li, G. (2004) Modelling and forecasting UK tourism demand in Western Europe: illustrations of TVP-LAIDS models' superiority over other econometric approaches. *PhD thesis*. Guildford: University of Surrey.

Lietz, C. (2003) *Consumer-centric Marketing: How leading consumer packaged good companies are transforming the way they market. A Fair Isaac White Paper.* http://www.fairisaac.com/NR/rdonlyres/20104EED-F186-4058-9608-26B54B57AB14/0/ConsumerCentricMktgWP.pdf (accessed 9 September, 2004).

Lindridge, A. and Dibb, S. (2003) Is 'culture' a justifiable variable for market segmentation? A cross-cultural example. *Journal of Consumer Behavior*, **2**(3), 269–287.

Lipman, G. (2004) *Papers on Liberalization with a Human Face*. Madrid: World Tourism Organization.

Little, J.D.C. (1979) Decision support systems for marketing managers. *Journal of Marketing*, **43**(3), 9–26.

Long, N. (2001) *Development Sociology. Actor Perspectives*. London: Routledge.

Lorenz, E.N. (1963) Deterministic non-periodic flow. *Journal of the Atmospheric Sciences*, **20**(2), 130–141.

Luhrman, D. (ed) (1999) *Shining in the Media Spotlight*. Madrid: World Tourism Organization.

Luhrman, D. (2003) Crisis Guidelines for the Tourism Industry, *Asia-Pacific Ministerial Summit on Crisis Management*, Manila, 18 June, 2003.

Luhrman, D. (1999) Introduction to the round table on crisis communications. In *Observations on International Tourism Communications, First World Conference on Tourism Communications* (Klancnik R, ed.), Madrid, 29–30 January, pp. 169–171.

Lynch, R. and Veal, A.J. (1996) *Australian Leisure*. South Melbourne: Longman Australia.

Macnaughten, P. and Urry, J. (1998) *Contested Natures*. London: Sage.

Manente, M (2003) *The Impact that restrictive measures applied to tourism supply growth would have on the Canary Islands' economic system*. University of Venice: Centro Internazionale di Studi sull' Economia Turistica (CISET).

Maney, R., Flink, C. and Lietz, C. (2002) White paper on Consumer Centric Marketing: How leading consumer packaged good companies are transforming the way they market. Seurat Company http://www.dmreview.com/whitepaper/WID494.pdf

Manidis Roberts Consultants (1997) *Developing A Tourism Optimisation Management Model*. Surrey Hills: Manidis Roberts Consultants.

Marcussen, C. (2003) Trends in European Internet Distribution of Travel and Tourism, Denmark http://crm.ittoolbox.com/documents/document.asp?i = 2835.

Marin, B. and Mayntz, R. (eds) (1991) Introduction: studying networks. In: *Policy Network. Empirical Evidence and Theoretical Considerations*. Boulder: Westview, pp. 11–23.

Marsh, D. and Rhodes, R.A.W. (eds) (1992) *Policy Networks in British Government*. Oxford: Oxford University Press.

Massey, D. (1991) A global sense of place. *Marxism Today*, June, pp. 24–29.

Mathews, K.M., White, M.C. and Long, R.G. (1999) The problem of prediction and control in theoretical diversity and the promise of complexity sciences. *Journal of Management Inquiry*, **8**(1), 17–31.

Mattila, A.S. (1999) The role of culture and purchase motivation in service encounter evaluations. *Journal of Services Marketing*, **13**(4/5), 376–389.

Maxwell, S. (2001) An expanded price/brand effect model: A demonstration of heterogeneity in global consumption. *International Marketing Review*, **18**(3), 325–343.

Mazanec, J.A. (1986) Allocating an advertising budget to international travel markets. *Annals of Tourism Research*, **13**, 609–634.

McKercher, B. (1999) A chaos approach to tourism. *Tourism Management*, **20**, 425–434.

McKercher, B. and Hui, E.L.L. (2003) Terrorism, economic uncertainty and outbound travel from Hong Kong. *Journal of Travel and Tourism Marketing*, **15**(2/3), 99–115.

McPherson, B.D. (1998) *Ageing as a Social Process: An Introduction to Individual and Population Ageing*, 3rd edn. Toronto: Harcourt Brace and Company.

Meadows, D.H. (1998) *Indicators and Information Systems for Sustainable Development: A Report To The Balaton Group*. Hartland: The Sustainability Institute.

Mercer, D. (2004) Tourist and resource management. In: *A Companion to Tourism* (Lew, A., Hall, C.M. and Williams, A. eds). Oxford: Blackwell Publishing, pp. 463–472.

Middelkoop, M. van (2001) Merlin: a decision support system for outdoor leisure planning. Development and test of a rule-based microsimulation model for the evaluation of alternative scenarios and planning options. PhD thesis. Eindhoven: Technical University.

Middleton, V.T.C. and Hawkins, R. (1998) *Sustainable Tourism. A Marketing Perspective*. Oxford: Butterworth-Heinemann.

Mill, R.C. and Morrison, A.M. (1985) *The Tourism System: An Introductory Text*. New Jersey: Prentice-Hall.

Miller, G. (2001) The development of indicators for sustainable tourism: results of a Delphi survey of tourism researchers. *Tourism Management*, **22**, 351–362.

Miller, G. and Twining-Ward, L. (2005). *Monitoring for a Sustainable Tourism Transition*. Oxford: CAB International.

Mills, M. (2000) Providing space for time: The impact of temporality on life course research. *Time and Society*, **9**(1), 91–127.

Mintel (2003) Film Tourism – The Global Picture. *Travel & Tourism Analyst*, October.

Mintzberg, H. (1991) The effective organization: forces and forms. In *Organization Development and Transformation: Managing Effective Change*, 4th edn (French WL, Bell CH, Zawacki RA, eds). Burr Ridge: Irwin, pp. 588–604.

Mitchell, B. (1989) *Geography and Resource Analysis*. New York: Longman.

Mitchell, B. (1997) *Resource and Environmental Management*. Longman: Harlow.

Mok, C. and Armstrong, R. (1998) Expectations for hotel service quality: do they differ from culture to culture? *Journal of Vacation Marketing*, **4**(4), 381–391.

Morris, C. (2004) Networks of agri-environmental policy implementation: A case study of England's Countryside Stewardship Scheme. *Land Use Policy*, **21**, 177–191.

Morris, J.A. (2003) Emotional labor in the hospitality and tourism industry. In *Managing Employee Attitudes and Behaviors in the Tourism and Hospitality Industry* (Kusluvan S, ed.). New York: Nova Science Publishers.

Morrison, A.J. (1994), Marketing strategic alliances: the small hotel firm. *International Journal of Contemporary Hospitality Management*, **6**(3), 25–30.

Morrison, A.J., Rimmington, M. and Williams, C. (1999) *Entrepreneurship in the Hospitality, Tourism and Leisure Industries*. London; Butterworth-Heinemann.

Moutinho, L., Rita, P. and Curry, B. (1996) *Expert Systems in Tourism Marketing*. New York: Routledge.

Mowforth, A. and Munt, I. (1998) *Tourism and Sustainability: New Tourism In The Third World*. London: Routledge.

Mulhern, F.J. and Williams, J.D. (1994) A comparative analysis of shopping behaviour in Hispanic and non-Hispanic marketing areas. *Journal of Retailing*, **70**(3), 231–251.

Müller, H. (1998) Long-haul tourism 2005 – Delphi study. *Journal of Vacation Marketing*, **4**, 192–201.

Murdoch, J. (1998) The spaces of actor-network theory. *Geoforum*, **29**(4), 357–374.

Murdoch, J. and Marsden, T. (1995) The spatialization of politics: Local and national actor-spaces in environmental conflict. *Transactions of the Institute of British Geographers*, **20**, 368–380.

Murphy, M. (1987) Measuring the family life cycle: concept, data and methods. In *Rethinking the Life Cycle*, Bryman A, Bytheway B, Allatt P, Keil T (eds). Basingstoke: Macmillan, pp.30–50.

Murphy, P.M. (1985) *Tourism a Community Approach*. London: Routledge.

Navarro, J.R. and Rubio, J.Q. (2000) DATATUR: Tourism Statistics Information System – the Experience of Spain. In: *Proceedings of the International Conference on Information and Communication Technologies in Tourism*, (Fesenmaier, D.R., Klein, S. and Buhalis, D. eds). Vienna: Springer, pp. 126–146

Nelson, E. and Dannefer, D. (1992) Aged heterogeneity: fact or fiction? The fate of diversity in gerontological research. *The Gerontologist*, **32**(1), 17–23.

Nelson, J.G., Butler, R. and Wall, G. (eds) (1993) *Tourism and Sustainable Development: Monitoring, Planning, Managing*. University of Waterloo: Department of Geography, Publication Series Number 37.

Nickson, D. and Warhurst, C. (2003) The New 'Labour Aristocracy'? Aesthetic Labour in the Service Economy. Paper to *3rd Critical Management Studies Conference*, Lancaster.

Nielsen, C. (2001) *Tourism and the Media*. Melbourne: Hospitality Press.

Niininen, O. and Riley, M. (2004) Towards the conceptualization of tourism destination loyalty. In *Consumer Psychology of Tourism Hospitality and Leisure* (Crouch G, Perdue R, Timmermans H, Uysal M, eds). Wallingford: CAB International, pp. 275–284.

Observatory of European SMEs 2002 (2003) http://europa.eu.int/comm/enterprise/enterprise_policy/analysis/observatory.htm, date: 1.11.2004.

O'Connor, P. (1999) *Electronic Information Distribution in Tourism & Hospitality*. Oxford: CAB.

O'Connor, P. (2003) *Online Intermediaries – Revolutionizing Travel Distribution*. London: EIU Travel and Tourism Analyst.

Odgers, P. and Baum, T. (2001) *Benchmarking of Best Practice in Hotel Front Office*. Dublin: CERT.

Olsen, M.D. and Connolly, D.J. (2000) Experience-based travel. *Cornell Hotel and Restaurant Administration Quarterly,* pp. 30–40.

Onyeiwu, S. and Joners, R. (2003) An institutional perception of cooperative behaviour. *Journal of Socio-economics,* **32,** 233–248.

O'Rand, A. and Krecker, M. (1990) Concept of the life cycle: The history, meanings and uses in the social sciences. *Annual Review of Sociology,* **16,** 214–262.

O'Riordan, T. (1981) *Environmentalism,* 2nd edn. London: Pion.

Orwell, G. (1933) *Down and out in Paris and London.* London: Penguin.

Pacific Asia Travel Association (2003) Crisis: It Won't Happen to Us! PATA.

Pacific Asia Travel Association (2004) PATA 2004 www.pata.org

Papatheodorou, A. (2002) Civil aviation regimes and leisure tourism in Europe. *Journal of Air Transport Management,* **8**(6), 381–388.

Papatheodorou, A. (2003) Deregulation. In *Encyclopaedia of Leisure and Outdoor Recreation* (Pigram J, Jenkins J, eds). London: Routledge.

Papatheodorou, A. (2004) Exploring the evolution of tourism resorts. *Annals of Tourism Research,* **31**(1), 219–237.

Paraskevas, A. and Buhalis, D. (2002) Information communication technologies decision-making: The ASP outsourcing model from the small hotel owner/manager perspective. *The Cornell Hotel Restaurant Administration Quarterly,* **43**(2), 27–39.

Pausch, H. *An Essay on Benjamin's Passagen-Werk (Arcades Project 1927).* http://www.litencyc.com/php/sworks.php?rec=true&UID=5738 (accessed 18 June, 2004).

Pavlovich, K. (2003a) The evolution and transformation of a tourism destination network: The Waitomo Caves, New Zealand. *Tourism Management,* **24,** 203–216.

Pavlovich, K. (2003b) Pyramids, pubs, and pizzas: An interpretation of tourism network structures. *Tourism, Culture and Communication,* **4,** 41–48.

Pearce, D. (1992) *Tourist Organisations.* Harlow: Longman Group UK Ltd.

Pearce, D. and Stringer, P. (1990) Psychology and tourism. *Annals of Tourism Research,* **11,** 343–352.

Pesaran, M.H. and Shin, Y. (1995) An autoregressive distributed lag modelling approach to cointegration analysis. In: *Centennial Volume of Rangar Frisch, Econometric Society Monograph* (Strom, S., Holly, A. and Diamond, P. eds). Cambridge: Cambridge University Press.

Peter, J.P. and Olson, J.C. (1998) *Consumer Behavior and Marketing Strategy.* Boston: McGraw-Hill.

Peters, M., Weiermair, K. and Leimegger, R. (2004) Employees' evaluation of entrepreneurial leadership in small tourism businesses. In *Small and Medium Sized Enterprises in Tourism* (Bieger T, Keller P, eds). St Gallen: AIEST.

Pettigrew, A.M. and Fenton, E.M. (2000) *The Innovating Organization.* London: Sage Publications.

Pine, J. and Gilmore, J. (1999) *The Experience Economy.* Boston: Harvard Business School Press.

Pizam, A. (1993) Managing cross-cultural hospitality enterprises. In: *The International Hospitality Industry: Organizational and Operational Issues* (Jones, P. and Pizam, A. eds). London: Pitman.

Pizam, A (1999) A comprehensive approach to classifying acts of crime and violence at tourism destinations. *Journal of Travel Research,* **38**(1), 5–12.

Pizam, A. and Jeong, G. (1996) Cross-cultural tourist behavior: perceptions of Korean tour guides. *International Journal of Tourism Management*, **17**(4), 277–286.

Pizam, A. and Mansfeld, Y. (eds) (1996) *Tourism, Crime and International Security Issues*. Chichester: Wiley.

Pizam, A. and Reichel, A. (1996) The effect of nationality on tourist behavior: Israeli tour guides' perceptions. *Journal of Hospitality and Leisure Marketing*, **4**(1), 23–49.

Pizam, A. and Sussmann, S. (1995) Does nationality affect tourist behavior? *Annals of Tourism Research*, **22**(4), 901–917.

Pizam, A., Jansen-Verbeke, M. and Steel, L. (1997) Are all tourists alike regardless of nationality? The perceptions of Dutch tour guides. *Journal of International Hospitality, Leisure and Tourism Management*, **1**(1), 19–40.

Plog, S. (1974) Why destination areas rise and fall in popularity. *Cornell Hotel and Restaurant Administration Quarterly*, November 13–16.

Plummer, R. and FitzGibbon, J. (2004) Some observations on the terminology in co-operative environment management. *Journal of Environmental Management*, **70**(1), 63–72.

Poon, A. (1993) *Tourism, Technology and Competitive Strategies*. Oxford: CAB International.

Population Reference Bureau (2004) 2004 World Population Data Sheet. Washington DC: Population Reference Bureau.

Prahalad, C.K. and Ramaswamy, V. (2000) Co-opting customer competence. *Harvard Business Review*, January–February, 79–87.

Prideaux, B., Laws, E. and Faulkner, B. (2003) Events in Indonesia: exploring the limits to formal tourism trends forecasting methods in complex crisis situations. *Tourism Management*, **24**, 475–487.

Prigogine, I. and Stengers, I. (1985) *Order Out of Chaos*. London: Flamingo.

Quinion, M. (1998) World Wide Words: coopetition. http://www.worldwidewords.org/turnsofphrase/tp-coo2.htm (accessed 27 August, 2004).

Quinn, J.B., Anderson, S. and Finkelstein, S. (1996) New forms of organizing. In: *The Strategy Process* (Mintzberg, H. and Quinn, J.B. eds). Upper Saddle River: Prentice Hall, pp. 350–362.

Quinn, R.E. and Spreitzer, G.M. (1997) The road to empowerment: seven questions every leader should consider. *Organizational Dynamics*, **26**(2), 37–49.

Rahman, S.S., Waddock, S., Andriof, J. and Husted, B. (2002) *Unfolding Stakeholder Thinking: Theory, Responsibility and Engagement*. Sheffield: Greanleaf Publishing Ltd.

Reilly, R. (1990) *Effective Communication in the Travel Industry*. Delmar Publishers, Merton House Travel and Tourism Publishers, Albany, New York.

Ricci, F. (2004) Travel Recommender Systems. *IEEE Intelligent Systems*, November/December, 55–57.

Riddington, G. (1999) Forecasting ski demand: comparing learning curve and time varying parameter approaches. *Journal of Forecasting*, **18**, 205–214.

Riley, M. (1996) *Human Resource Management in the Hospitality and Tourism Industry*, 2nd edn. Oxford: Butterworth-Heinemann.

Riley, M. (1999) Re-defining the debate on hospitality productivity. *Tourism and Hospitality Research*, **1**(2), 182–186.

Riley, M., Ladkin, A. and Szivas, E. (2002) *Tourism Employment Analysis and Planning*. Clevedon: Channel View Publications.

Rita, P. (1993) A knowledge-based system for promotion budget allocation by national tourism organizations. PhD Thesis. Cardiff: University of Wales, College of Cardiff.

Ritchie, B.W., Dorrell, H., Miller, D. and Miller, G.A. (2003) Crisis communication and recovery for the tourism industry: lessons from the 2001 foot and mouth disease outbreak in the United Kingdom. *Journal of Travel and Tourism Marketing*, **15**(2/3), 199–216.

Ritchie, J.R. and Crouch, G.I. (2003) *The Competitive Destination: A Sustainable Tourism Perspective*. Oxford: CAB International.

Ritchie, R.J.B. and Ritchie, J.R.B. (2002) A framework for an industry supported destination marketing information system. *Tourism Management*, **23**(5), 439–454.

Ritzer, G. (1993) *The McDonaldization of Society*. Thousand Oaks: Pine Forge Press.

Ritzer, G. (1998) *The McDonaldization Thesis*. London: Sage Publications.

Robbins, P.T. (2001) *Greening the Corporation: Management Strategy and the Environmental Challenge*. London: Earthscan.

Russell, R. and Faulkner, B. (1999) Movers and shakers: chaos makers in tourism development. *Tourism Management*, **20**, 411–423.

Ryder, N.B. (1965) The cohort as a concept in the study of social change. *American Sociological Review*, **20**, 843–861.

Saayman, M. and Slabert, E. *Tourism Entrepreneurs: Opportunities and Threats. A South African Perspective*. http://66.102.9.104/search?q = cache: xdBZ7jLj_ ZwJ:www.saesba.co.za/old_website/papers/11-Saayman.pdf+super-segmentation&hl = en&ie = UTF-8 (accessed 27 August, 2004).

Scherer, F.M. and Ross, D. (1990) *Industrial Market Structure and Economic Performance*. Boston: Houghton Mifflin Company.

Schramm, W. (1960) *Mass Communication*. Chicago: University of Illinois Press.

Schumpeter, J.A. (1961) *The Theory of Economic Development*. New York: Oxford University Press.

Schumpeter, J.A. (1983) *Theory of Economic Development: An Inquiry into Profits, Capital, Credit, Interest and the Business Cycle*. London: Transaction Publishers.

Scott, D., McBoyle, G. and Mills, B. (2003) Climate change and the skiing industry in Southern Ontario (Canada): Exploring the importance of snowmaking as a technical adaptation. *Climate Research*, **23**, 171–181.

Seymour, D. (2000) Emotional labour: a comparison between fast food and traditional service work. *International Journal of Hospitality Management* **19**(2), 159–171.

Sharpley, R. (2002) The consumption of tourism. In: *Tourism and Development: Concepts and Issues* (Sharpley, R. and Telfer, D. eds). Clevedon: Channel View Publications, pp. 300–318.

Shaw, G. and Williams, A.M. (1990) Tourism economic development and the role of entrepreneurial activity. In *Progress in Tourism, Recreation and Hospitality Management*, Vol. 2 (Cooper CP, ed.). London: Bellhaven, pp. 67–81.

Shaw, G. and Williams, A.M. (1998) Entrepreneurship, small business culture and tourism development. In: *The Economic Geography of the Tourism Industry* (Ioannides, D. and Debbage, K.D. eds). London: Routledge, pp. 235–255.

Shaw, G. and Williams, A.M. (2004) From lifestyle consumption to lifestyle production: changing patterns of tourism entrepreneurship. In: *Small Firms in Tourism: International Perspectives* (Thomas, R. ed.). Amsterdam: Elsevier, pp. 99–113.

Sheldon, P. (1997) *Information Technologies for Tourism*. Oxford: CAB.

Shepherdson, N. (2000) New kids on the lot. *American Demographics*, **22**, 44–47.

Sinclair, T.M. and Stabler, M. (1997) *The Economics of Tourism*. London: Routledge.

Sirakaya, E., Sasidharan, V. and Sonmez, S. (1999) Re-defining eco-tourism: the need for a supply side. *Journal of Travel Research*, **38**, 168–172.

Sirakaya, E., Jamal, T.B. and Choi, H.S. (2001) Developing indicators for destination sustainability. In: *The Encyclopedia of Ecotourism* (Weaver, D.B. ed.) AB International: Oxford, pp. 411–431.

Smale, B.J.A. and Candance, N.I.J. (2001) *Tourism generating regions in Canada: factors associated with travel patterns and tourist behaviours*. World Tourism Organization, Madrid.

Smeral, E. (1996) *AIEST Congress Report 46*, Vol 38, New Zealand, St Gall (see www.wifo.ac.at/Egon.Smeral/AIEST_NewZealand_1996.htm)

Smith, K. (1993) The influence of weather and climate on recreation and tourism. *Weather*, **48**(12), 398–404.

Smith, L.P. (1999) Intercultural network theory: A cross-paradigmatic approach to acculturation. *International Journal of Intercultural Relations*, **23**(4), pp. 629–658.

Smith, V. (ed.) (1977) *Hosts ad Guests*. University of Pennsylvania Press, Philadelphia.

Soemodinoto, A., Wong, P.P. and Saleh, M. (2001) Effect of prolonged political unrest on tourism. *Annals of Tourism Research*, **28**, 1056–1060.

Sofield, T. (2003) *Empowerment for Sustainable Tourism Development*. London: Pergamon.

Song, H. and Witt, S.F. (2000) *Tourism Demand Modelling and Forecasting: Modern Econometric Approaches*. Oxford: Pergamon.

Song, H. and Wong, K.F. (2003) Tourism demand modeling – a time varying parameter approach. *Journal of Travel Research*, **42**, 57–64.

Song, H., Witt, S F and Jensen, T.C. (2003a) Tourism forecasting: accuracy of alternative econometric models. *International Journal of Forecasting*, **19**, 123–141.

Song, H., Wong, K.F. and Chon, K. (2003b) Modelling and forecasting the demand for Hong Kong tourism. *International Journal of Hospitality Management*, **22**, 435–451.

Sönmez, S. (1998) Tourism, terrorism and political instability. *Annals of Tourism Research*, **25**, 416–456.

Sönmez, S.F. and Graefe, A.R. (1998) Influence of terrorism risk on foreign tourism decisions. *Annals of Tourism Research*, **1**, 112–144.

Sönmez, S., Apostolopoulos, Y. and Tarlow, P. (1999) Tourism in crisis: managing the effects of terrorism. *Journal of Travel Research*, **38**(1), 13–18.

Sönmez, S.F., Backman, S.J. and Allen, L.R. (1994) *Managing Tourism Crises*. Clemson University.

Stacey, R.D. (1992) *Managing Chaos*. London: Kogan Page.

Stafford, G., Yu, L. and Armoo, A.K. (2001) Crisis management and recovery: How Washington, DC, hotels responded to terrorism. *Cornell Hotel and Restaurant Administration Quarterly*, **43**, 27–40.

Stallard, J. (2004) *The Next Jet Set*. http://www.pbs.org/wnet/innovation/episode5_essay1.html (accessed 6 October, 2004).

Statistics Canada (1998) Estimates of government revenue attributable to tourism, 1992. Part I.

Stoker, G. and Young, S. (1993) *Cities in the 1990s*. Harlow: Longman.

Sundbo, J., Fussing Jensen, C. and Mattsson, J. (2003a) Tourist Firms' Entrepreneurial Network Approach. Conference paper to Nordisk Företaks Förenings, August 14–16, 2003, Reykyavik.

Sundbo, J., Mattsson, J., Fussing Jensen, C., Herlau, H. and Tetzner, H. (2003b) Strategic Innovation in Tourism: Drawers as key to Innovation. Working paper from Danish Centre for Tourism Research (www.geo.ruc.dk/trcd/projekter.htm. (accessed 20 August, 2004).

Swarbrooke, J. (1999) *Sustainable Tourism Management*. London: CABI Publishing.

Telfer, D.J. (2002) Evolution of tourism and development theory. In *Tourism and Development: Concepts and Issues* (Sharpley R, Telfer D, eds). Clevedon: Channel View Publications, pp. 35–78.

Thapa, B. (2003) Tourism in Nepal: Shangri-La's troubled times. *Journal of Travel and Tourism Marketing*, **15**(2/3), 117–138.

The Economist (1998) A better Way to Fly. 19 February (web edition).

The Economist (2003) New Routes to the Beach. 31 July.

The Economist (2003) New Routes to the Beach. 31 July (web edition).

The Economist (2004) Turbulent Skies. 10 July (web edition).

Thietart, R.A. and Forgues, B. (1995) Chaos theory and organization. *Organization Science*, **6**(1), 19–1.

Thomas, R. (ed.) (2004) *Small Firms in Tourism: International Perspectives*. London: Elsevier Science.

Tichy, N.M. and Sherman, S. (1993) *Control your destiny or someone else will*. New York: Harper.

Toohey, B. (1994) *Tumbling Dice*. Melbourne: Heinemann.

Torkildsen, G. (1999) *Leisure and Recreation Management*, 4th edn. London: E&FN Spon.

Townley, B. (2002) The role of competing rationalities in institutional change. *Academy of Management Journal*, **45**(1), 163–180.

Trist, E.L. (1983) Referent organisations and the development of interorganisational domains. *Human Relations*, **36**, 247–268.

Tulder, R. (ed.) (1999) *Redrawing organisational boundaries*. Rotterdam: Rotterdam School of Management (Department of Public Management).

Turner, L.W. and Witt, S.F. (2001) Forecasting tourism using univariate and multivariate structural time series models. *Tourism Economics*, **7**, 135–147.

Twining-Ward, L. (2002) *Monitoring sustainable tourism development: a comprehensive, stakeholder-driven, adaptive approach*. PhD Thesis, University of Surrey, Guildford.

Tyler, D. and Dinan, C. (2001) The role of interested groups in England's emerging tourism policy network. *Current Issues in Tourism*, **4**(2–4), 210–252.

Ucbasaran, D., Wright, M. and Westhead, P. (2003) A longitudinal study of habitual entrepreneurs: starters and acquirers. *Entrepreneurship and Regional Development*, **15**, 207–228.

UN, Organisation for Economic Co-operation and Development and Commission of the European Communities (Eurostat) (2001) *Tourism Satellite Account: Recommended Methodological Framework*. New York: United Nations, World Tourism Organization.

United Nations Division for Social Policy and Development (1998) *The Ageing of the World's Population*. New York: United Nations.

United Nations Population Division (1998) *World Population Projections to 2150*. New York: United Nations.

United States Census Bureau (2004) *World Population Information*. International Data Base, various, http://www.census.gov/ipc/www/idbnew.html (accessed 17 October, 2004).

Urban Strategies Inc. The Tourism Company (1998) Niagara Falls Tourism Development Strategy.

Urry, J. (1990) *The Tourist Gaze*. London: Sage.

US Department of State (2004) Travel Warnings. <http://www.state.gov/travel/> (accessed 15 September, 2004).

Usunier, J.C. (2000) *Marketing Across Cultures*, 3rd edn. London: Prentice Hall.

Verbole, A. (2000) Actors, discourses and interfaces of rural tourism development at the local community level in Slovenia: Social and political dimensions of the rural tourism development process, *Journal of Sustainable Tourism*, **8**(6), 479–490.

Viner, D. and Amelung, B. (2003) *Climate change, the Environment and Tourism: The Interactions*. Proceedings of the ESF-LESC Workshop, June 4–6, Milan.

Waldrop, M. (1992) *Complexity: The Emerging Science and the Edge of Order and Chaos*. London: Simon and Schuster/Penguin.

Walker, P.A., Greiner, R., McDonald, D. and Lyne, V. (1999) The tourism futures simulator: systems thinking approach. *Environmental Modelling and Software*, **14**, 59–67.

Walton, J. (2001) *The Victorian Seaside* http://www.bbc.co.uk/history/society_culture/society/seaside_06.shtml (accessed 30 July, 2004).

Wanhill, S.R.C. (1994) The measurement of tourist income multipliers. *Tourism Management*, **15**(4), 281–283.

Warhurst, C., Nickson, D., Witz, A. and Cullen, A.M. (2000) Aesthetic labour in interactive service work: some case study evidence from the 'New Glasgow'. *Service Industries Journal*, **20**(3), 1–18.

WCED (World Commission on Environment and Development) (1987) *Our Common Future*. New York: Oxford University Press.

Weaver, D.B. (ed.) (1998) Introduction to ecotourism. In *Ecotourism in the Less Developed World*. Oxford: CAB International, pp. 1–33.

Weaver, D. and Oppermann, M. (2000) *Tourism Management*. Brisbane: John Wiley and Sons.

Weiermair, K. (2001) The growth of tourism enterprises. *Tourism Review*, **56**(3/4), 17–25.

Wenger, E., McDermott, R. and Snyder, W.M. (2002) *Cultivating Communities of Practice*. Boston: Harvard Business School Press.

Werthner, H. and Klein, S. (1999) *IT and Tourism: a Challenging Relationship*. Vienna: Springer Verlag.

Wickens, M.R. and Breusch, T.S. (1988) Dynamic specification, the long-run and the estimation of transformed regression model. *Economic Journal*, **98** Conference, 189–205.

Wierenga, B. and van Bruggen, G. (2000) *Marketing Management Support Systems. Principles, Tools and Implementation*. Boston: Kluwer.

Wight, P. (1998) Tools for sustainability analysis in planning and managing tourism and recreation in the destination. In: *Sustainable Tourism: A*

Geographical Perspective (Hall, C.M. and Lew, A. eds). Harlow: Longman, pp. 75–91.

Williams, A.M. and Hall, C.M. (2002) Tourism, migration, circulation and mobility: the contingencies of time and place. In: *Tourism and Migration: New Relationships Between Production and Consumption* (Hall, C.M. and Williams, A.M. eds). Dordrecht: Kluwer, pp. 1–52.

Williams, A.M., Shaw, G. and Greenwood, J. (1989) From tourist to tourism entrepreneur, from consumption to production: evidence from Cornwall, England. *Environment and Planning*, **A**(21), 1639–1653.

Wilton, D. (2004) *A Research Report Prepared for the Canadian Tourism Commission. Recent Developments in the National Tourism Indicators.* University of Waterloo, Canada.

Witkowski, T.H., Ma, Y. and Zheng, D. (2003) Cross-cultural influences on brand identity impressions: KFC in China and the United States. *Asia Pacific, Journal of Marketing and Logistics*, **15**(1/2), 74–88.

Witt, S.F. and Witt, C.A. (1992) *Modeling and Forecasting Demand in Tourism.* London: Academic Press.

Wöber, K.W. (1998) TourMIS: an adaptive distributed marketing information system for strategic decision support in national, regional, or city tourist offices. *Pacific Tourism Review*, **2**(3/4), 273–286.

Wöber, K.W. (2000) Benchmarking hotel operations on the Internet: a data envelopment analysis approach. *Information Technology and Tourism*, **3**(3/4), 195–212.

Wöber, K.W. (2001) Identifying competing tourism destinations using group decision support systems. In *Information and Communication Technologies in Tourism. ENTER 2001. Proceedings of the International Conference in Montreal, Canada* (Sheldon P, Wöber K, Fesenmaier D, eds). Vienna, New York: Springer, pp. 1–12.

Wöber, K.W. (2003) Information supply in tourism management by marketing decision support systems. *Tourism Management*, **24**(3), 241–255.

Woods, M.J. (1997) Discourses of power and rurality: Local politics in Somerset in the 20th Century. *Political Geography*, **16**, 453–478.

World Commission on Environment and Development (1987) *Our Common Future.* New York: Oxford University Press.

World Tourism Organization (1997a) *Agenda 21 for the Travel and Tourism Industry: Towards Environmentally Sustainable Development.* Madrid: World Tourism Organization, World Travel and Tourism Council and the Earth Council.

World Tourism Organization (WTO) (1997b) *International Tourism: A Global Perspective.* Madrid: WTO.

World Tourism Organization (WTO) (2001) *Vision 2020.* Madrid: WTO.

World Tourism Organization (WTO) (2003) *World Overview and Market Trends.* Madrid: WTO.

World Tourism Organization (2004) *Long-term Prospects: Tourism 2020 Vision.* http://www.world-tourism.org/facts/2020.html (accessed 26 January, 2005).

World Watch (2004) World Watch special issue Population and its Discontents. September/October.

WTO (1980) Physical Planning and Area Development for Tourism in the Six WTO Regions 1980. Madrid: WTO.

WTO (2001) *Basic References on Tourism Statistics*. Madrid: World Tourism Organization.

WTO (2003) *World Tourism Barometer*. **1**(1), June.

WTO (2004) Indicators of Sustainable Development for Tourism Destinations – A Guidebook. Madrid: WTO.

Yale, P. (1995) *The Business of Tour Operations*. London: Longman.

Zamecka, A. and Buchanan, G. (2000) *Disaster Risk Management*. Queensland Government, Australia: Department of Emergency Services.

Zimmermann, E.W. (1933) *World Resources and Industries*, revised 1951. New York: Harper Brothers.

Index